IMAGES
of America

NASHVILLE'S HILLSBORO VILLAGE

ON THE COVER: This was a one-time event that occurred in August 1957 in front of the Sweet Shop. Local high school fraternities and sororities met at the Sweet Shop to celebrate their new pledges. Neighbors reported the noise from the horns blasting, and the crowd grew to around 500 high school students. When the police showed up, the crowd grew. The officers took over two hours to gain control of the rowdy crowd. (Courtesy of Nashville Public Library Special Collections.)

IMAGES
of America

NASHVILLE'S HILLSBORO VILLAGE

Yvonne Eaves

ARCADIA
PUBLISHING

ISBN 978-1-4671-0864-5

Published by Arcadia Publishing
Charleston, South Carolina

Printed in the United States of America

Library of Congress Control Number: 2022934955

For all general information, please contact Arcadia Publishing:
Telephone 843-853-2070
Fax 843-853-0044
E-mail sales@arcadiapublishing.com
For customer service and orders:
Toll-Free 1-888-313-2665

Visit us on the Internet at www.arcadiapublishing.com

Dedicated to the fantastic employees past and present at Cornerstone Financial Credit Union in Hillsboro Village. Thanks for the great memories.

Contents

ACKNOWLEDGMENTS

Just a couple of weeks after I decided to work on the history of Hillsboro Village, the world experienced the COVID outbreak. Research became a little difficult. Some individuals were concerned with talking to anyone outside their own families. A lot of the research for this book was accomplished using the website Newspaper.com. Nashville is so fortunate to have some great places for research: the Tennessee State Library & Archives, the Metro Library, and Metro Archives. All three have an enormous amount of material for research and a very knowledgeable staff. A special thanks at the state library to Lindsay Hagar, who was very patient. Thanks for dealing with me understanding the proper way for ordering copies of photographs. Thank you to the Special Collections department at the Metro Library. Dixie Johnson and Kathleen Feduccia, many thanks to you both. Retired Beth Odle, many thanks to you as well. Metro Archives, thanks for the knowledge of photographs your staff has. I much appreciate the Metro Archives' assistance, especially Sarah Arntz, Ken Fieth, and Kelly Sirko. The Metro Archives has an enormous collection of images. A special thank-you goes to LaDonya Weber at Scarritt Center, an organization with some very interesting photographs. Thanks to Betty Jane Taylor for her information on the Belmont Methodist Church. I would also like to thank my aunt June Hedge—your encouragement is always priceless.

INTRODUCTION

As early as the ice age, humans have occupied the Middle Tennessee area. Some evidence of the inhabitation still lingers. Along the Cumberland River and many of the creek beds in the area, arrowheads can be found. Remains of the Archaic Indian culture can be seen in shell mounds along the Cumberland River. About 3,000 years ago, the Woodland peoples left proof of their existence. They buried their deceased loved ones in stone-lined graves with their possessions. Examples of the contents of the graves were stone pottery, pipes, and beads. About 900 AD, some of the southern states were home to the Mississippian culture. The Mississippians created living quarters. They had places they would gather to practice religious ceremonies and other activities. For unknown reasons, all of these cultures have died off. When the settlers came to this area, they discovered how fertile the soil was. They also discovered an area that was a large salt lick that attracted various wildlife. The tribes in Middle Tennessee during the 1700s were mostly the Creeks, Cherokees, Chickasaws, and Shawnees. The different tribes of Native Americans did not accept the pioneers, as they were concerned about their hunting grounds. None of these tribes lived near the Nashville area. The Indians were pushed back beyond the Duck River in Maury County. There is no evidence of any Native American ever in the Hillsboro Village. It is possible because of the small creeks running through the area that prehistoric Native Americans existed here, but their existence cannot be proven.

In the late 1700s, two groups of pioneers left their homes for unsettled lands. James Robertson led a group of men by land, while John Donelson's group was made up of mostly women and children. Donelson's group traveled by waterway. Robertson and his men arrived near the future Fort Nashborough on Christmas Day 1779. The day the men arrived, they walked across the frozen Cumberland River. Donelson and his group arrived on April 24, 1780. The group of settlers built Fort Nashborough. The pioneers had many battles with the Native American warriors. Eventually, the pioneers were rewarded for their efforts of enduring the trip to unsettled grounds. Records show Elijah Robertson, James Robertson's brother, was given 640 acres of land. A piece of the property awarded to Elijah would one day become Hillsboro Village. Elijah never built a home on this property. A hand-drawn map from 1798 indicates a path for a road was being cleared. The road was going through Elijah's lands from Hillsboro Pike toward Brown's Station. Located a couple of miles southwest of today's Hillsboro Village was Hillsboro Road. Some historians believe the road created by Elijah was to connect Hillsboro Road to the Natchez Trace. In Nashville, the final destination of Natchez Trace was Cockrill Springs (Centennial Park).

During the Civil War, the Union troops occupied a few homes close to the area now known as Hillsboro Village. Glen Oak and Rokeby were still intact after the war was over.

Before the 1900s, what is Hillsboro Village today was mostly farmlands. A map of 1896 shows the village area was not within the city limits. It appears in an 1877 Nashville City map that Hillsboro Road ended before Grand Avenue. The naming of Twenty-First Avenue South occurred sometime between 1910 and 1920. The roadway would have been incorporated into Nashville

City. Where Hillsboro Village is located today, a small creek once traveled up today's Twenty-First Avenue South. The path of the creek rambled toward the north of the village and eventually drained into a low spot where Blakemore Avenue and Twenty-First Avenue South intersect.

By the early 1900s, Nashville was beginning to experience growing pains. Families were leaving overcrowded downtown Nashville for the suburbs. Rural family farmers were moving closer to the cities, and factory and manufactory jobs were flourishing. Land companies were dividing large parcels of land to create neighborhoods. Belmont Land Company was the largest close to the future Hillsboro Village. Most of Belmont Land Company's holdings were on the east side of Twenty-First Avenue South. The land companies determined what restrictions would be placed on future property owners. Belmont required houses have a 35-foot setback. Belmont Land Company also prohibited any liquor sales on any property it sold. In 1913, Belmont Realty took over the Belmont Land Company. On the west side of Twenty-First Avenue South, Edgar Jones determined his limitations for anyone who purchased his land and used the 35-foot setback. He also required any house that was built to cost at least $1,200. Jones insisted if anyone purchased one of his lots, they had to agree that they would not bring live swine with them.

There was public transportation in the future Hillsboro Village area. By 1910, electric streetcars were the most popular means of transportation. The streetcars were active, most likely due to Vanderbilt and other schools in the area. Before the electric streetcars, Nashvillians were transported by horse-drawn trolleys. Automobiles were not seen in the area before the 1920s. During the 1940s, buses replaced electric streetcars.

Vanderbilt was growing with job openings at the university and hospital. From time to time, Vanderbilt offered a special incentive for employees who bought homes in the 37212 zip code. At one time, an estimated 10 percent of the residents of 37212 were employed by Vanderbilt.

The Belmont Methodist Church has also been in the area since the 1910s. By 1920, the commercial district began to take shape. The first year saw a pharmacy and two grocery stores within a block of the church. By the mid-1920s, Hillsboro Village was becoming a commercial district with 19 businesses, including a post office, dry cleaners, and a bank. Much of the property was owned by H.G. Hill Realty. The naming of Hillsboro Village to the commercial district along Twenty-First Avenue South cannot be found before the 1940s. It could be possible the business owners decided the naming of Hillsboro Village was to copy New York's Greenwich Village.

For years, Nashville's nickname has been "Athens of the South." The nickname was due to Nashville, from 1864 to 1930, experiencing 10 schools of higher education opening. Half of the 10 were located close to Hillsboro Village.

Before Tennessee became a state, the western edge of North Carolina reached the Mississippi River. The river was also on the western edge of America. Settlers came to Middle Tennessee and beyond for farmland. A group of families moved from Hillsborough, North Carolina, to Williamson County, Tennessee. The farmers wanted to name their community Hillsborough. The US Post Office rejected the naming of Williamson County's Hillsborough. Coffee County, Tennessee, had a community named Hillsborough, and the post office refused the name due to possible confusion between the two Tennessee communities. Williamson County's Hillsborough became Leiper's Fork. Before the Civil War, America had about two dozen counties, villages, and post offices that were named Hillsborough. By 1771, Tennessee had a Hillsborough. There are 44 cities, towns, or locations that have shortened the name to Hillsboro.

A little past Hillsboro Village on the south is Four-Forty Parkway. The purpose of Interstate 440 was to bypass downtown traffic. Interstate 440's construction was the most expensive on record. The cost was $178.3 million, and the interstate's length was 7.64 miles. The site of Interstate 440 was on abandoned Tennessee Central Railroad tracks. There were several hard-fought court battles with opposition to the parkway. Plans for Interstate 440 began in the 1950s. Construction on the project started in 1982 and did not see completion until 1987. The original design of Interstate 440 was to handle 64,000 vehicles a day. By 1999, it was estimated Interstate 440 had 100,000 vehicles a day. Many people think the opening of Interstate 440 separated the Hillsboro Village and Green Hills communities. To some, the street name changes close to Interstate 440.

Anything north of the Four-Forty Parkway is considered Twenty-First Avenue South and south is Hillsboro Pike or Road.

To the east of Hillsboro Village is Belmont, the former home of Adelicia and Joseph Acklen. The childhood home of Adelicia was close by too. Adelicia's parents, the Hayeses, lived in Rokeby, and the property became home to the Upper Room. The Belmont mansion was built after the Acklens' European honeymoon. *Bell monte* is Italian for "beautiful mountain." The massive mansion had 36 rooms in 20,000 square feet, and there was a zoo and an aviary on the grounds. In 1890, the property around Belmont was sold. In Adelicia's will, the mansion was left to become Belmont College, a school for young ladies. After a few years, the name was changed to Ward-Belmont. The view from the front entrance of Belmont looking north is today's Music Row.

Hillsboro Village's largest contender has always been to the north of the village. Vanderbilt University's name was changed from Central University, and in the beginning, it had strong Methodist connections. In the beginning, the faculty and most of the students were Methodist. In 1875, Vanderbilt University was officially dedicated thanks to a million-dollar donation from Cornelius Vanderbilt. The donation was due to financial hardship left in Nashville after the Civil War. At about the same time, University School's medical program became Vanderbilt's Medical University. After the 1900s, Vanderbilt continued to grow, and its expansion has been nonstop. The campus has grown to over 300 acres. Over the years, Vanderbilt has been notorious for snatching homes and property in the area. Many families and businesses have lost land due to Vanderbilt's growth. No one was spared from Vanderbilt land acquisitions; even employees were displaced from their homes.

One

The Village

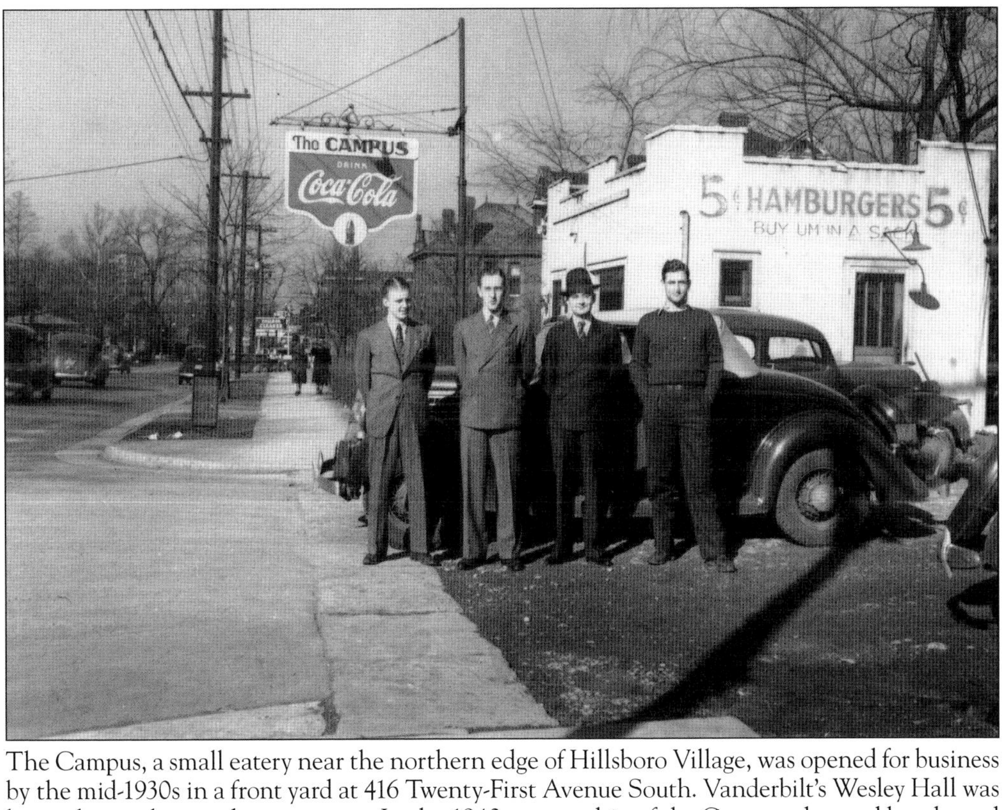

The Campus, a small eatery near the northern edge of Hillsboro Village, was opened for business by the mid-1930s in a front yard at 416 Twenty-First Avenue South. Vanderbilt's Wesley Hall was located very close to the restaurant. In the 1940s, ownership of the Campus changed hands, and it was renamed the Campus Grill. (Courtesy of Tennessee State Library & Archives.)

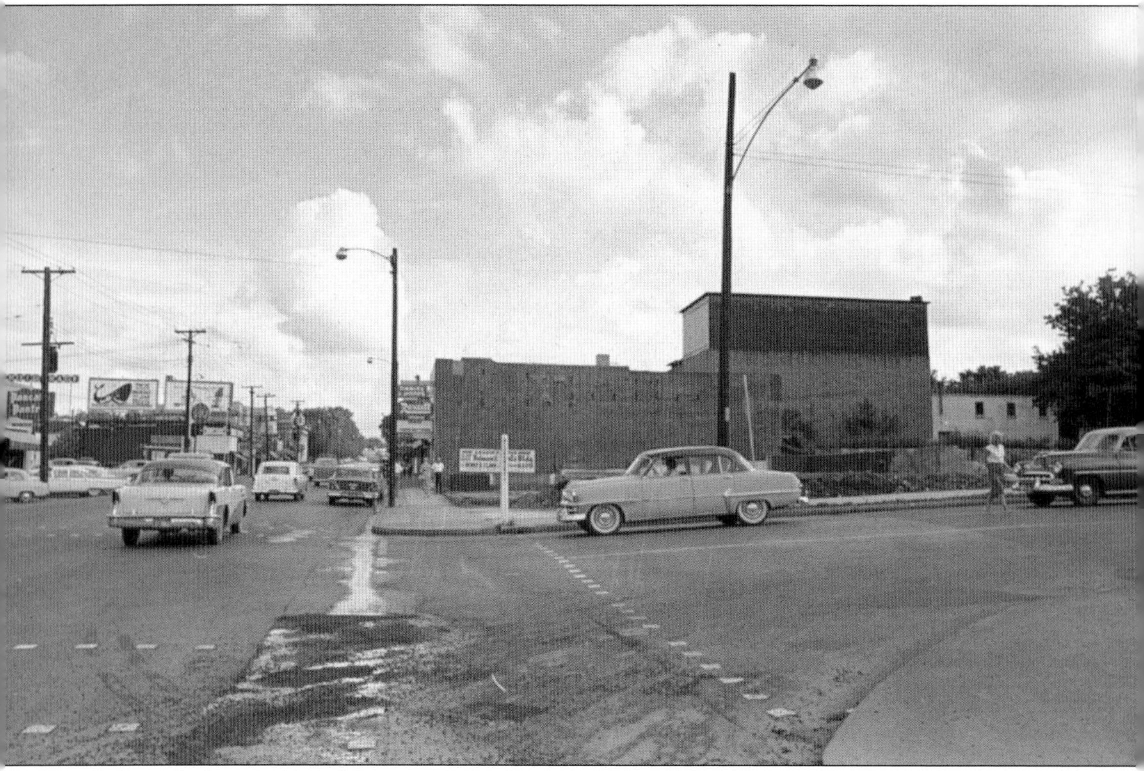

The Whitley Building became a permanent structure in Hillsboro Village after the Belmont Theatre was demolished. The new property owners were Belmont Investments, made up of Marshall Whitley, Margaret Lawson Whitley, Peter Curlin, Mary Curlin, and Robert McCampbell. The stucco building was finished in 1962. When opened, it was the first modern office building in Hillsboro Village and was named for Marshall and Margaret Whitley. Most of the first floor was retail stores. There was also a pharmacy, a dentist, and a sportswear store. The three upper floors were used for offices. A couple of organizations that were in the building were to help disadvantaged individuals, such as Outlook Nashville, which worked with handicapped students. (Courtesy of Metro Archives.)

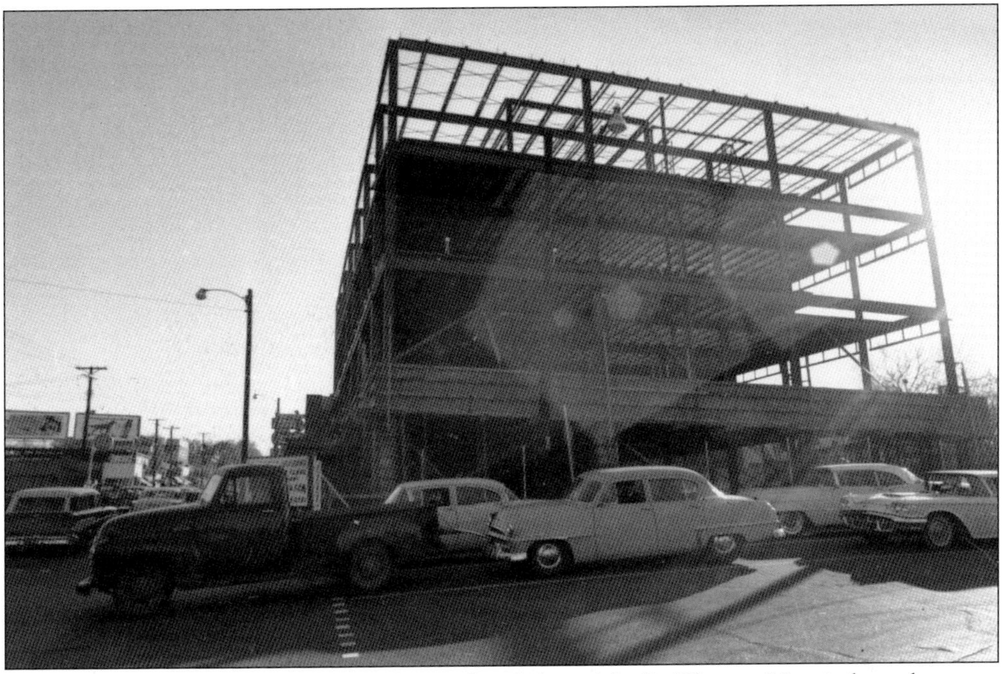

In the late 1960s, property had been acquired and cleared for St. Thomas Hospital to relocate to Blakemore Avenue. Belmont Investments had filed an appeal with Metro Zoning with the hope of adding 11 stories to the existing four floors of the Whitley Building. St. Thomas decided to build on Harding Road. (Courtesy of Metro Archives.)

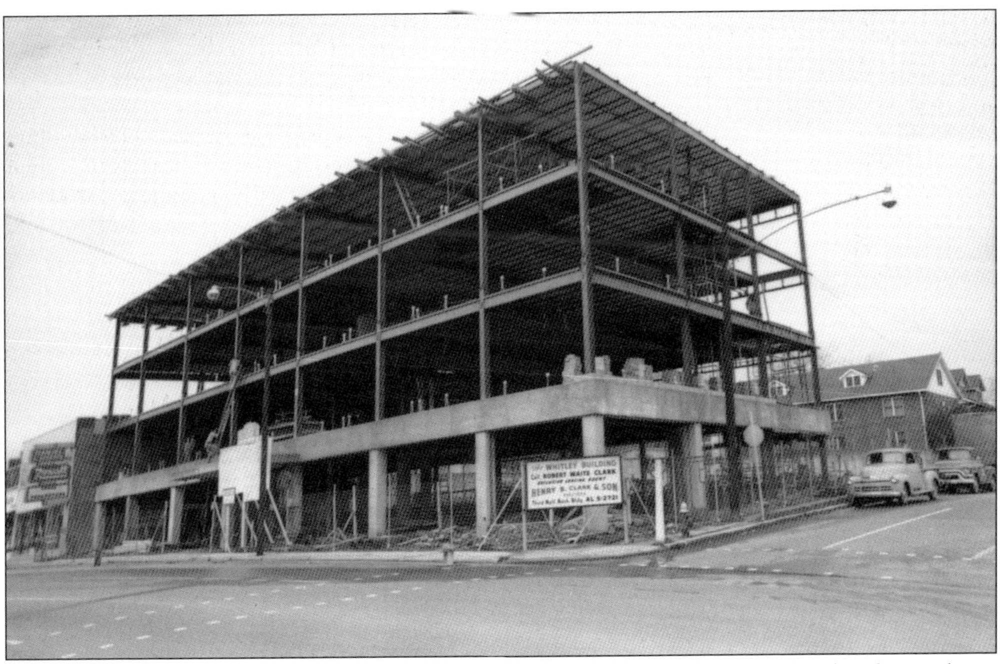

Metro Zoning did not approve the addition to the Whitley Building. A couple of years later, Belmont Investments sold the Whitley Building to Mid-State Educators Credit Union. Eventually, the credit union was renamed Cornerstone Financial Credit Union. (Courtesy of Metro Archives.)

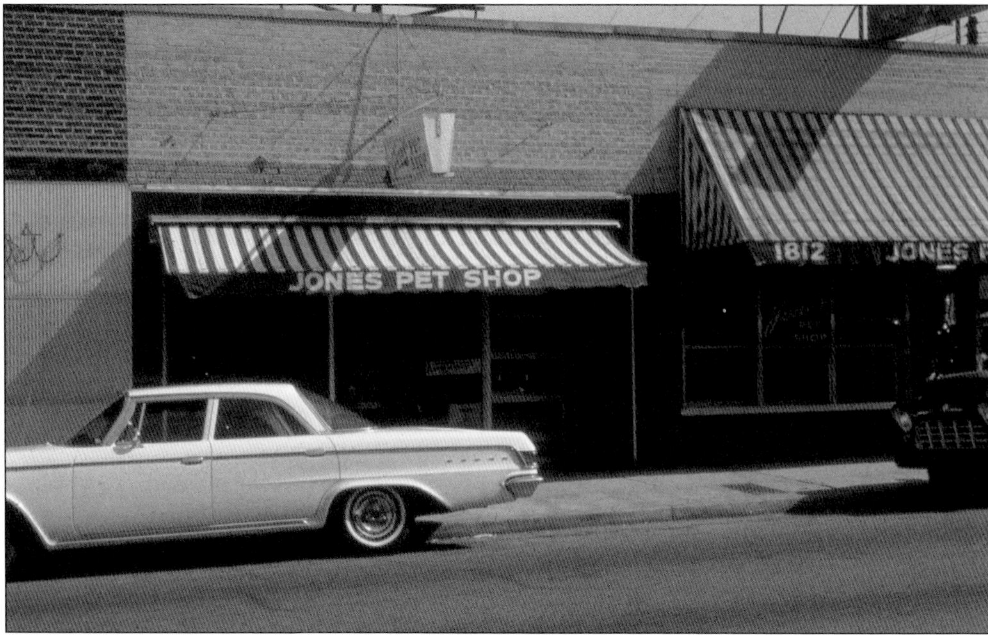

Jones Pet Shop opened in the late 1930s. It was always considered by many a favorite place to visit in Hillsboro Village. Anything a pet owner needed could be found at the pet shop. Jones Pet Shop had a wide variety of all kinds of aquatic life, birds, hamsters, turtles, and sometimes puppies and kittens. The staff was all very knowledgeable and helpful. The pet shop closed in November 1994, and the building took on a different role in Hillsboro Village—it became Fidos, a coffee shop. (Courtesy of Metro Archives.)

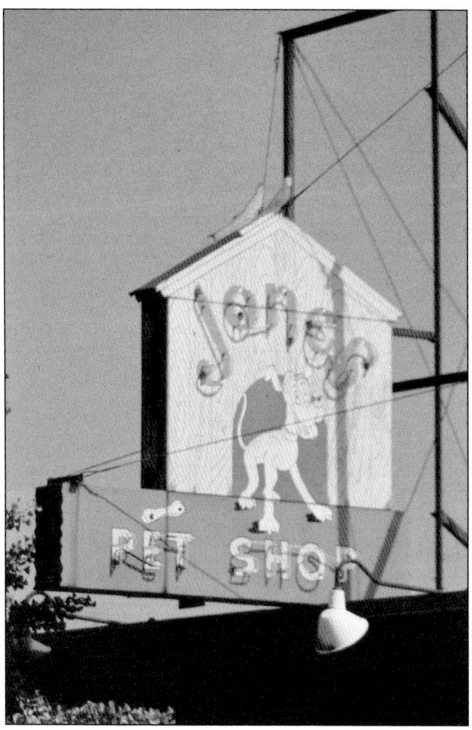

The building that was home to Jones Pet Shop had an outside sign for a long time. In 1992, a Metro Zoning ordinance was passed. The Metro Government had decided outdoor signs could not be attached to the building. The community was worried after the ownership changed hands the sign would have to be dissembled. After many letters and phone calls, Metro Zoning decided to make an exception. The Jones Pet Shop sign was allowed to remain part of Hillsboro Village. (Courtesy of Metro Archives.)

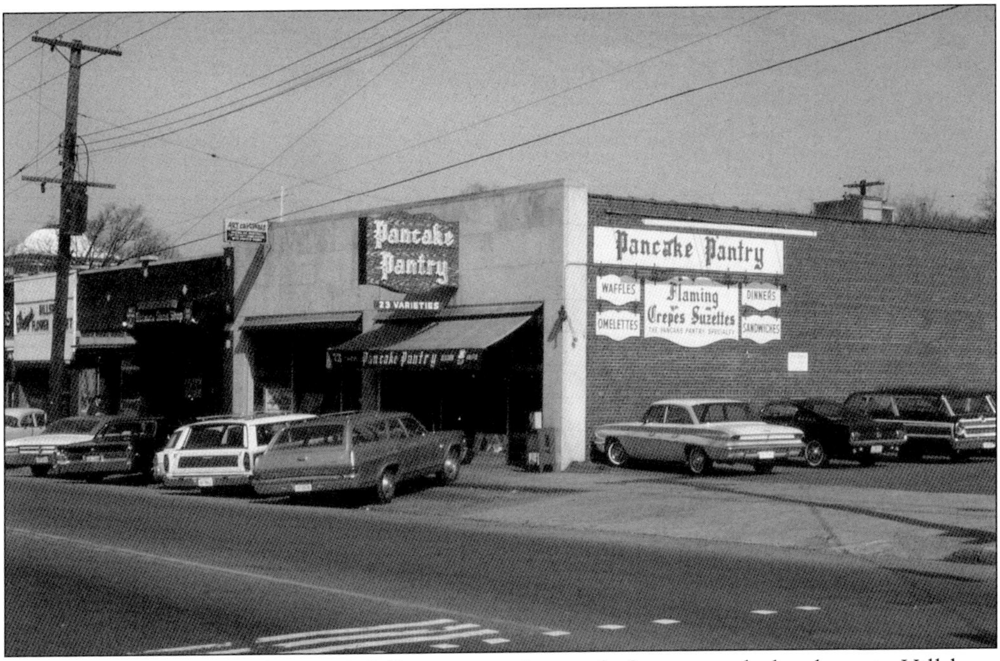

Pancake Pantry, famous for its 23 different pancakes made from scratch, has been in Hillsboro Village since 1961. Just as popular as Hillsboro Village's Pancake Pantry is Gatlinburg's Pancake Pantry, which is a couple of years older. After 61 years of being in Hillsboro Village, there is a wait to get inside most days, but the food is definitely worth it. (Courtesy of Metro Archives.)

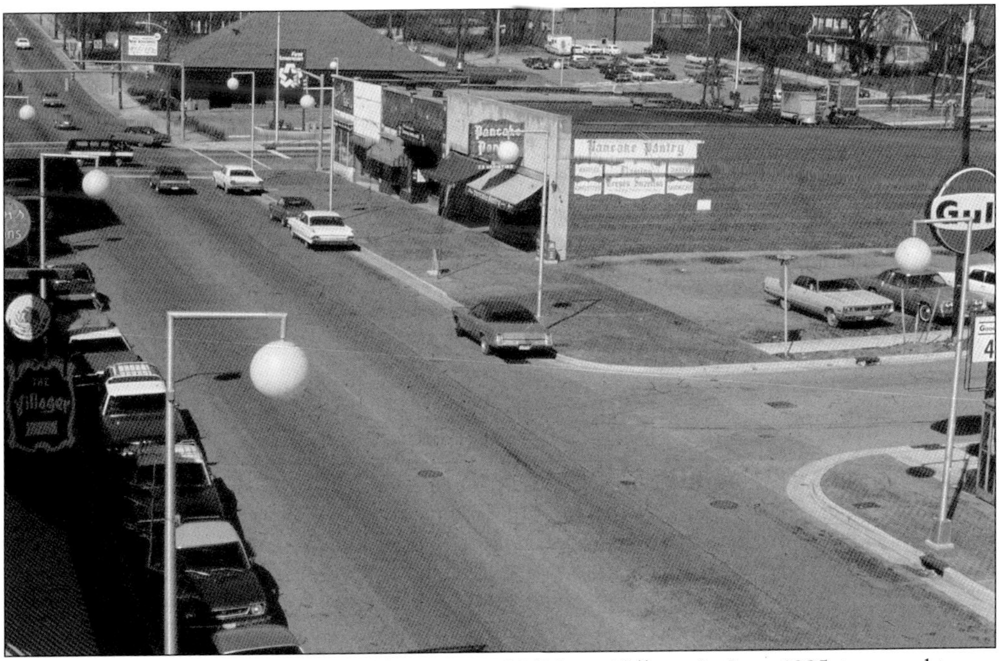

Pancake Pantry outgrew its original location in Hillsboro Village. In June 1995, it moved into a large building next door to the building at 1724 Twenty-First Avenue South. The larger Pancake Pantry was built where the parking is in the photograph. (Courtesy of Metro Archives.)

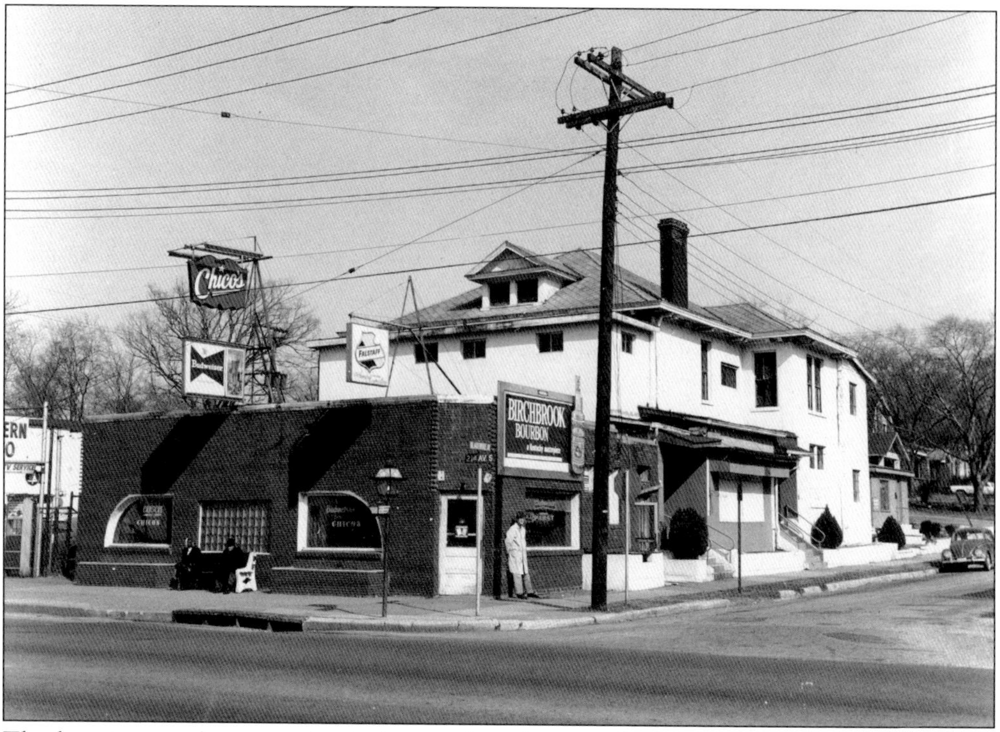

The location on the street sign indicates this photograph is the intersection of Blakemore Avenue and Twenty-First Avenue South. The property was demolished to enlarge and straighten Blakemore and Wedgewood Avenues where the streets cross Twenty-First Avenue South. (Courtesy of Metro Archives.)

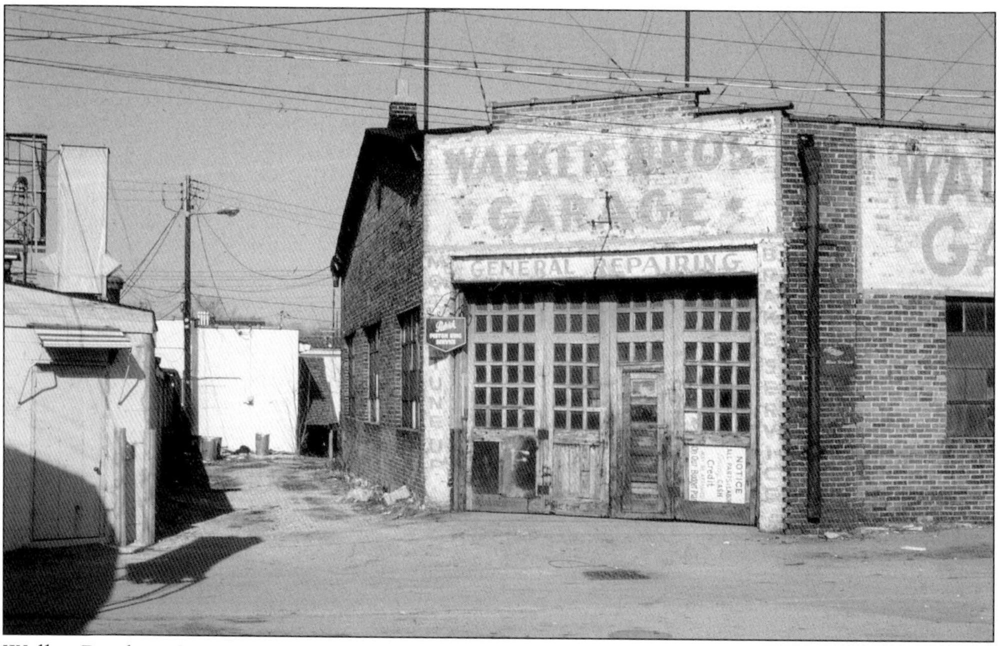

Walker Brothers Garage was located in the alley behind Jones Pet Shop. The garage was demolished to make way for a parking lot. (Courtesy of Metro Archives.)

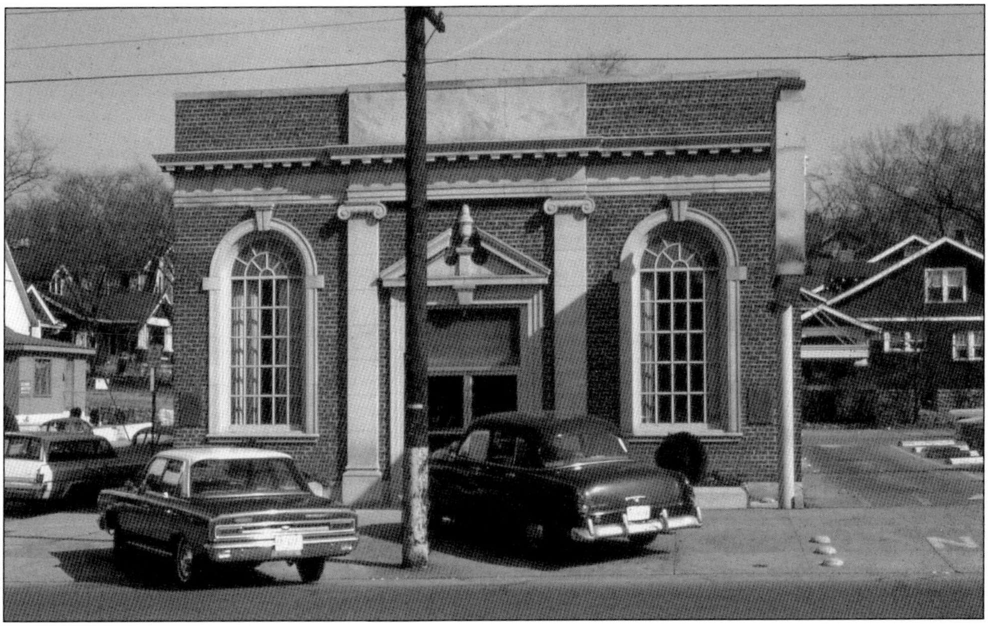

This was the earliest Hillsboro Village branch of First American National Bank, located at 1812 Twenty-First Avenue South. During the Depression, American National Bank consumed Fourth and First Bank and Trust. In the 1940s, American National Bank became First American National Bank. In 1999, AmSouth acquired First American. A few years later, AmSouth merged with Regions. This building was torn down to make room for the widening and straightening of Blakemore and Wedgewood Avenues. The second building, erected in the 1970s, was torn down in 2015. A larger mixed-use building with underground parking was constructed. Across Twenty-First Avenue South, a Third National Bank branch was also present in the village. In the late 1980s, Third National Bank became a branch of SunTrust Bank. (Courtesy of Metro Archives.)

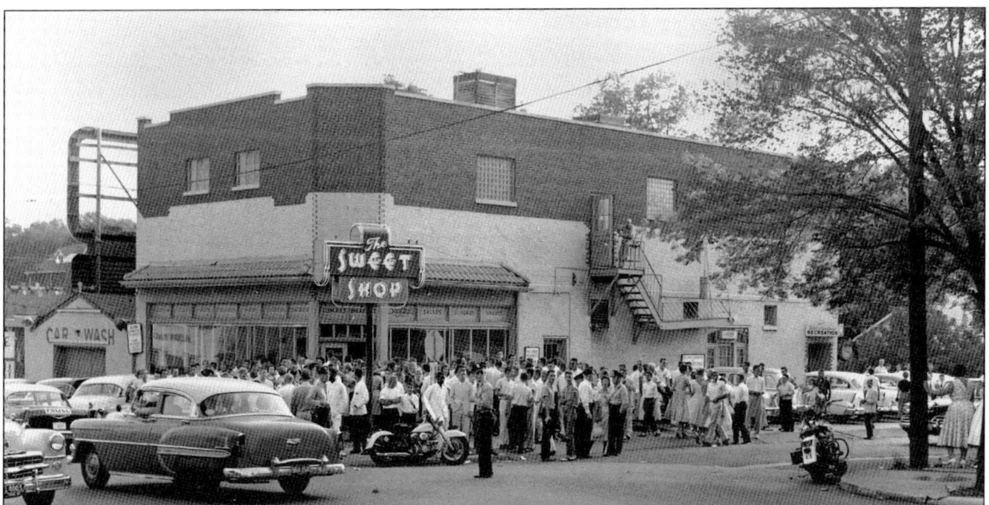

Located at 1601 Twenty-First Avenue South, the Sweet Shop was a typical soda shop. The building's second floor was a pool hall. Over the years, the building has been used for different eateries—Spats and Sportsman Grille are two of the better-known restaurants. (Courtesy of Nashville Public Library Special Collections.)

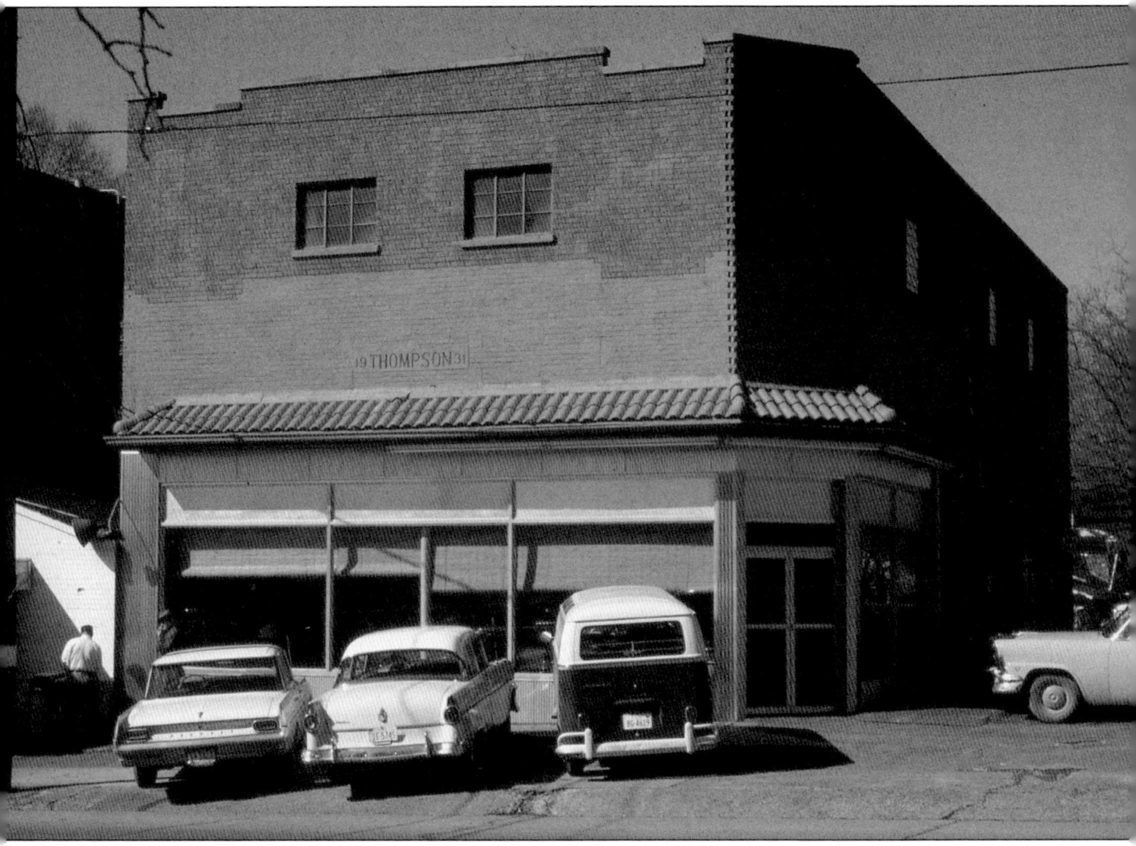

The Sportsman Grille opened in 1991, and after being in Hillsboro Village for 27 years, it closed. The interior of the Sportsman Grille was decorated in the spirit of a hunting lodge from the 1900s. Vanderbilt entered into a $2-million deal to purchase the building. The engraving on the top says "19 Thompson 31." Most recently, a barbecue chain is in the building. (Courtesy of Metro Archives.)

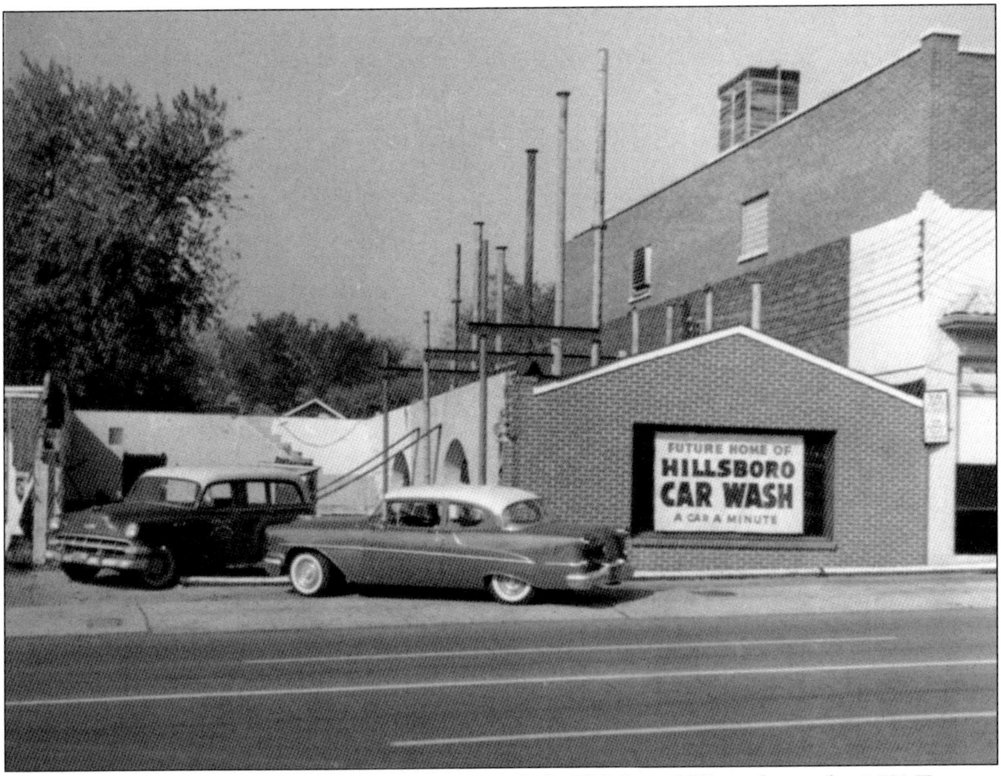

The image above, taken in 1956, is of a new car wash for Hillsboro Village, located at 1603 Twenty-First Avenue South. The Sweet Shop was located next door to the car wash. Currently, a bank parking lot is on the site where the car wash once stood. (Both, courtesy of Metro Archives.)

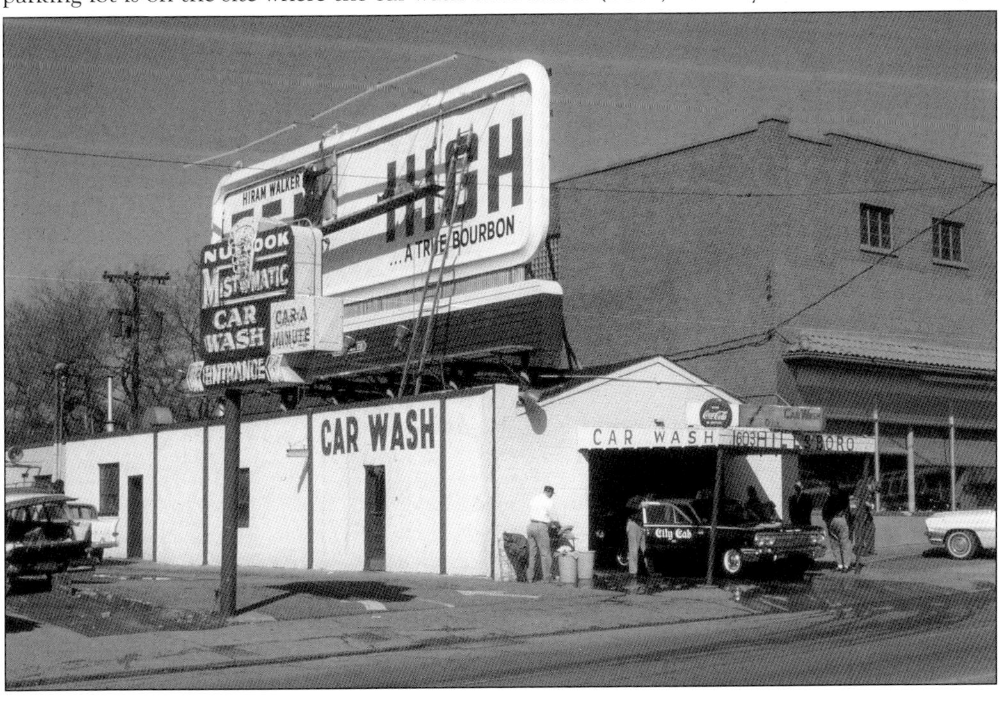

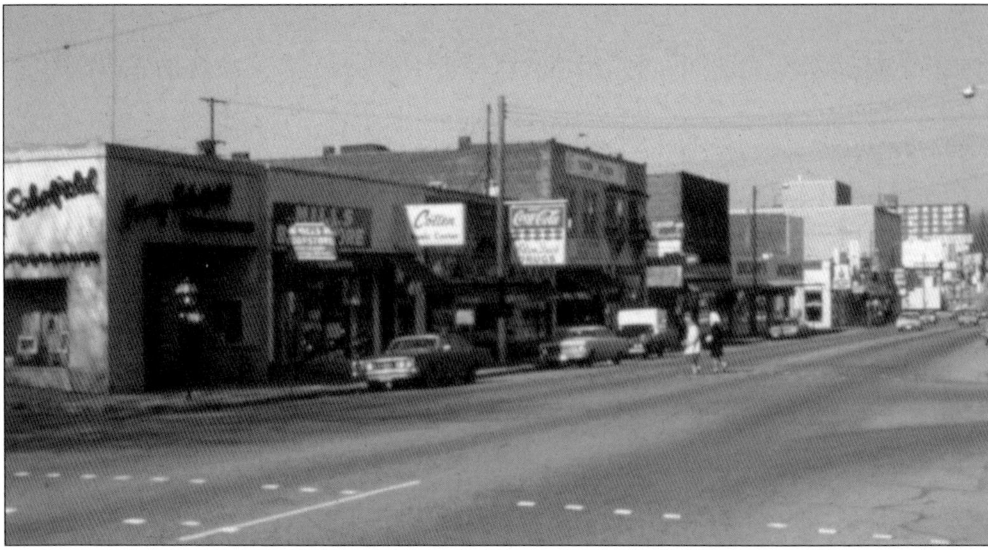

An early H.G. Hill Food Store in Hillsboro Village was at 1825 Twenty-First Avenue South. The open space behind Cotton Music Center looked like a burned-out building, but it was the H.G. Hill company's chicken yard. Chickens were slaughtered and cleaned before they were sent to area stores to be purchased. In the 1920s and 1930s, H.G. Hill had almost 100 stores in the Nashville area. Another H.G. Hill store opened at 1710 Twenty-First Avenue South in Hillsboro Village, followed by one just south of Blair Boulevard. Piggly Wiggly, A&P, and Kroger also had stores in Hillsboro Village. (Courtesy of Metro Archives.)

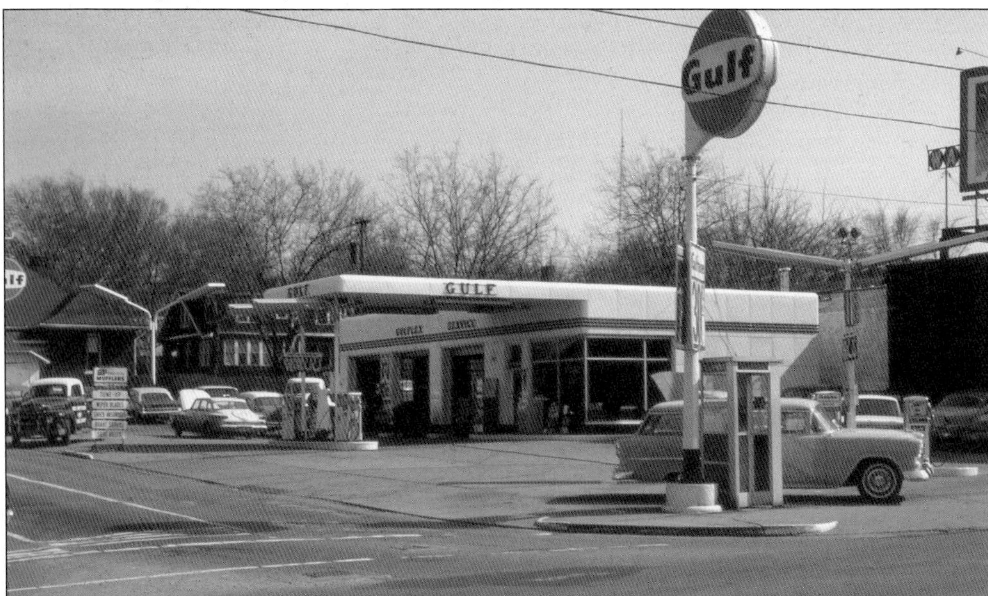

Hillsboro Village was home to Bob Smithson's Service Station from 1927 until 1993. Smithson purchased the station in 1964. Prior to being Bob Smithson's, it was a Standard Oil station. The customer service at this full-service station was impeccable. The station moved to a new location on Wedgewood Avenue close to Eight Avenue in 1993. American Gas, Waller Brothers Garage, and Western Auto were all located in Hillsboro Village to provide automobile maintenance. (Courtesy of Metro Archives.)

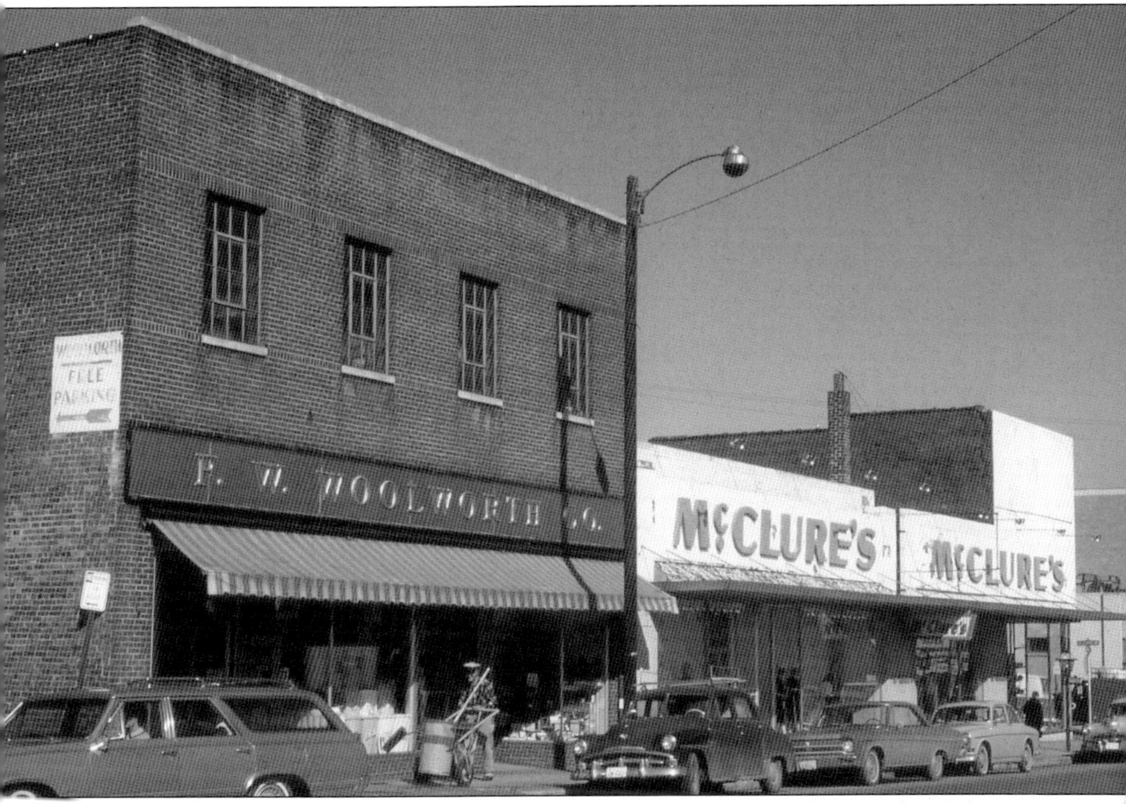

In 1936, Woolworth came to Hillsboro Village. The very first Woolworth opened in February 1879 and was located in Utica, New York, but it was not successful. A few months later, a second store opened in Lancaster, Pennsylvania, named Woolworth's Great Five Cent Store. In the early years, most of the merchandise in the store was sold for a nickel. Woolworth was created by brothers Frank and Charles Woolworth. Woolworth introduced another concept to the retail world: customers were able to pick and choose their own merchandise without the help of a store clerk. Prior to Woolworth, shoppers would hand their list to a store clerk, and the employee would gather the merchandise. Since the closing of Hillsboro Village's Woolworth in 1987, the building has been used for different dining establishments. (Courtesy of Metro Archives.)

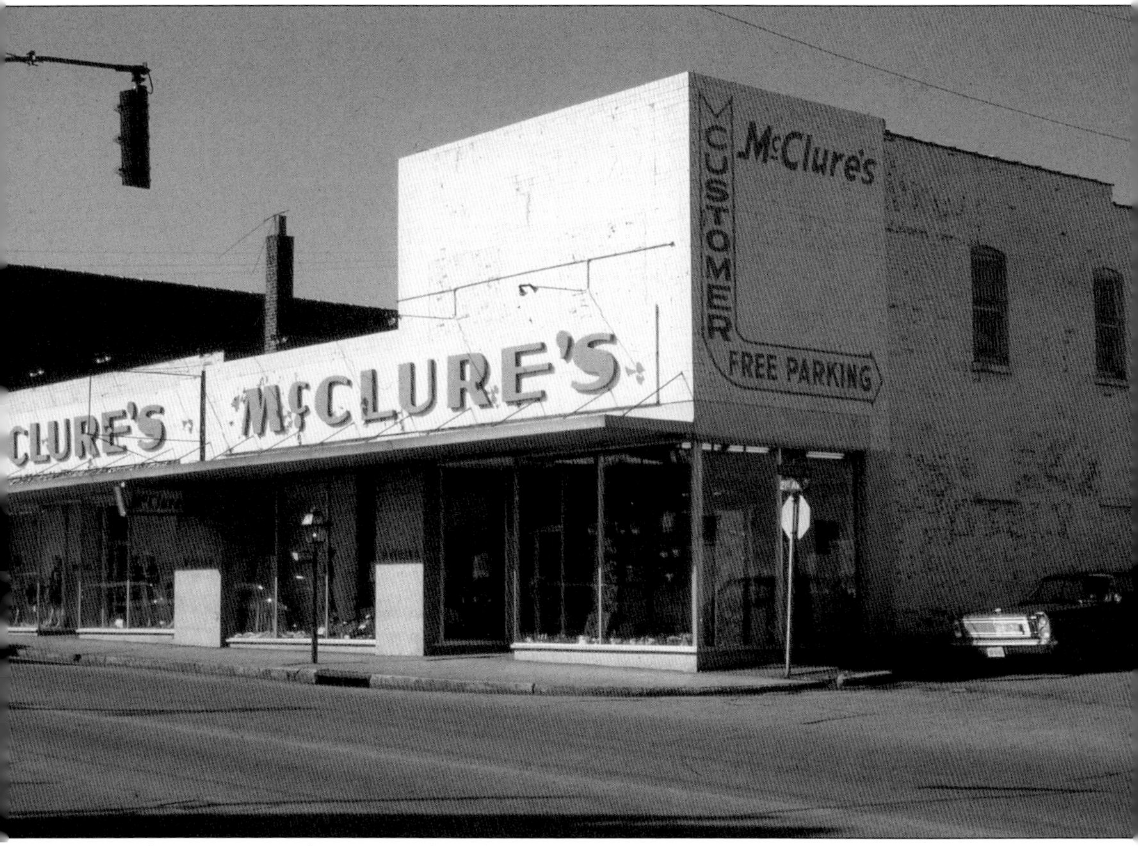

McClure's was next door to Woolworth at 1801 Twenty-First Avenue South in Hillsboro Village. The store opened in 1949, and it advertised itself as "Nashville's Largest Suburban Department Store." The store was a definite favorite with Nashvillians. McClure's was a local family-owned retail business started by Sam Harwell. The business was a spinoff of a wholesale dry goods business. McClure's was started as an outlet for Neely, Harwell, and Company. In the 1950s, Harwell's daughter's family was running McClure's. The number of stores had increased to four, including the one in Hillsboro Village. The three other locations were in Madison Square and Franklin, with a furniture store in Madison. In the next 20-plus years, two more McClure's opened, with one in Belle Meade and the other in Brentwood. The one in Belle Meade was larger than the four earlier stores. McClure's was always known for outstanding customer service. In the spring, the store would have live bunnies, and it was always a treat to go visit the rabbits. (Courtesy of Metro Archives.)

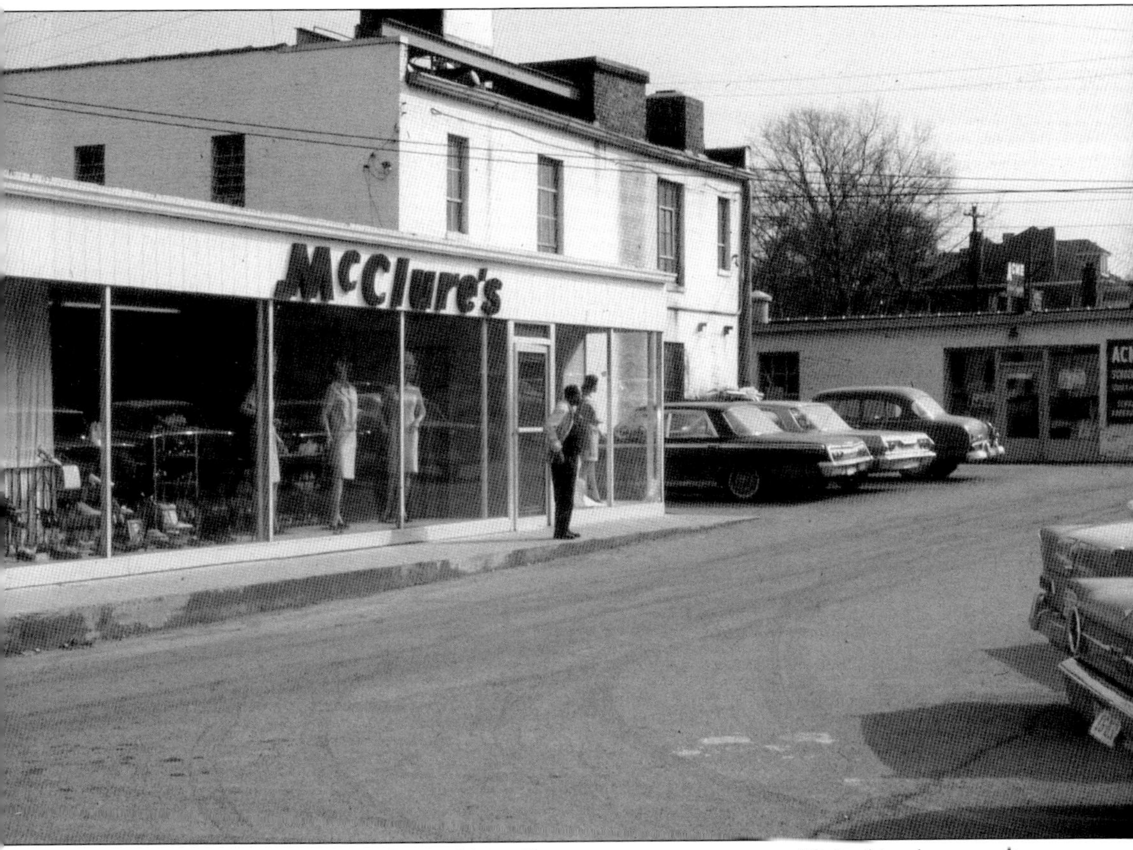

In the 1950s, brothers Owen and Harold Bradley were trying to get established in the recording business. They found property off Twenty-First Avenue South behind McClure's and the Woolworth store in Hillsboro Village. A historical marker is close to the site with the inscription "Owen and Harold Bradley operated a one-story, concrete block film and recording studio located behind this Hillsboro Village storefront from 1953–1955." "Queen of Country Music" Kitty Wells, bluegrass legends Bill Monroe and the Stanley Brothers, and popular vocalist Pat Boone—making his studio debut—were among the artists who recorded there. The structure later served as a school-supply store and a ceramics studio. The building was demolished in 2014. On the right-hand side of the photograph, a sign is visible for Acme School Supply. After leaving Hillsboro Village, the Bradley brothers started the first recording studio on Sixteenth Avenue South. To many, this was considered the birth of Music Row. (Courtesy of Metro Archives.)

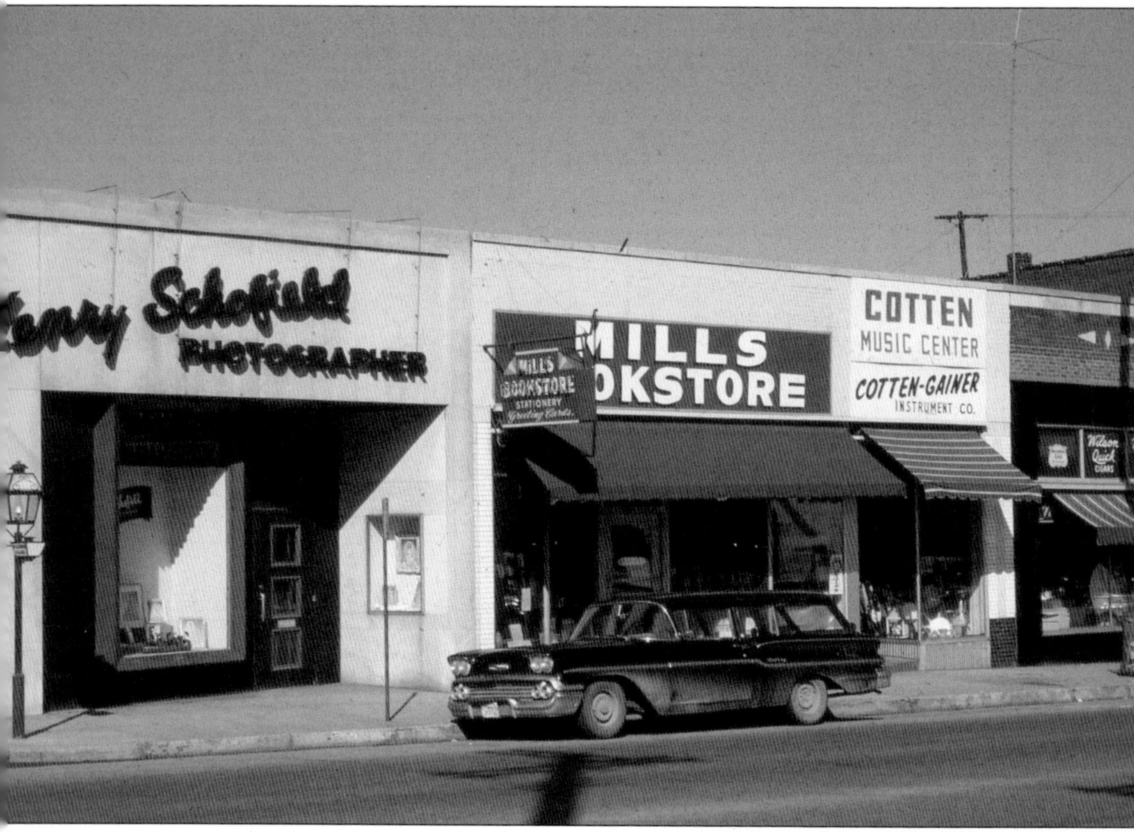

Hillsboro Village's Mills Bookstore was a good example of an old family business. In 1892, eighteen-year-old Reuben Mills opened Mills Bookstore in downtown Nashville. During the Depression, Mills started selling photography supplies and equipment in his bookstore. His wife started baking cookies to sell at the store. By 1928, the Millses' 12-year-old daughter Adelaide "Adele" started working with her dad in the bookstore. One day, while working in the bookstore, Adele met a soldier while he was browsing the collection of books. Bernie Schweid and Adele were married in 1943, and both worked at the bookstore together. In 1970, Mills, located on Church Street, closed and moved to Hillsboro Village. There were two additional Mills Bookstores in Nashville: one in Belle Meade Plaza Shopping Center and the other at 100 Oaks Shopping Center. The memory of the Millses and Schweids continues—Nashville's main library created a space named the Schweid/Mills Writer's Room. (Courtesy of Metro Archives.)

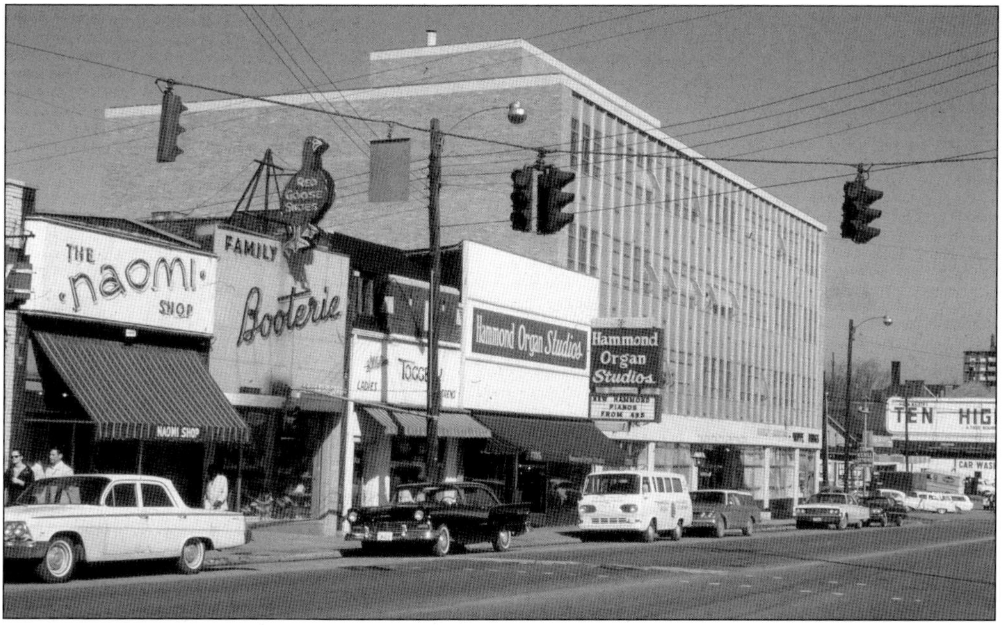

This was the second Family Booterie opened in Nashville; the first one was in the downtown area. Family Booterie was known for Red Goose Shoes. The jingle for Red Goose Shoes was "Half the fun of having feet is Red Goose Shoes." After purchase, the customer would pull down on the neck of a red plastic goose, and a golden egg would be the reward. Favorite shoe styles in the 1960s were leather penny loafers, saddle oxfords, moccasins, and go-go boots. Popular shoes for children were Buster Browns. An advertisement before Christmas one year offered skates for $15 a pair. Roller-skating was very popular during the 1950s and 1960s. A local skating rink, the Hippodrome, was a favorite with Nashvillians young and old. The Hippodrome was located on West End Avenue until 1968, when it was replaced by the Holiday Inn–Vanderbilt. (Courtesy of Metro Archives.)

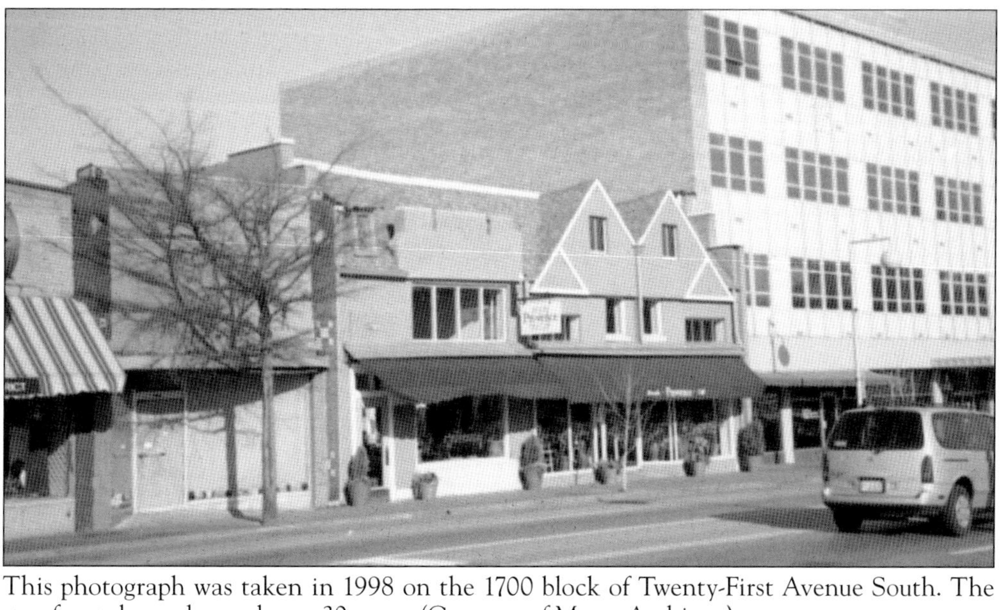

This photograph was taken in 1998 on the 1700 block of Twenty-First Avenue South. The storefronts have changed over 30 years. (Courtesy of Metro Archives.)

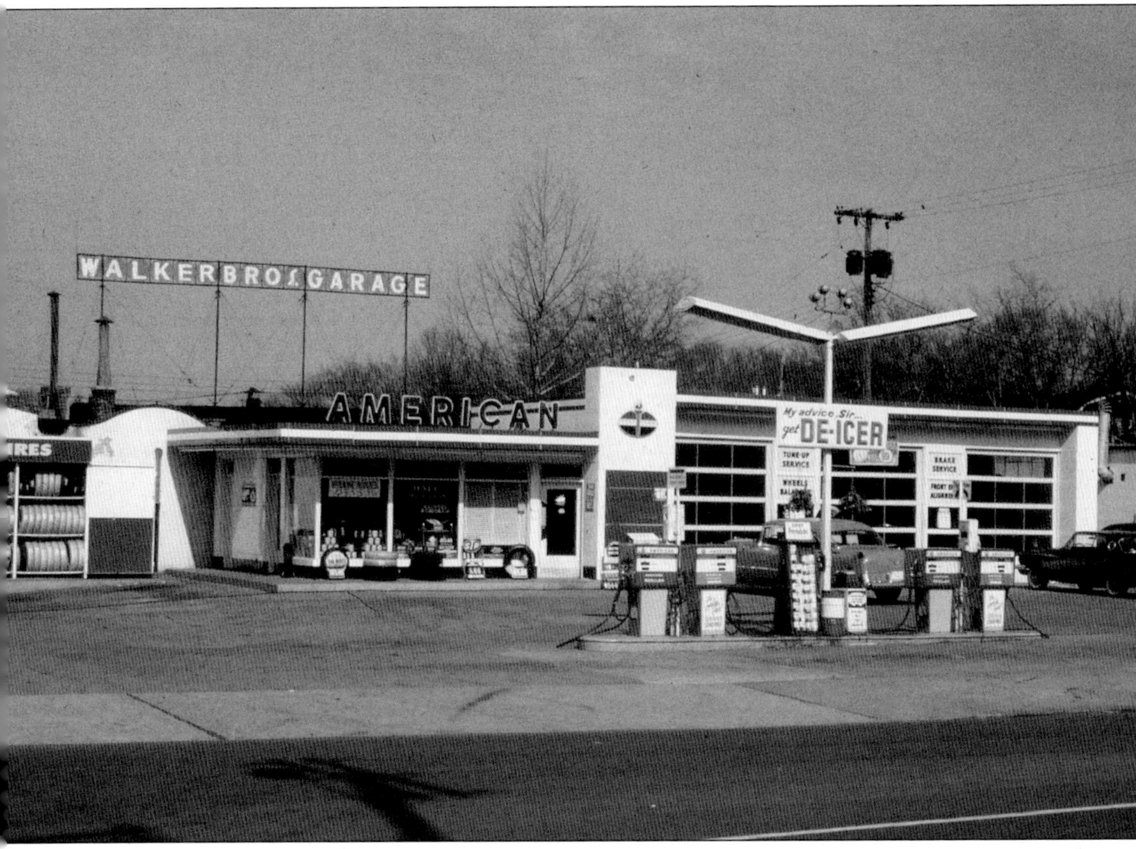

In the 1960s, a popular brand of gasoline was known as American. At the time of this photograph, this station was full-service. A gas station employee would approach the vehicle and put gas in the tank. The service station attendant would offer to clean the windows and check the air in the tires and the fluid levels under the hood. The price of gas was less than 50¢ a gallon. The building is still located on the corner of Acklen Avenue and Twenty-First Avenue South. Currently, the station, Hillsboro Village Auto Service, offers to service cars and trucks. It is very convenient for individuals who work near the village. In the early times of Hillsboro Village, residents close by could use a trolley to go downtown. In a few years, more families owned their own automobiles for transportation. The sign in the picture dates the station between 1961–1970. American eventually became Amoco. (Courtesy of Metro Archives.)

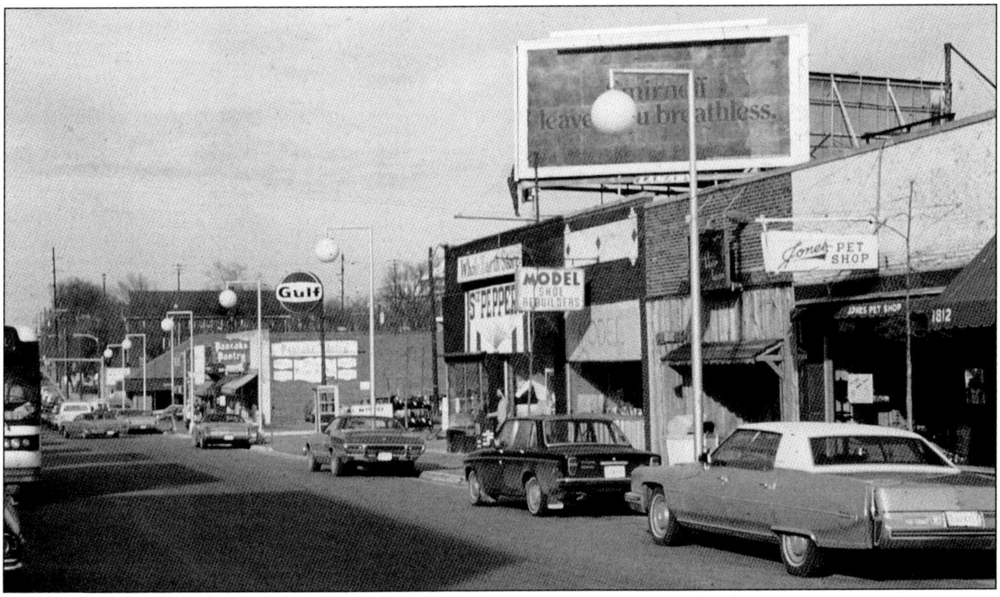

Sgt. Pepper's Whole Earth Store, named after the Beatles song, was a couple of doors away from Jones Pet Shop. In the early 1970s, Ringo Starr made several trips to Nashville to record an album. While sightseeing, his Nashville friend was driving through Hillsboro Village. Ringo spotted the Sgt. Pepper's sign and insisted on visiting the store. The store sold hip and trendy merchandise for the time, as well as tickets for upcoming concerts and vinyl records. The store owners filed for bankruptcy in 1977. (Courtesy of Metro Archives.)

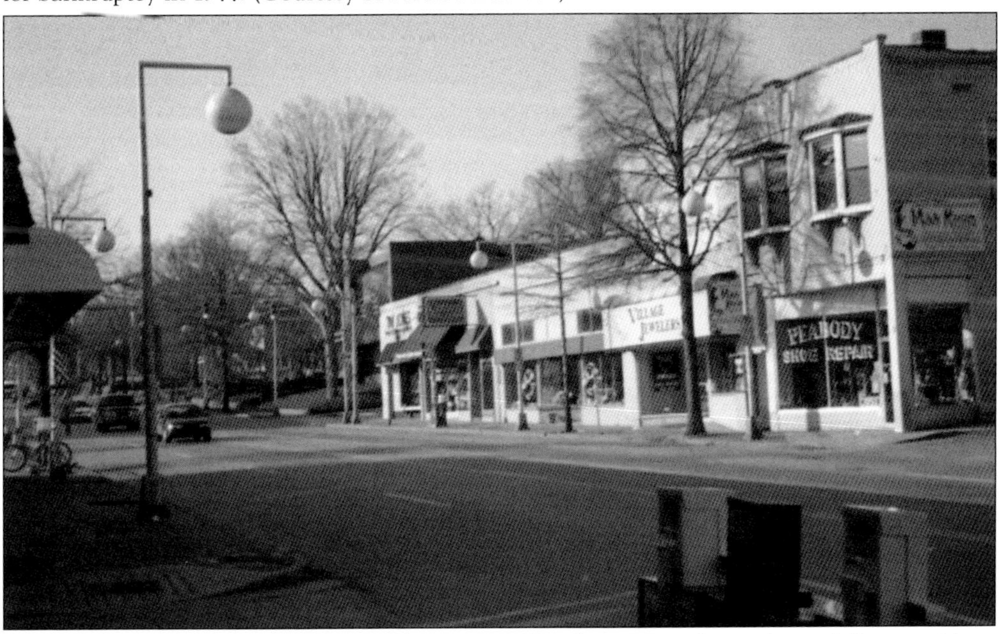

Village Jewelers came to Hillsboro Village in 1947 but has since relocated to a different address in the village. Around 1935, Peabody Shoe Repair came to Hillsboro Village. The exact date or original location of Peabody Shoe Repair is uncertain. The shoe repair service got its start in the basement of a building in the 1920s on Peabody's campus. Today, Peabody Shoe Repair is located near 100 Oaks Shopping Center. (Courtesy of Metro Archives.)

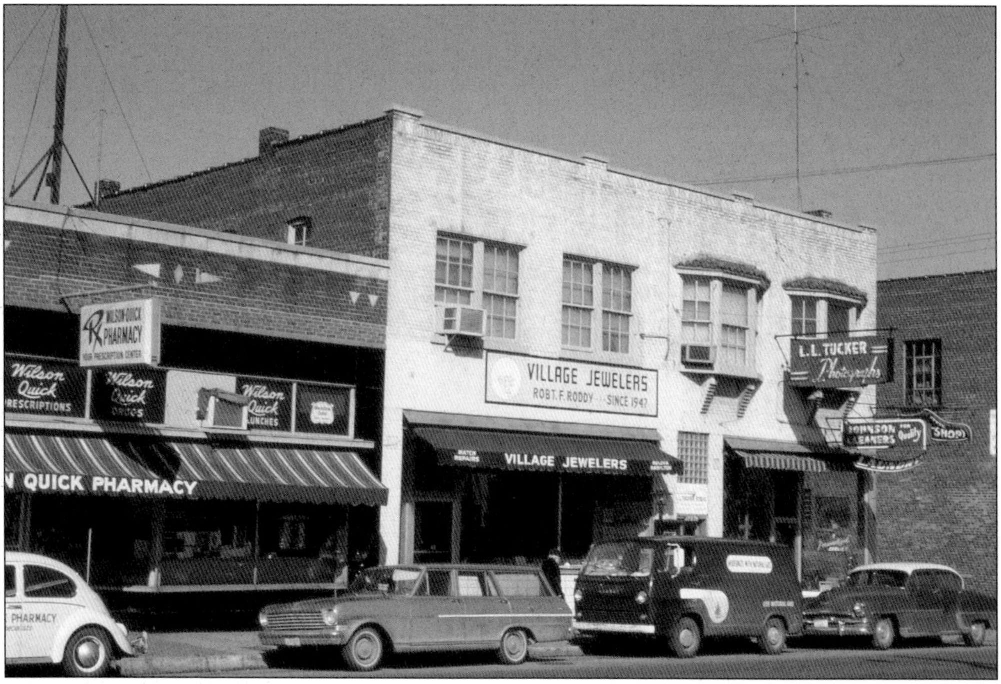

This photograph was taken a few years later and from a different angle. By 1988, the signs had changed, but Cotton Music, Peabody Shoe Repair, and the Village Jewelers were still in the village. (Courtesy of Metro Archives.)

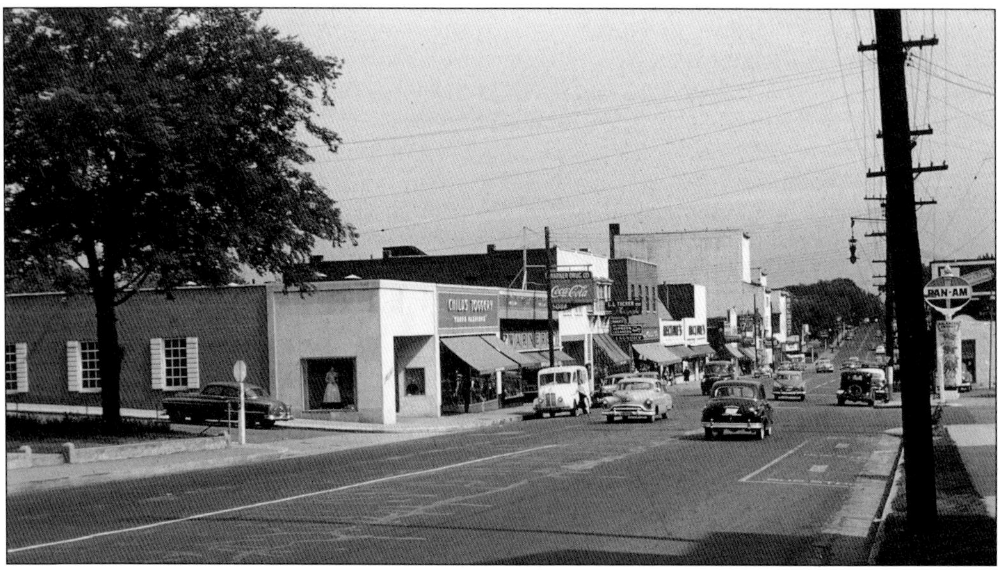

During the 1950s and 1960s, a shopper could get to Hillsboro Village riding the city bus. A day in the village could be a bite to eat at Browns, the Sweet Shop, or Pancake Pantry before going to one of the two theaters to watch a movie. A shopper could spend a few minutes browsing in a couple of the village's bookstores, Mills or Bookman. There was always McClure's or Woolworth. If a village visitor needed to have a shoe repaired, there was Peabody's Shoe Repair. The shopper could leave their vehicle to be repaired at Smithson's or the Pan Am. If the shopper was needing tires or a bike, Western Auto would be a good choice. (Courtesy of Metro Archives.)

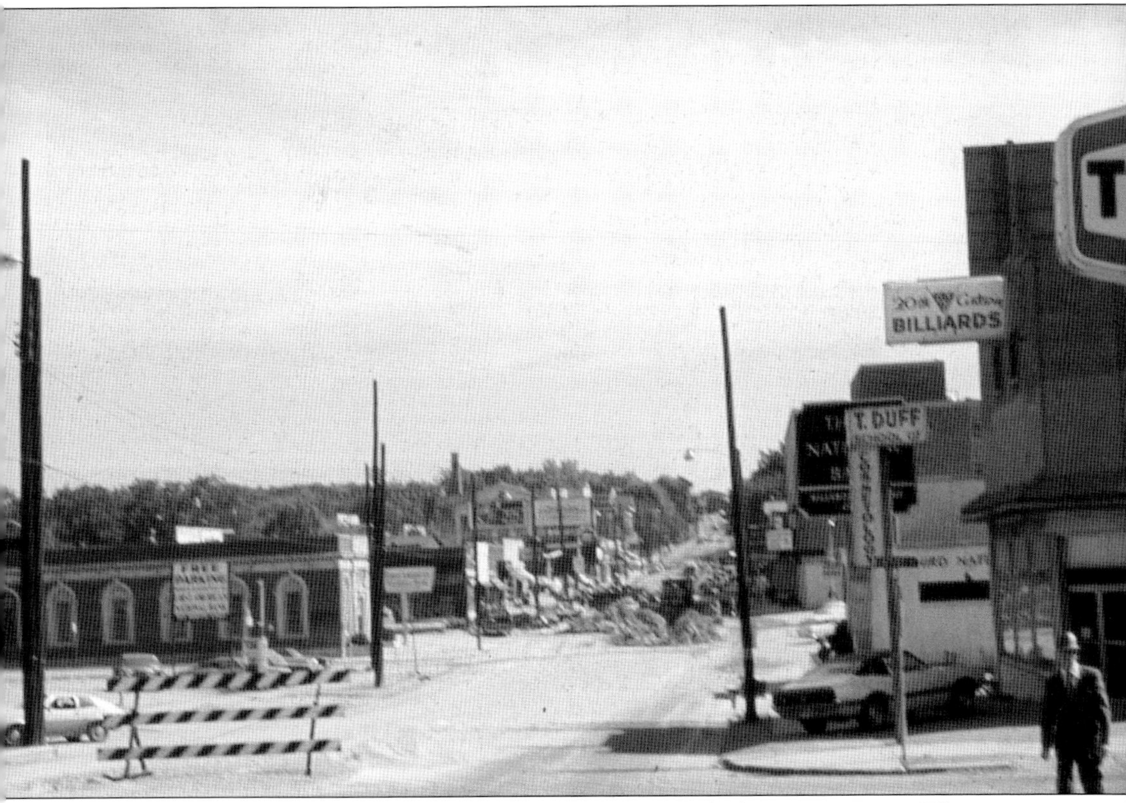

A trip to Hillsboro Village in the late 1960s or 1970s was a good afternoon getaway. There was First American Bank or Third National Bank to get some cash. Hillsboro Village always had a record store or two, and there was a nice jewelry store. Jones Pet Shop was always a must-stop, as the aquariums at the pet shop were amazing and could have a calming effect on a weary shopper. A Baskin Robbins was a couple of doors away from the pet shop, and across the street, one could drop by the Villager Tavern for a quick dart game. A well-known family business in Hillsboro Village was Davis Cookware and Cutlery. The Davis family store was in Hillsboro Village for over 50 years. At one time, the village always had a couple of drugstores. (Courtesy of Metro Archives.)

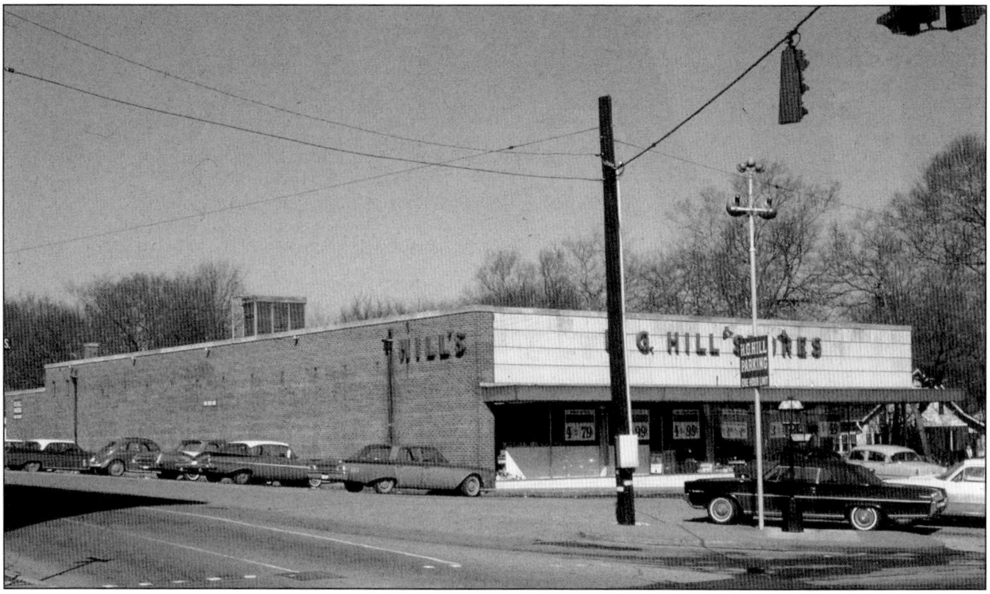

Since 1920, Hillsboro Village has had several H.G. Hills Food Stores. This one was at the northwest corner of Blakemore Avenue and Twenty-First Avenue South. This was the last location of H.G. Hills Food Store in Hillsboro Village. All the H.G. Hills stores were located on the right going away from the city. Hills Realty owns quite a bit of property in Hillsboro Village. Vanderbilt acquired the property where this H.G. Hills was located. (Courtesy of Metro Archives.)

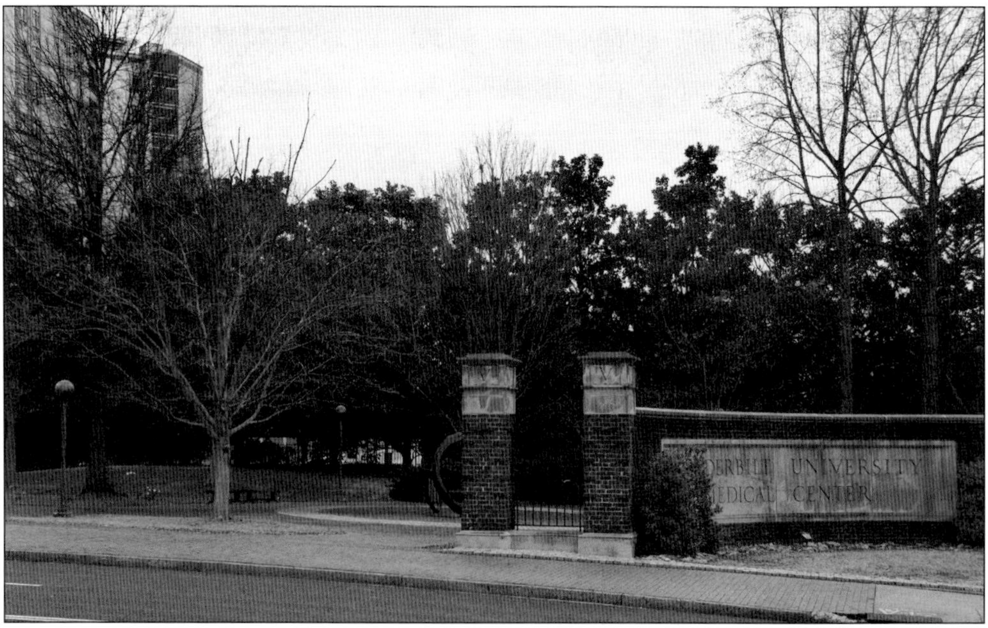

Vanderbilt decided to create a small park setting named Medical Gateway Park. The minipark provided patients' families a break from the sterile four walls of a hospital. Medical Gateway Park has park benches, a brick walkway, and several trees. People working or at the hospital can also benefit from the minipark. (Courtesy of Metro Archives.)

Two

A Fire Hall, Pie Wagon, and Tollgate

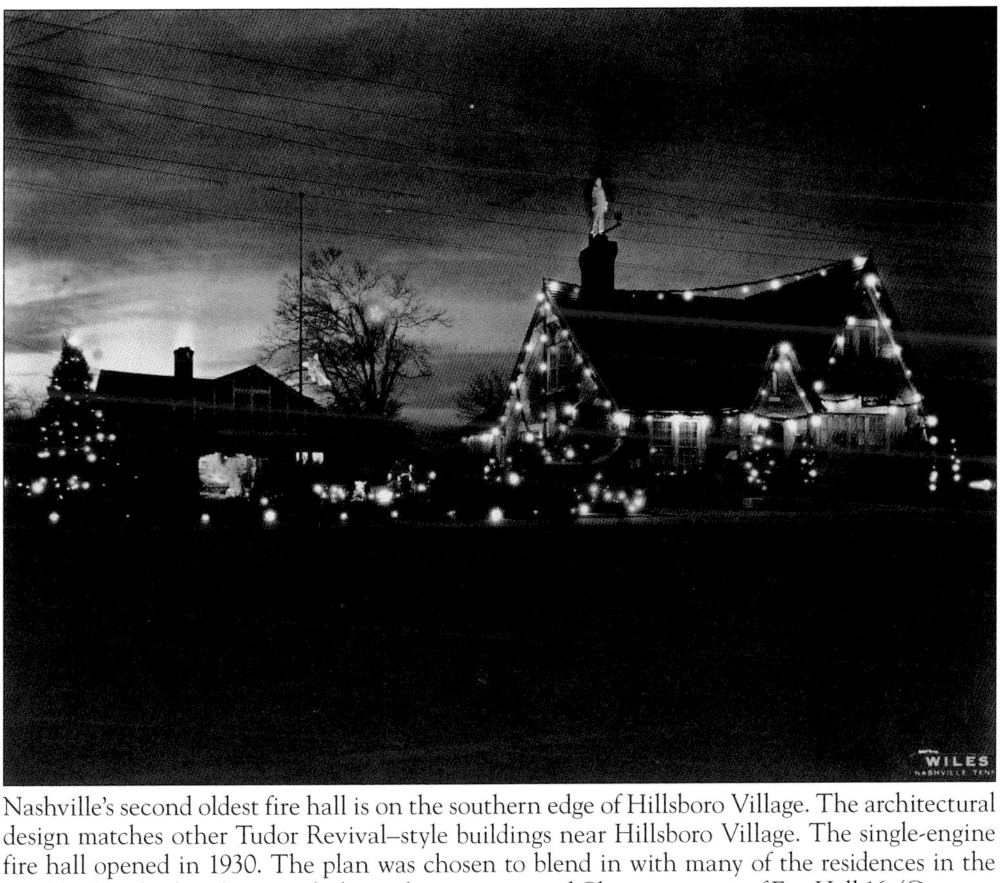

Nashville's second oldest fire hall is on the southern edge of Hillsboro Village. The architectural design matches other Tudor Revival–style buildings near Hillsboro Village. The single-engine fire hall opened in 1930. The plan was chosen to blend in with many of the residences in the neighborhood. This photograph shows the creativity and Christmas spirit of Fire Hall 16. (Courtesy of Metro Archives.)

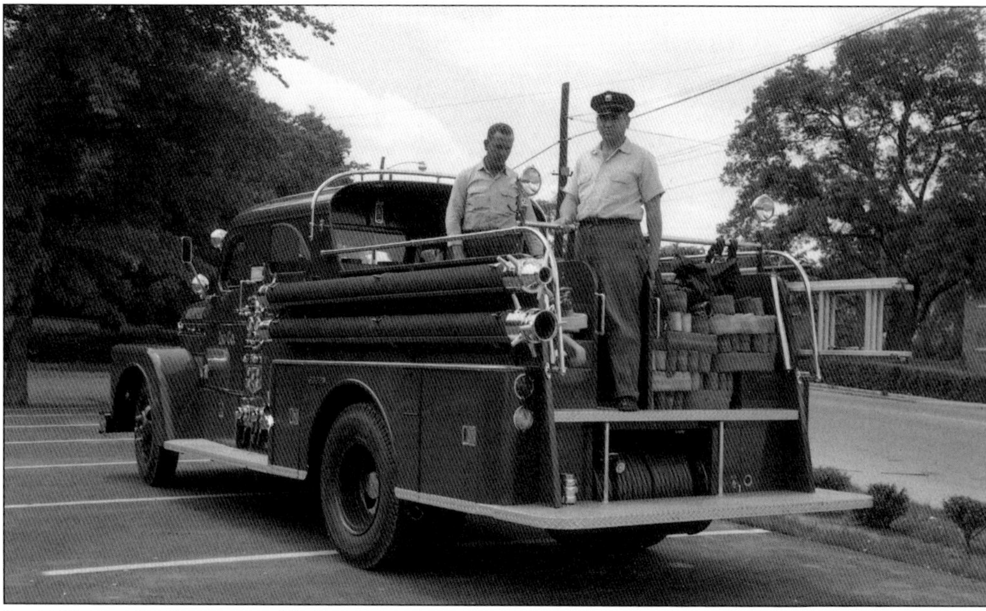

In 1993, Fire Hall 16 was added to the National Register of Historic Places. In 1990, a plaque was placed in the fire hall. The building was renamed in honor of Chief Frank Joseph Quinn, who had 44 years of service with the fire department. In 1930, he thought he was going to follow in his father's footsteps and become a cop, but he decided to fight fires instead. He worked his way through the ranks as lieutenant, captain, district chief, and eventually chief. During his career, he fought many fires. Two of the major fires he fought were at a Nashville Hardwood Co. in 1951 and the original Maxwell House fire in 1961. In his lifetime as a fireman, he experienced several close calls. One time, he was fighting a fire and a house collapsed on him. He spent six months in a cast up to his hips. At a fire at Steiner Lift, he fell into a deep hole of water, and the other firemen saved him from drowning. (Courtesy of Metro Archives.)

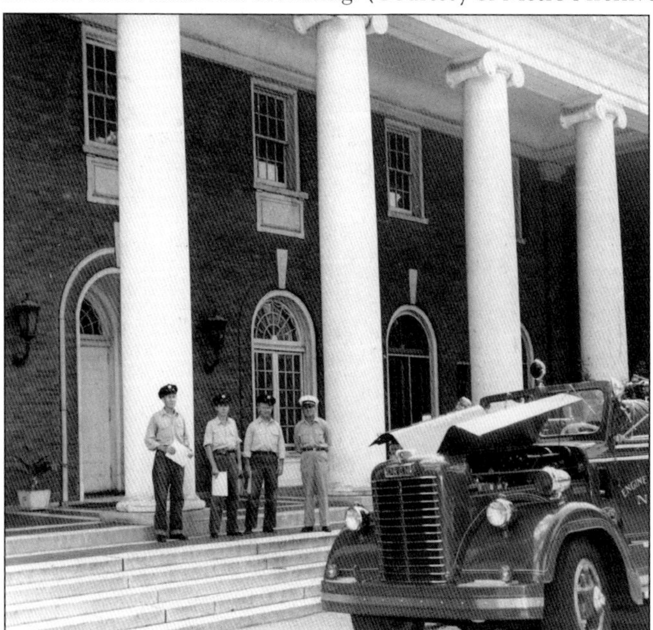

Fire Hall 16 is at Belmont College in 1956. The firemen are participating in Fire Prevention Week, when firemen would travel around to different schools or offices and make people aware of why fire prevention was so important. (Courtesy of Metro Archives.)

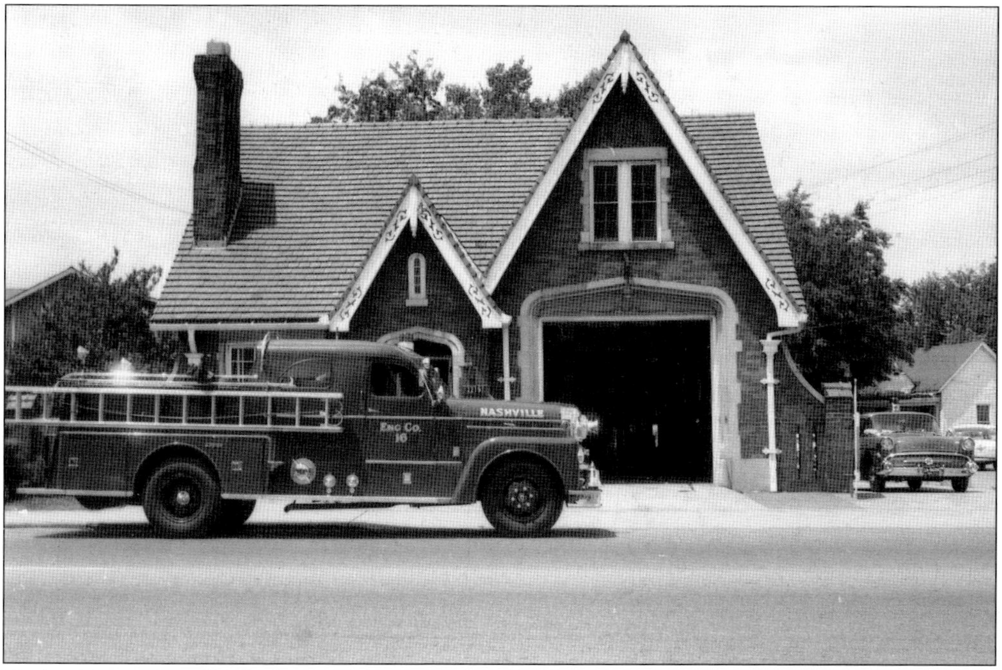

Nashville's earliest fire halls started on a volunteer basis in May 1807. In July 1860, firefighting became a paid service. The first fire chief in Nashville was John Dashiell. Until 1912, there was no motorized firefighting equipment. All vehicles were horse or mule driven. Many of the animals were trained that when an alarm sounded, they would go to a stall and step into the harness, waiting on the firemen. (Courtesy of Metro Archives.)

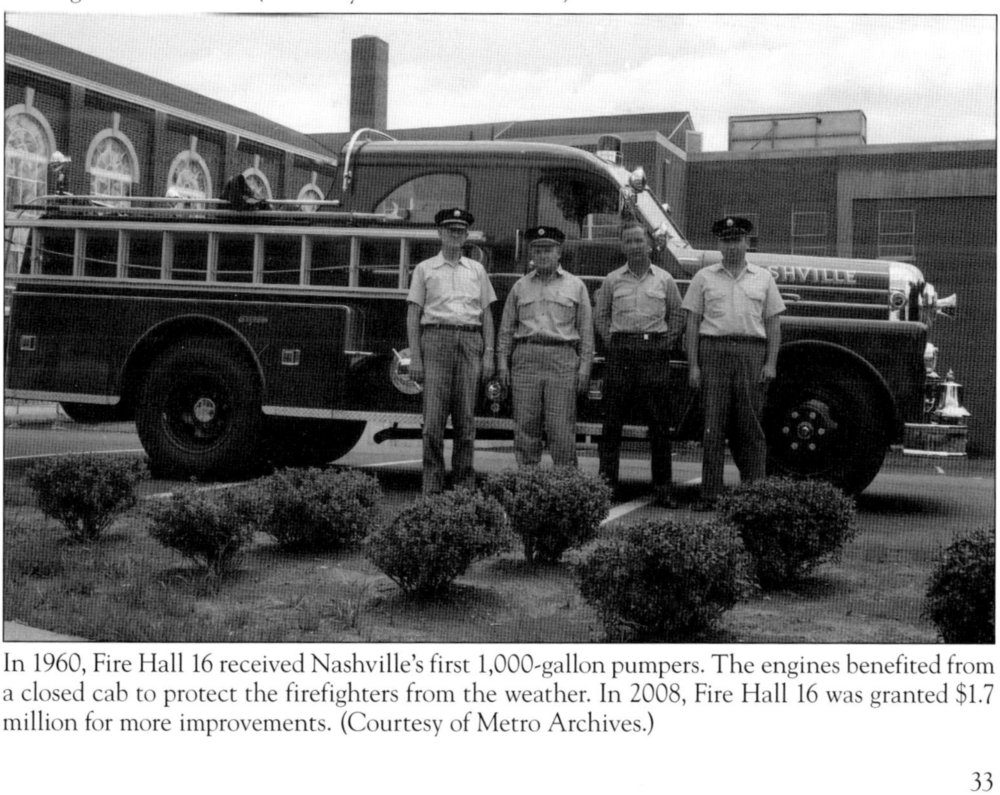

In 1960, Fire Hall 16 received Nashville's first 1,000-gallon pumpers. The engines benefited from a closed cab to protect the firefighters from the weather. In 2008, Fire Hall 16 was granted $1.7 million for more improvements. (Courtesy of Metro Archives.)

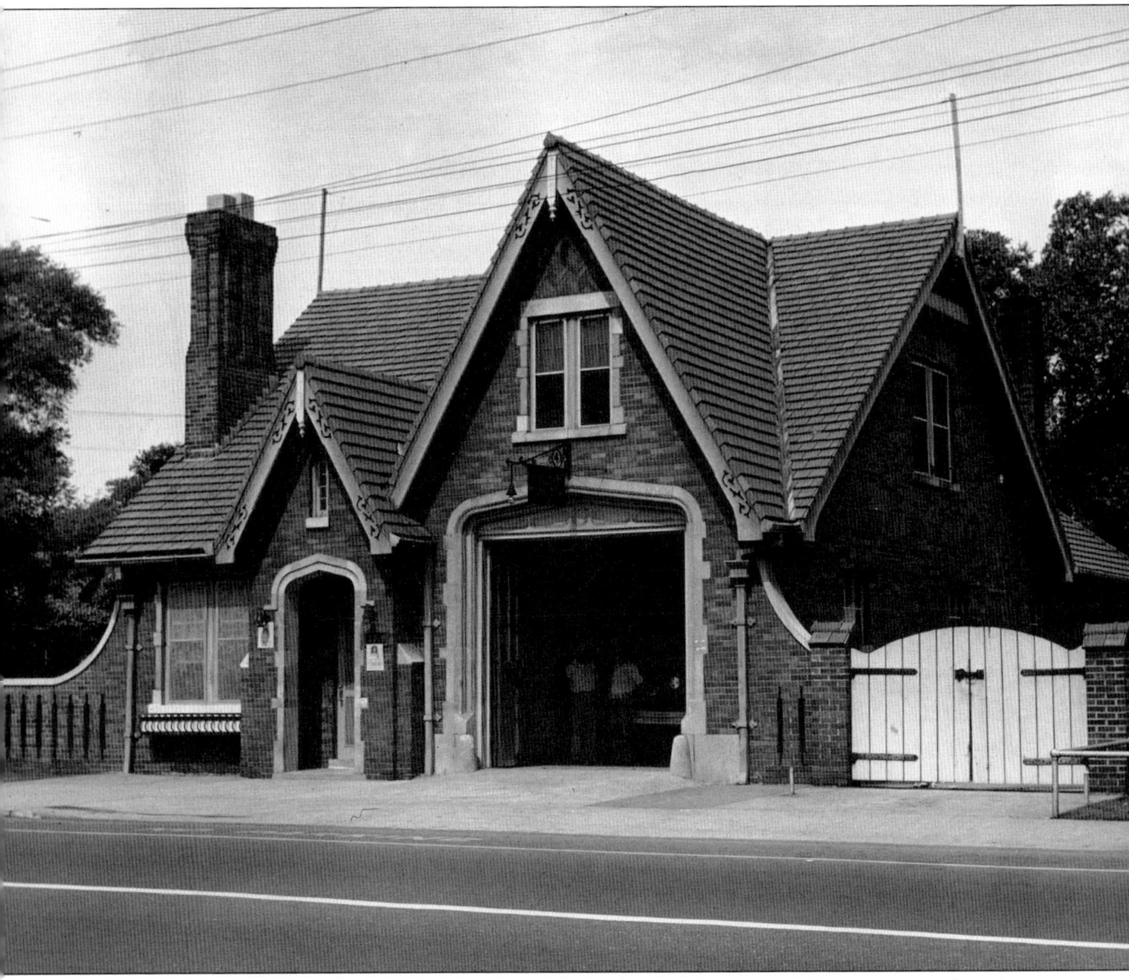

City directories indicate that this spot on Twenty-First Avenue South was once a lunch wagon. Garrett's Lunch Wagon was owned and operated by William Garrett until around 1930. Several grocery stores have been neighbors to the fire hall. A&P, Foodland, Harris Teeter, and Kroger's have been on the corner of Twenty-First Avenue South and Blair Boulevard. A dry cleaner and a pharmacy were also located close to the fire hall. Across Twenty-First Avenue South from the fire hall and Brown's Diner is "Kinnard's Corner." The large office building opened in 1982 with 55,000 square feet. Three months after opening, all but 1,400 square feet was rented. Before the opening of the five-story building, this address was home to Kinnard's Restaurant. In 1939, a 30-seat eatery known as the Tumble Inn was located at this address. By the early 1950s, plans were a family named Kinnard would be taking ownership. Over the years, the building saw 26 additions and grew to accommodate 250 customers. The family-owned eatery was closed in 1981. (Courtesy of Metro Archives.)

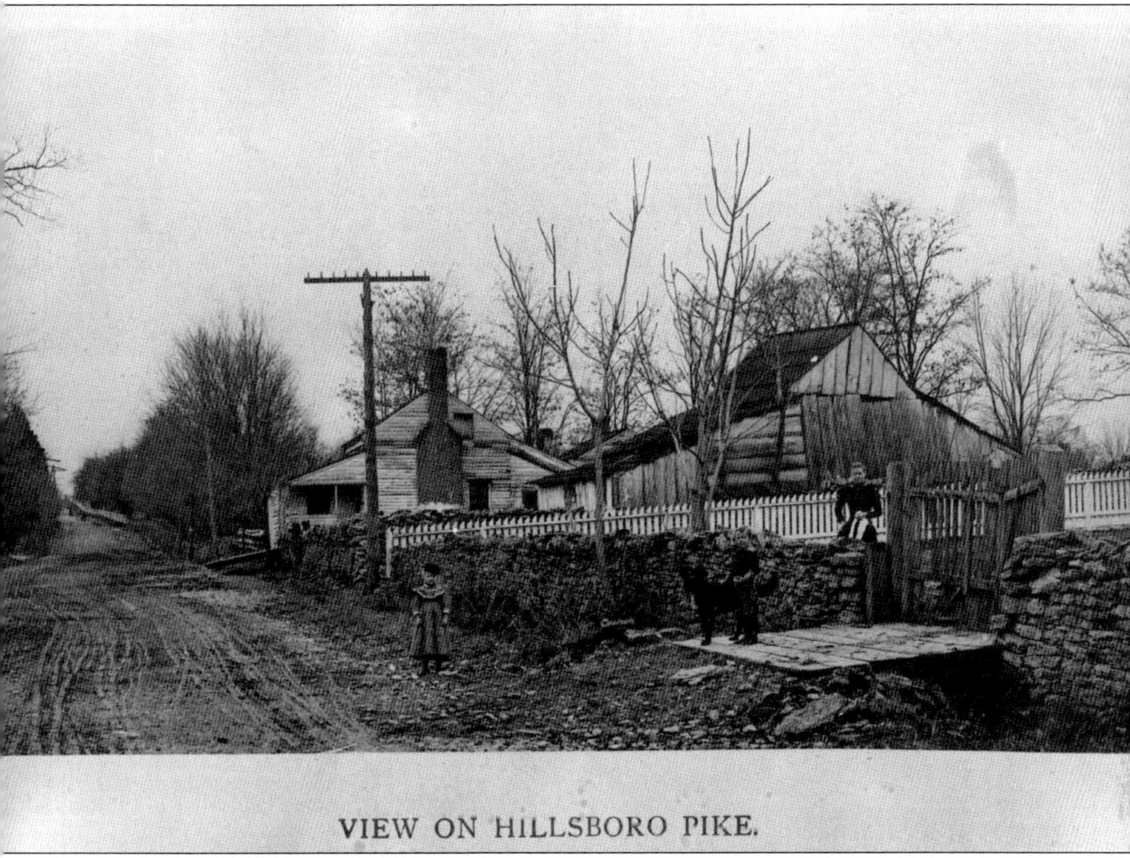

A few years before the fire hall was a fixture on Twenty-First Avenue South or Hillsboro Pike, the site was a toll gate. The name "Hillsboro" was from a rural village in Williamson County, and the rural community became known as Leiper's Fork. According to the historical marker, when farmers bought livestock to Nashville from rural Williamson County, the tolls could not exceed 3¢ for a horse or mule, 20¢ for 10 sheep, 25¢ for 20 meat cattle, and 25¢ for a carriage drawn by a pair of horses or mules. Tolls were taken every five miles, and the toll gate was in operation from 1848 until 1903. A map indicates an earlier toll gate on Twenty-First Avenue South operating close to Acklen Avenue. This toll gate near Blair Boulevard was the last known toll gate in Davidson County to be closed. (Courtesy of Tennessee State Library & Archives.)

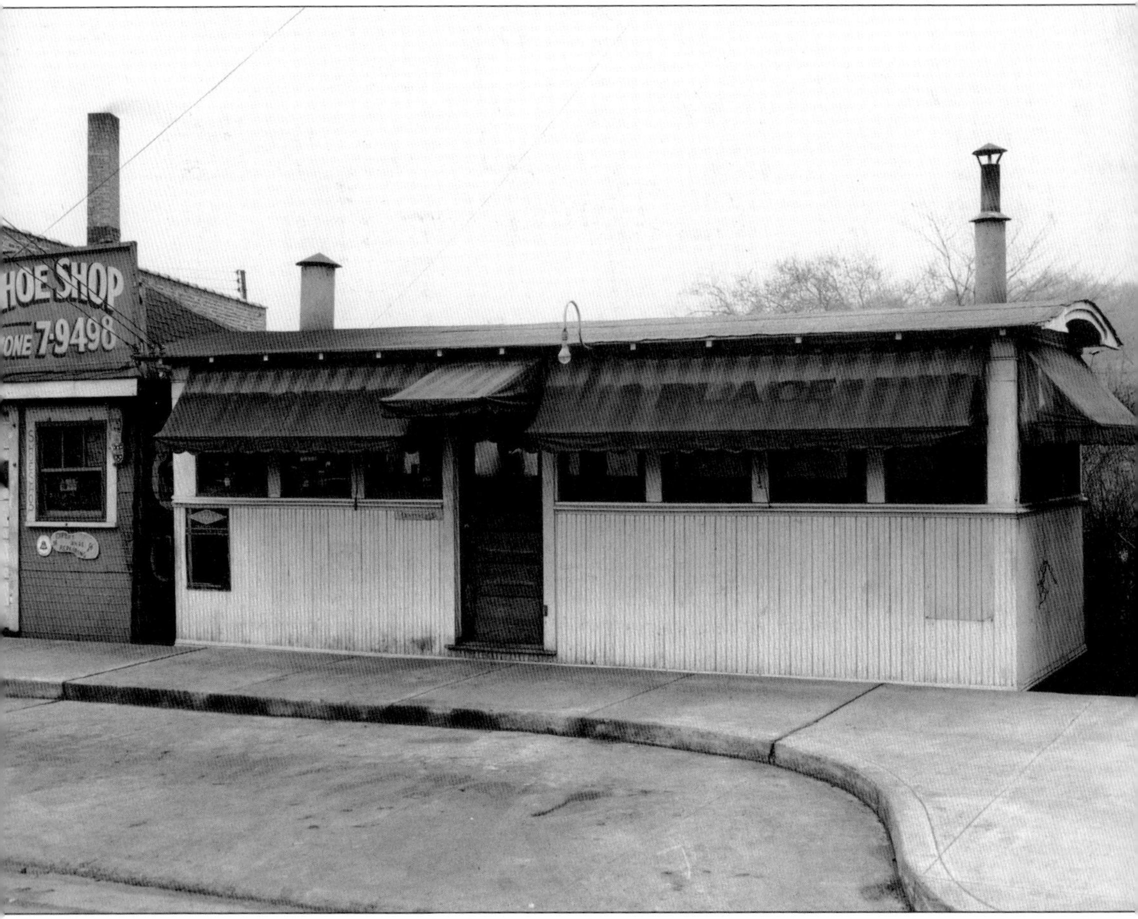

Charles Brown came to Hillsboro to open a pie wagon in 1927. Pie wagons were created from old mule-drawn trolleys and considered mobile. After a few years, an owner could often establish a permanent location. At first, Brown's Diner was on the east side of Twenty-First Avenue South and Blair Boulevard. In 1935, Brown's Diner moved across Twenty-First Avenue South to the current location. Originally, Brown's Diner was two trolley cars connected together, with the wheels still attached. One set of wheels was made of steel and oak. In the beginning, space at Brown's was limited to six booths. There were four booths in one trolley and two booths plus the bar in the other car. In 1986, the restaurant was expanded, and Brown's could seat up to 75 people. The location of Brown's Diner on Twenty-First Avenue South was once the last stop on one of the two streetcar lines on Hillsboro Pike. Brown's is probably best known for its delicious burgers. (Courtesy of Nashville Public Library Special Collections.)

Three

Two Theaters and a Dragon

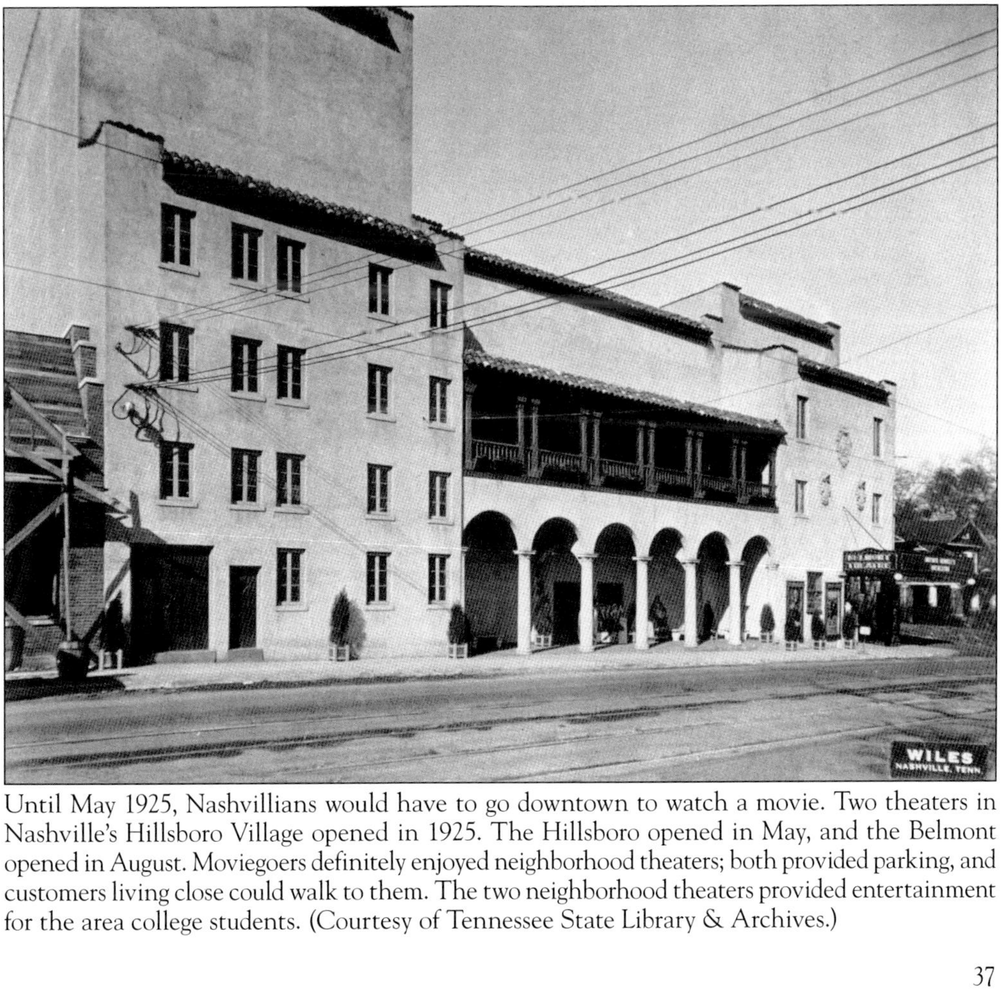

Until May 1925, Nashvillians would have to go downtown to watch a movie. Two theaters in Nashville's Hillsboro Village opened in 1925. The Hillsboro opened in May, and the Belmont opened in August. Moviegoers definitely enjoyed neighborhood theaters; both provided parking, and customers living close could walk to them. The two neighborhood theaters provided entertainment for the area college students. (Courtesy of Tennessee State Library & Archives.)

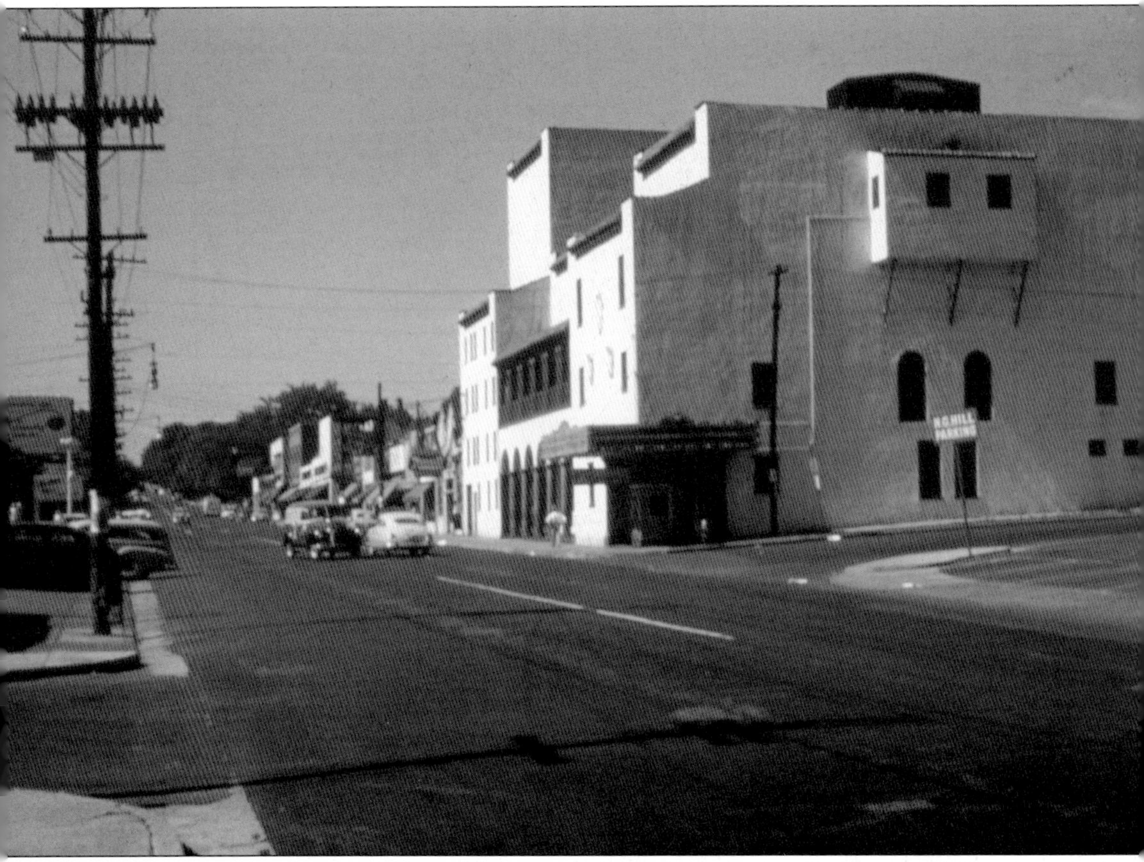

On August 25, 1925, the Belmont Theatre on Twenty-First Avenue South opened. Residents and students in the area had two theaters to choose from for entertainment. The theater had a parking lot that could accommodate 70 cars. Tony Sudekum was the mastermind behind the new motion picture theater. He was also the founder of Crescent Amusements. The Belmont was built on the site where the Blakemore family lived. Brothers Tony and Harry Sudekum were partners in Crescent Amusements. Crescent owned movie theaters all over the South. The Belmont Theatre was Crescent's 45th theater in three states and 15 cities. (Courtesy of Metro Archives.)

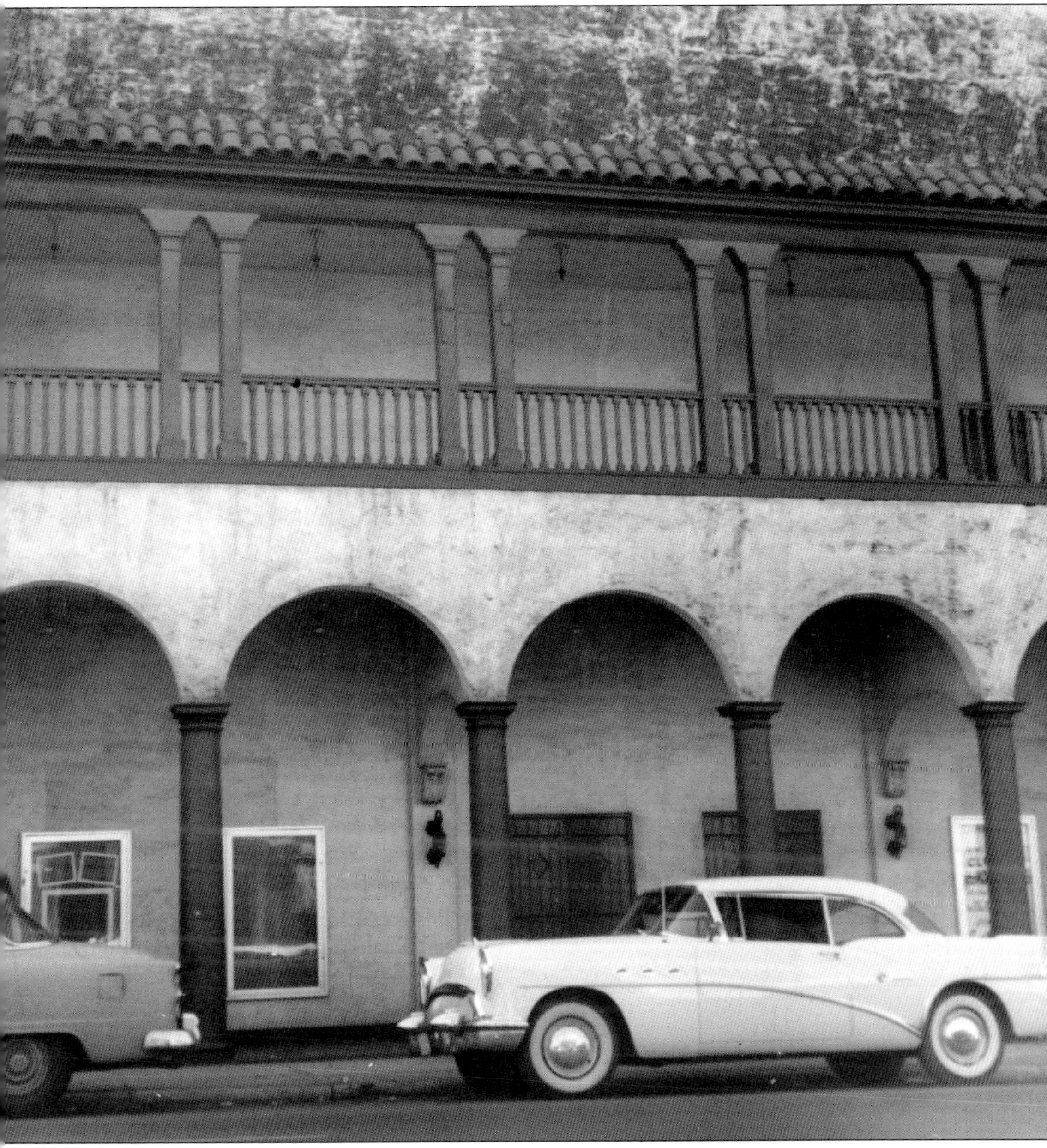

The design of the Belmont Theatre came to Tony Sudekum while on a Florida vacation with his family. He made a rough design of the theater in the sand. When Sudekum returned to Nashville, he consulted with architects Marr and Holman. The theater was of Spanish design, and the exterior was covered with stucco, an ode to Spanish Mission style and resembling the Alamo. (Courtesy of Tennessee State Library & Archives.)

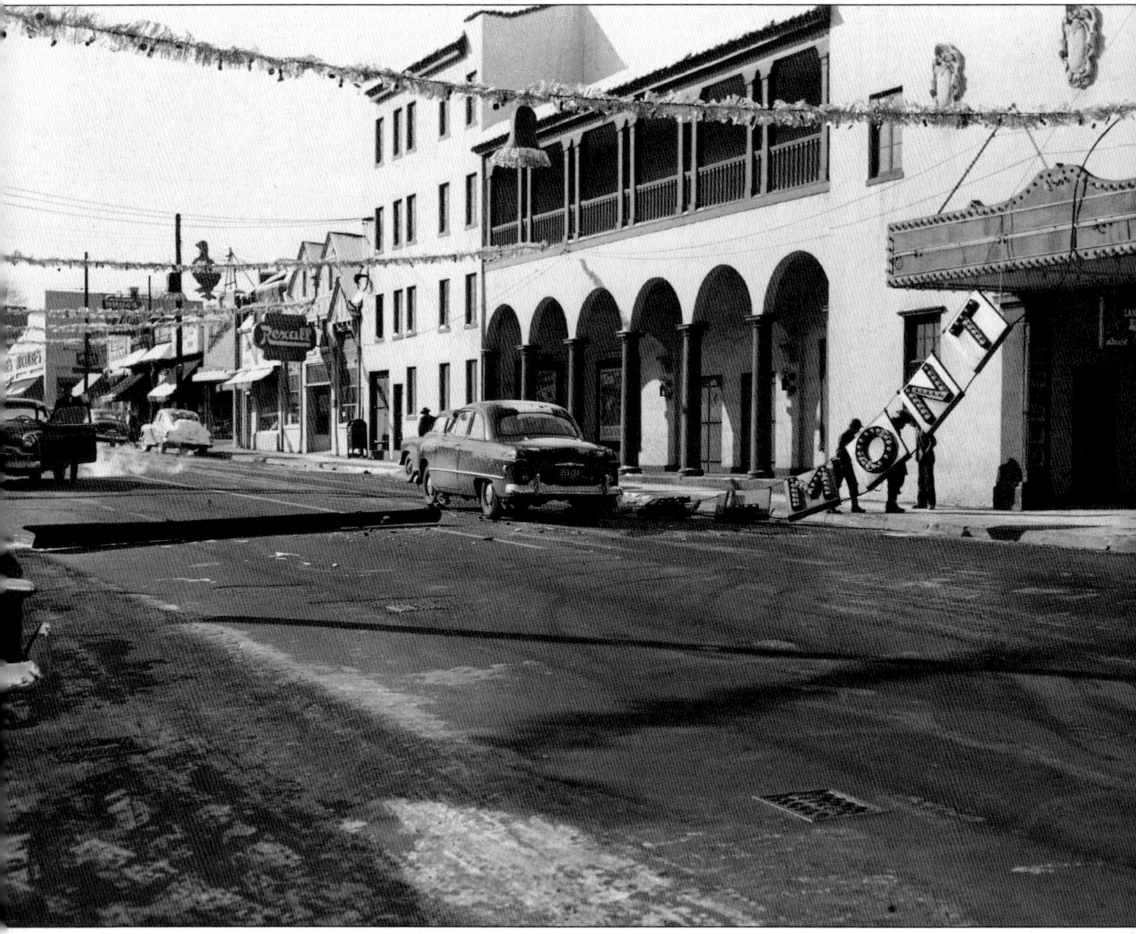

The outside of the building had a balcony that ran almost the length of the front of the building. A black-iron rail ran along the balcony. Inside the building off the balcony was a mezzanine with clubrooms. The same design team later designed the Belle Meade Theater on Harding Pike. The Belle Meade was more of a modern theme. (Courtesy of Metro Archives.)

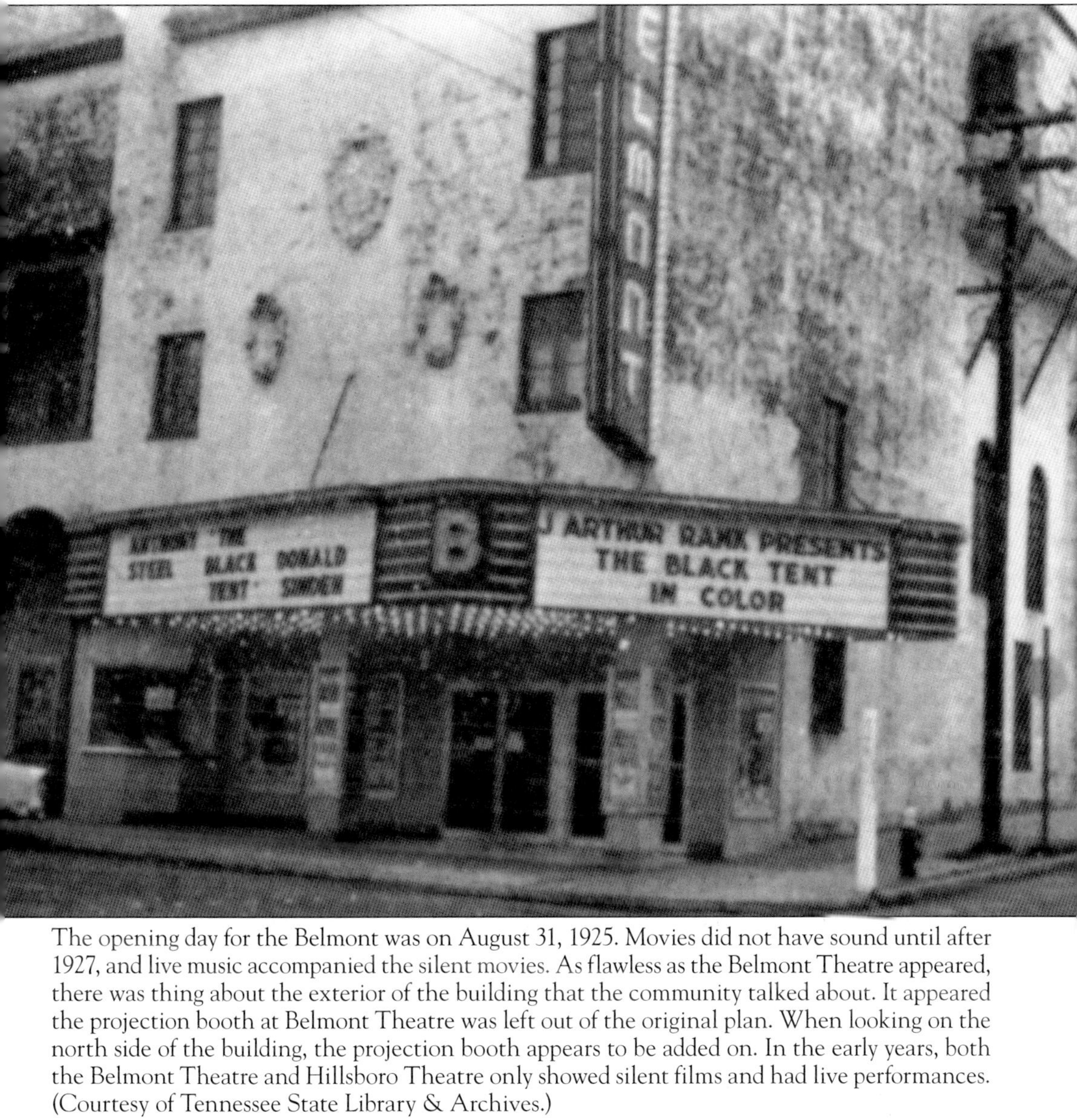

The opening day for the Belmont was on August 31, 1925. Movies did not have sound until after 1927, and live music accompanied the silent movies. As flawless as the Belmont Theatre appeared, there was thing about the exterior of the building that the community talked about. It appeared the projection booth at Belmont Theatre was left out of the original plan. When looking on the north side of the building, the projection booth appears to be added on. In the early years, both the Belmont Theatre and Hillsboro Theatre only showed silent films and had live performances. (Courtesy of Tennessee State Library & Archives.)

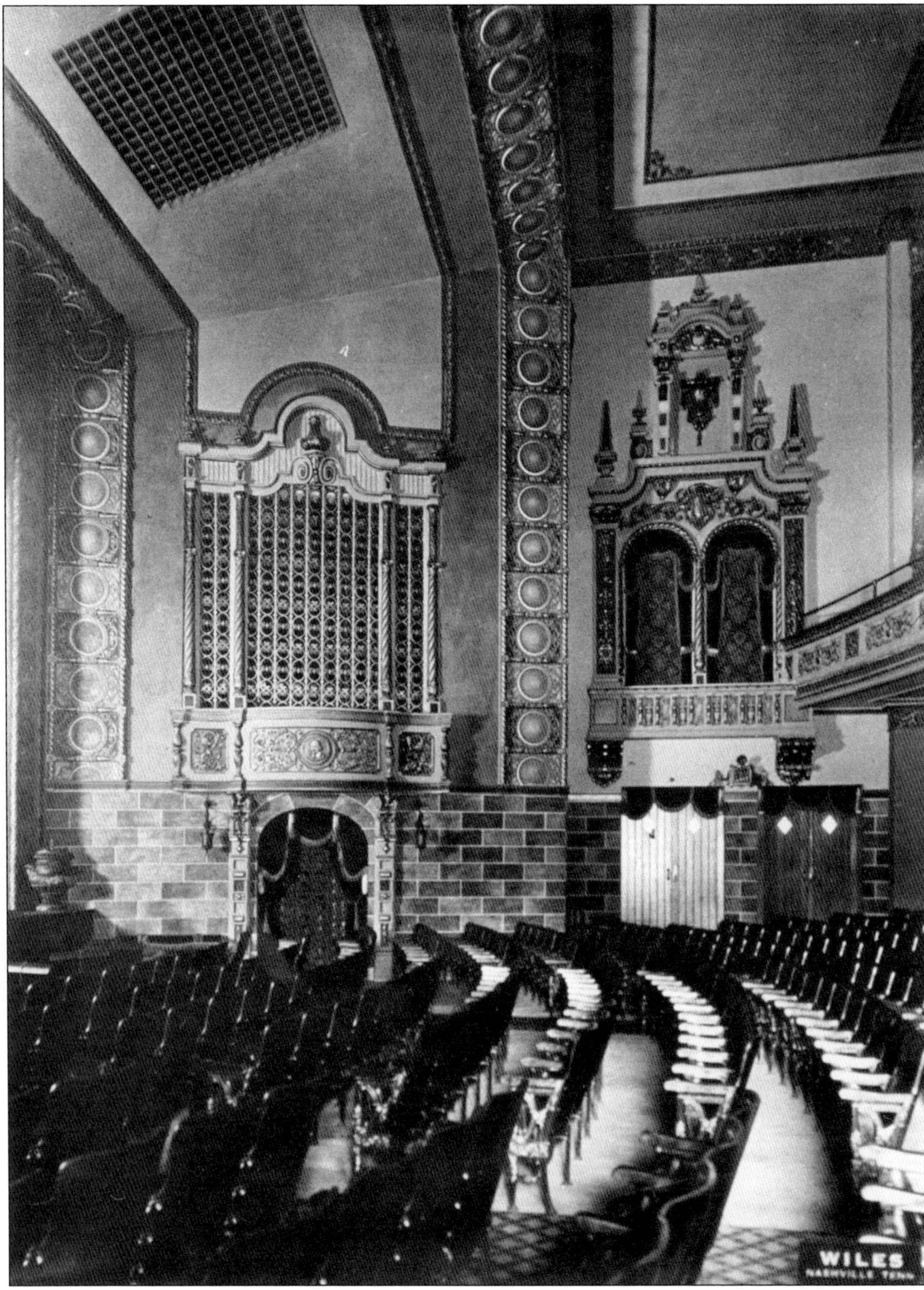

To continue with the Spanish theme, an advertisement was placed in Nashville newspapers. The Belmont was looking for young women with brown eyes, dark-brown hair, and darker skin tones to work as usherettes. (Courtesy of Tennessee State Library & Archives.)

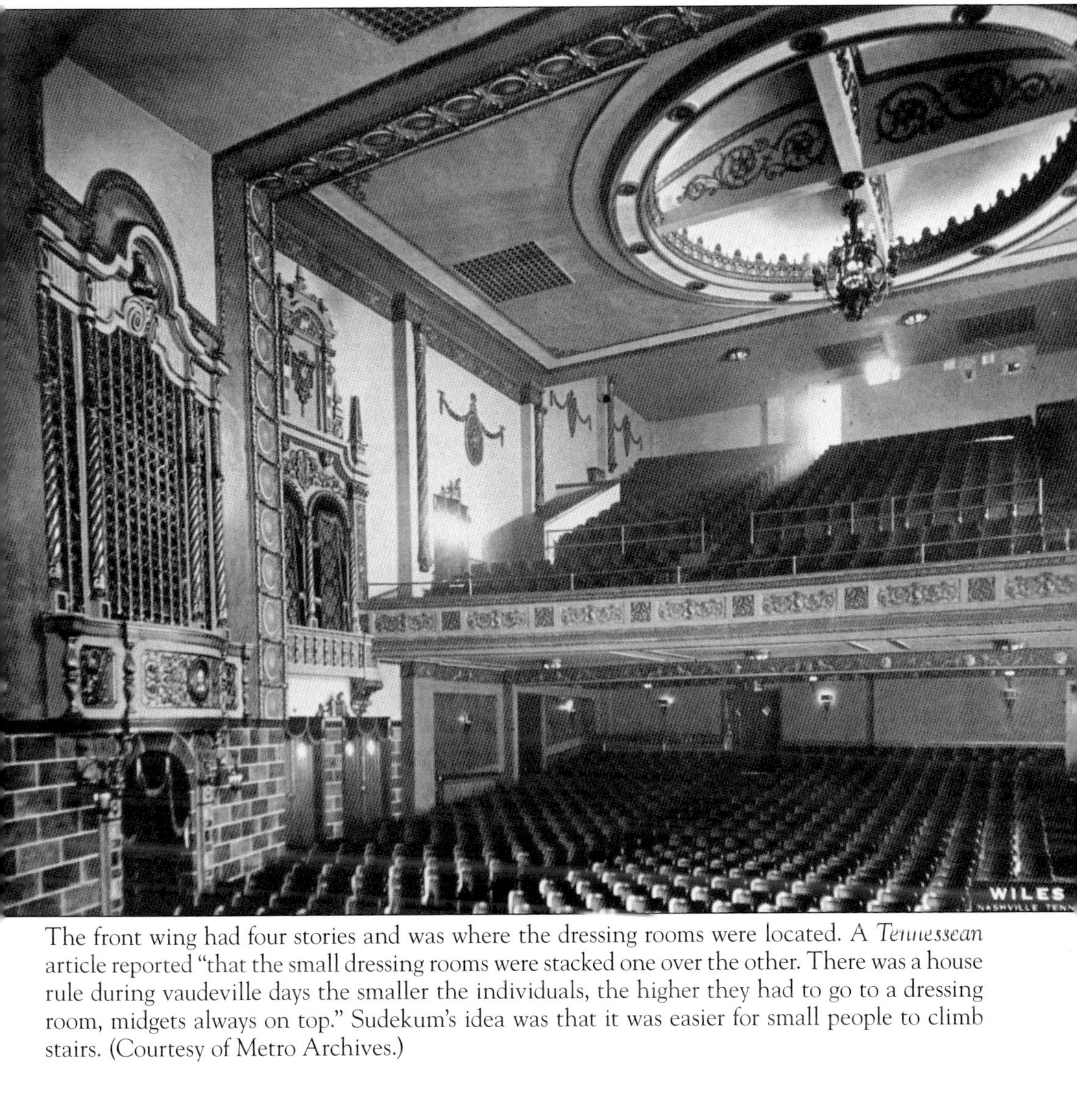

The front wing had four stories and was where the dressing rooms were located. A *Tennessean* article reported "that the small dressing rooms were stacked one over the other. There was a house rule during vaudeville days the smaller the individuals, the higher they had to go to a dressing room, midgets always on top." Sudekum's idea was that it was easier for small people to climb stairs. (Courtesy of Metro Archives.)

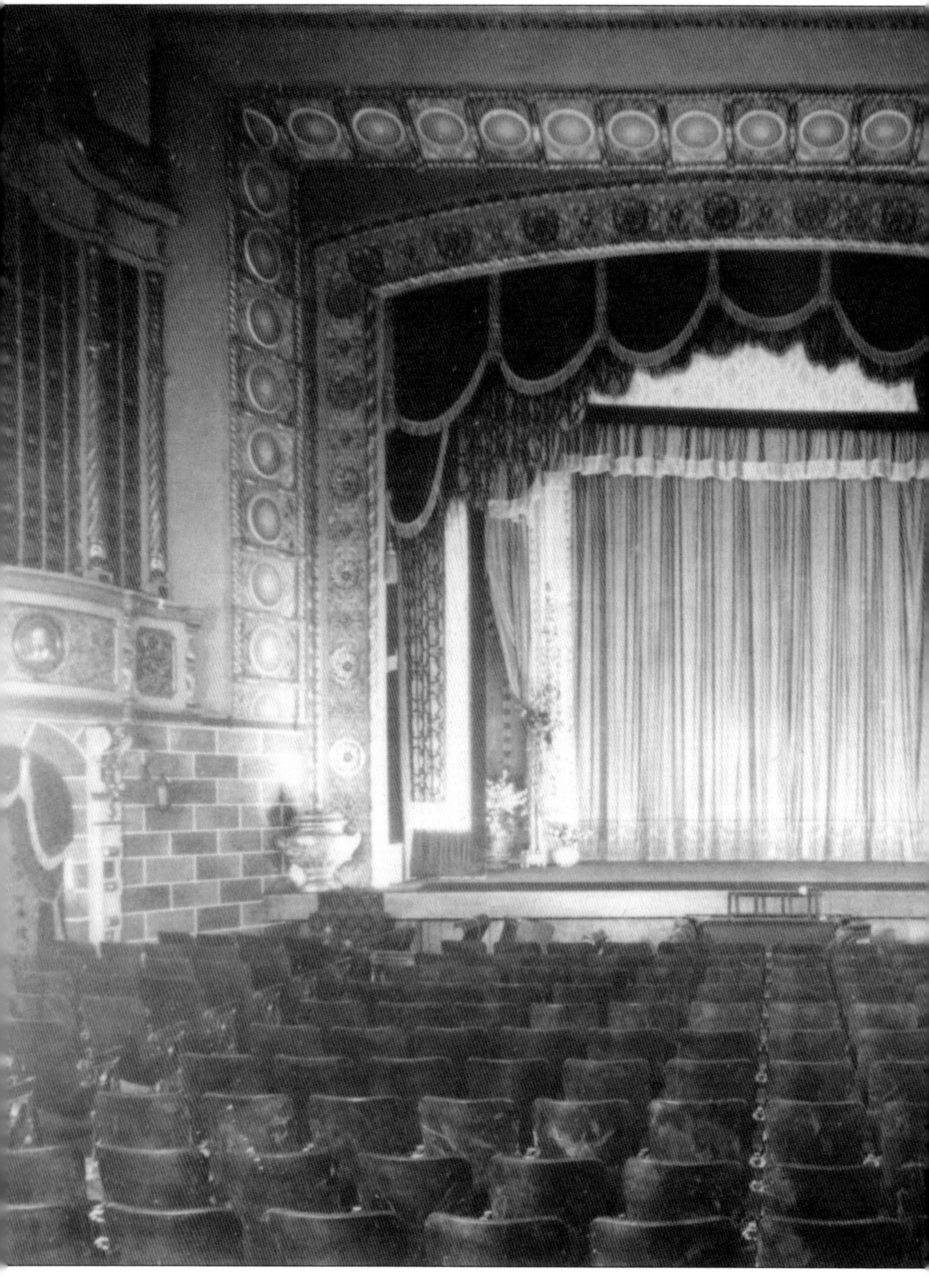

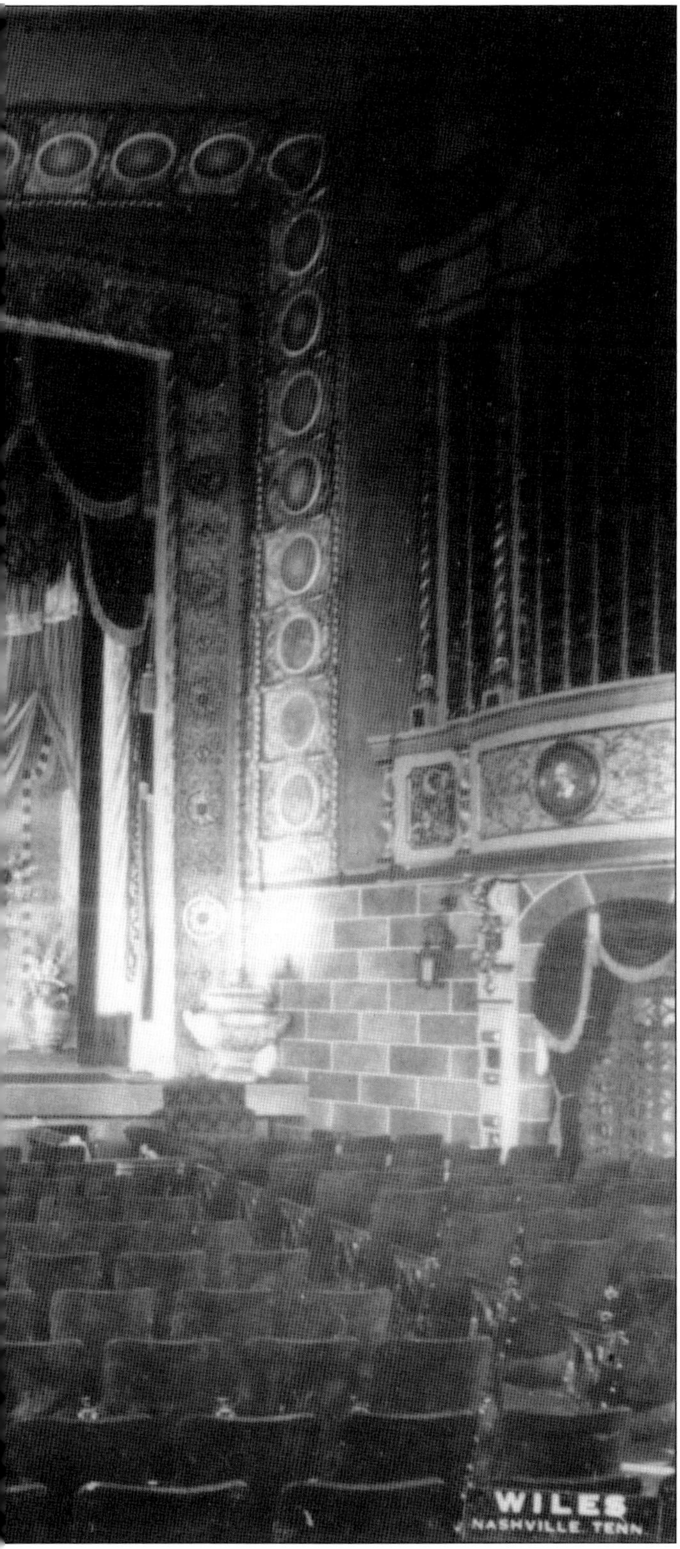

It is clear in this view looking toward the stage in the Belmont Theatre that there were no bad seats. Crescent Amusements spared no expense with any of its theaters. The interior of the Belmont was treated with a lot of gold leaf. All fabric looked like velvet or the best quality money could buy. The total cost of the theater was believed to be $100,000. Some who attended an event said it could be compared to any theater in the larger cities. Inside, the details of the motion picture house were as elaborate as the outside. (Courtesy of Tennessee State Library & Archives.)

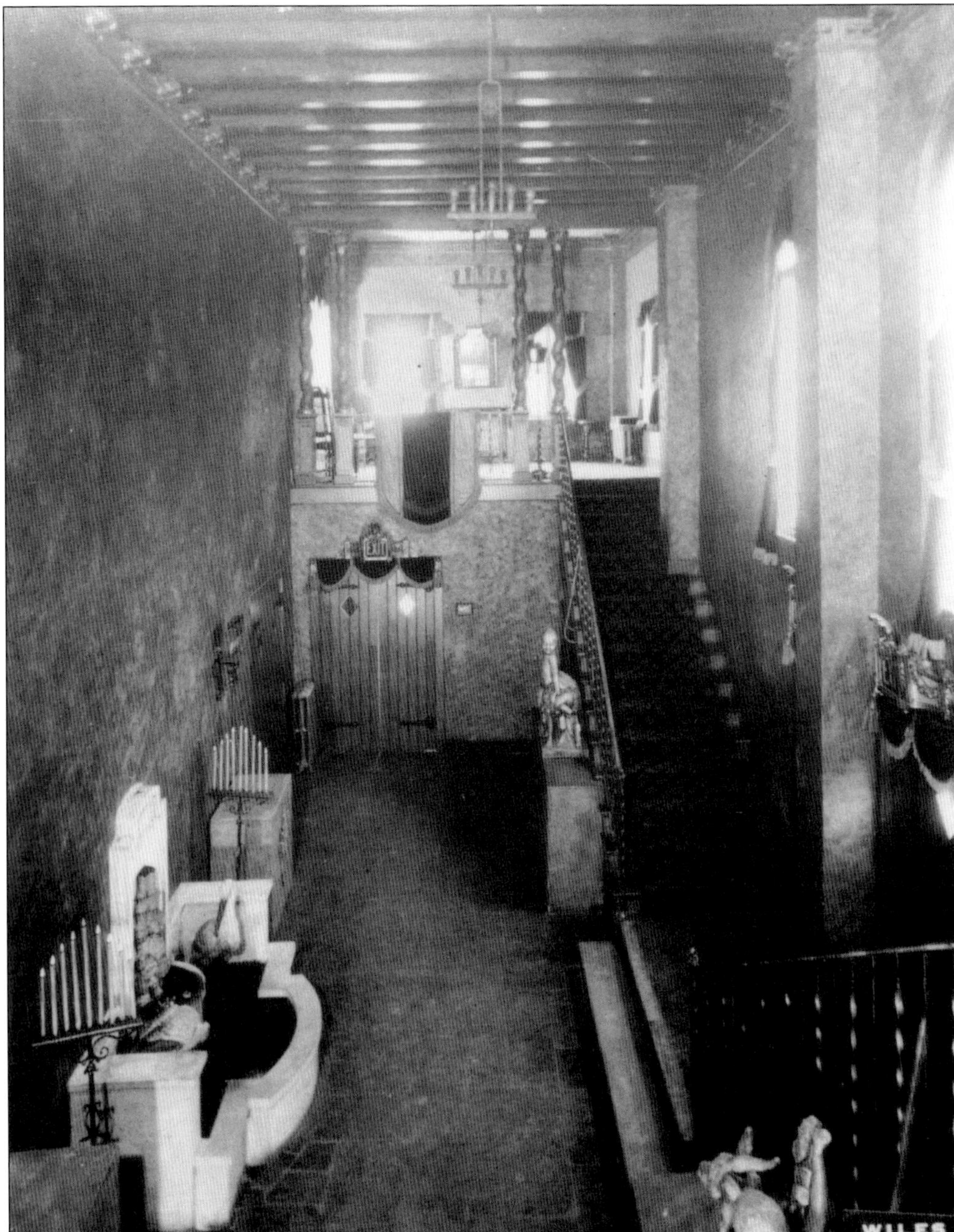

The lobby was decorated very ornately. The seating capacity was 1,350, there was a fish pond in the lobby, and doors with wrought iron decorations were part of the experience of the majestic movie house. (Courtesy of Metro Archives.)

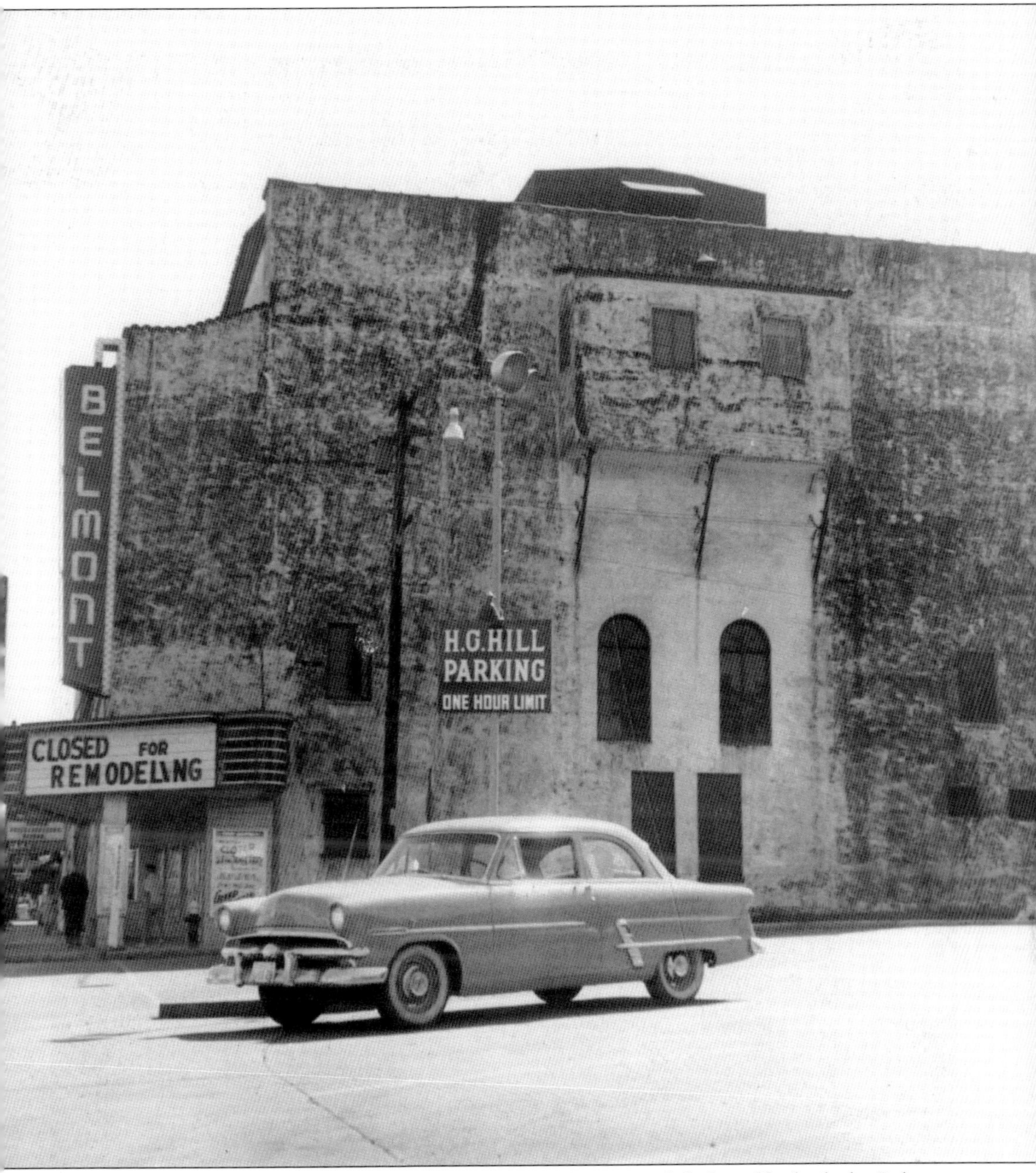

Tony Sudekum founded Crescent Amusements in 1908. Some people believed he built the Belmont to crush the Hillsboro Theater after opening in Hillsboro Village. Sudekum may have been jealous that someone else opened a neighborhood theater. After 35 years, the Belmont Theatre's final curtain call was March 15, 1961. Plans were to transform the building into the first modern office building in Hillsboro Village. (Courtesy of Metro Archives.)

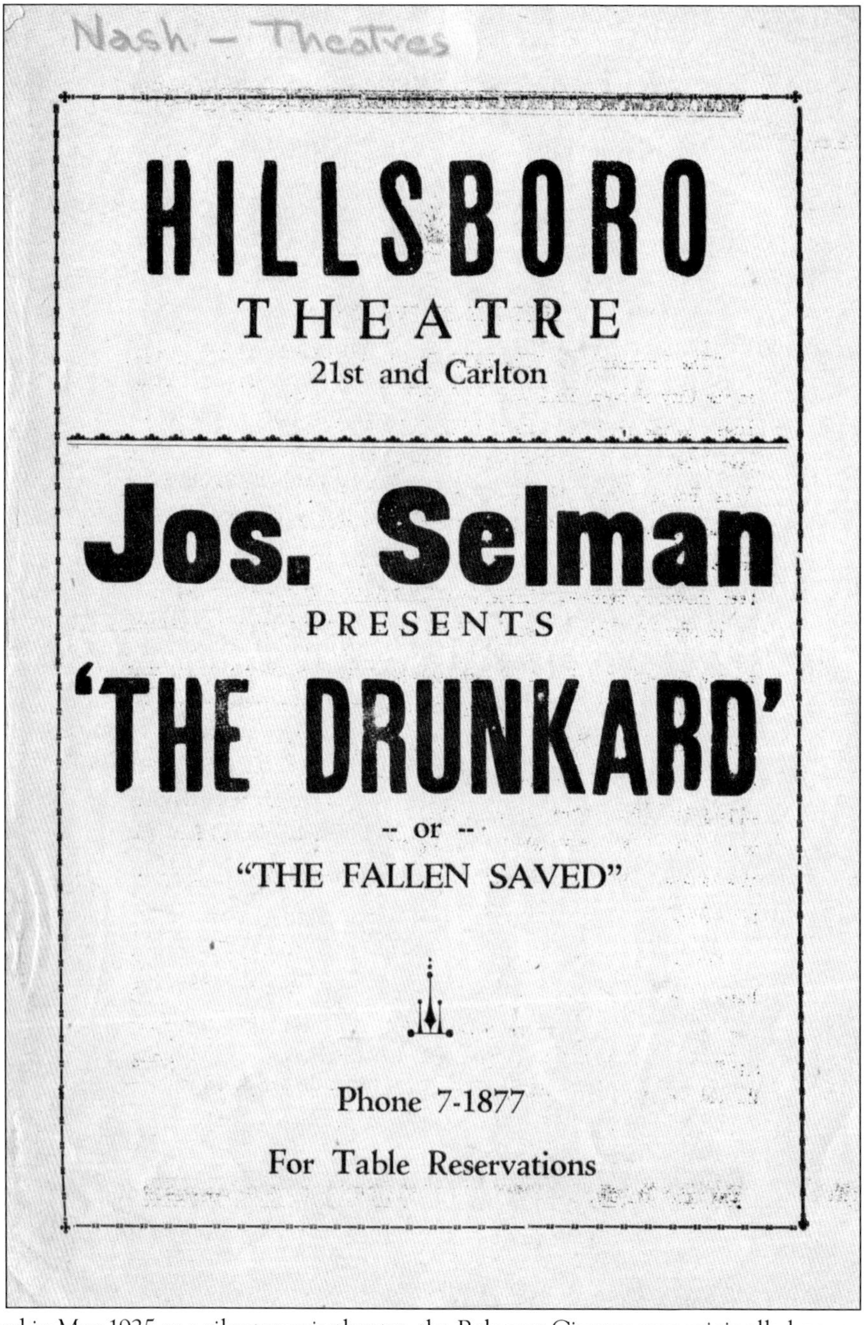

Opened in May 1925 as a silent movie theater, the Belcourt Cinema was originally known as the Hillsboro Theatre. The stage arch was created by Italian craftsman Raffaelo Mattei. As early as 1894, silent movies existed. By the 1930s, silent movies were being replaced by motion pictures with sound. Inside the theater was a Kimball pipe organ. During the era of silent movies, organs were commonly used in theaters, and this pipe organ could perform as a 25-piece orchestra. A program from one of the many live performances is pictured. For live entertainment, the Hillsboro's stage measured 60 by 25 feet. This was the largest stage in Nashville, and it was capable of managing any roadshow. (Courtesy of Metro Archives.)

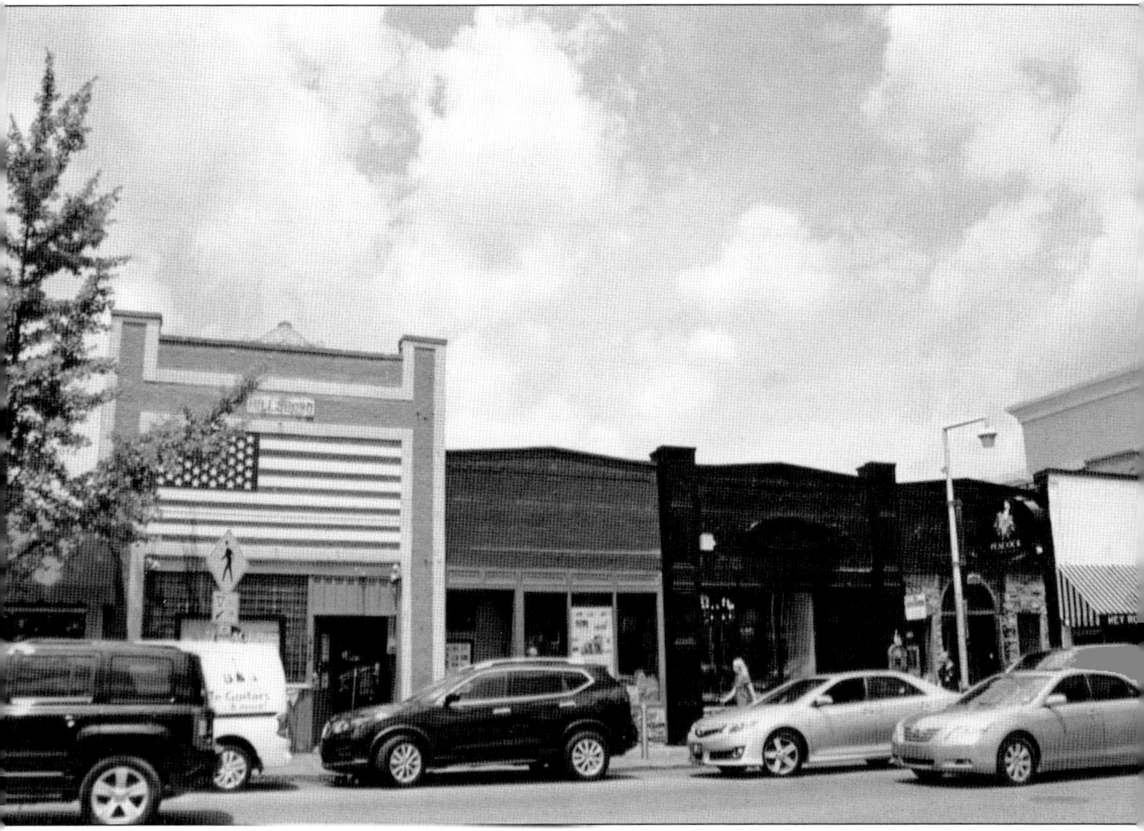

The entrance to the Hillsboro was at 1719 Twenty-First Avenue South. A sign on the outside of the building above the flag in the photograph still reads "Hillsboro." Before 1973, the Villager Tavern was known as the Golden Eagle. In the late 1920s and 1930, the building known as the Villager Tavern was the entrance to the Hillsboro Theatre. The Villager Tavern is on the National Historic Register. After all these years, the Villager Tavern is considered "where the locals go." (Courtesy of Metro Archives.)

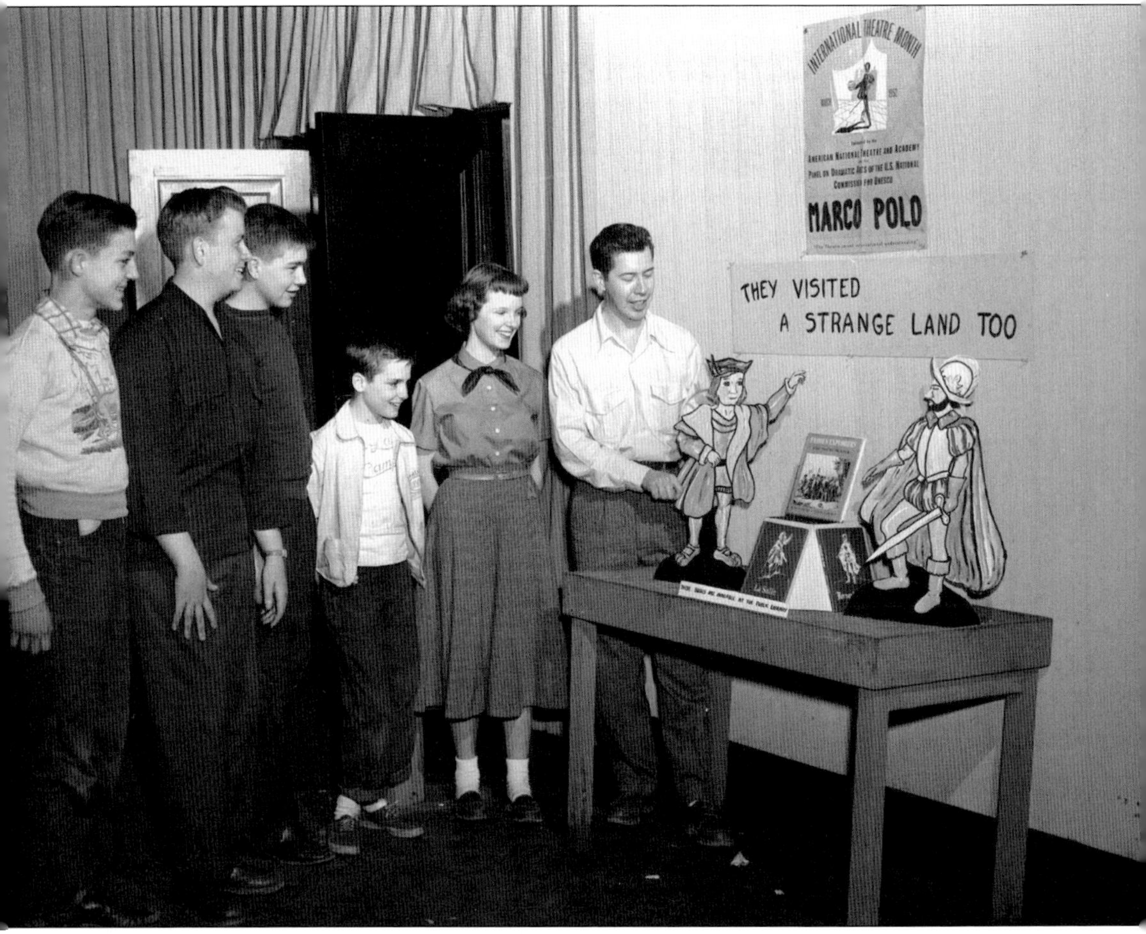

The Hillsboro had several uses through the years. The Hillsboro opened as a silent movie theater. The movies stopped, and live shows started. At one time, the Hillsboro Theatre became the Nashville Community Playhouse, and the theater stage was used for live performances. Productions for the children's theater were very active. While attending the shows, kids would get a behind-the-scenes experience. In this picture, students are getting an up-close experience with puppets used in a Marco Polo puppet show. (Courtesy of Metro Archives.)

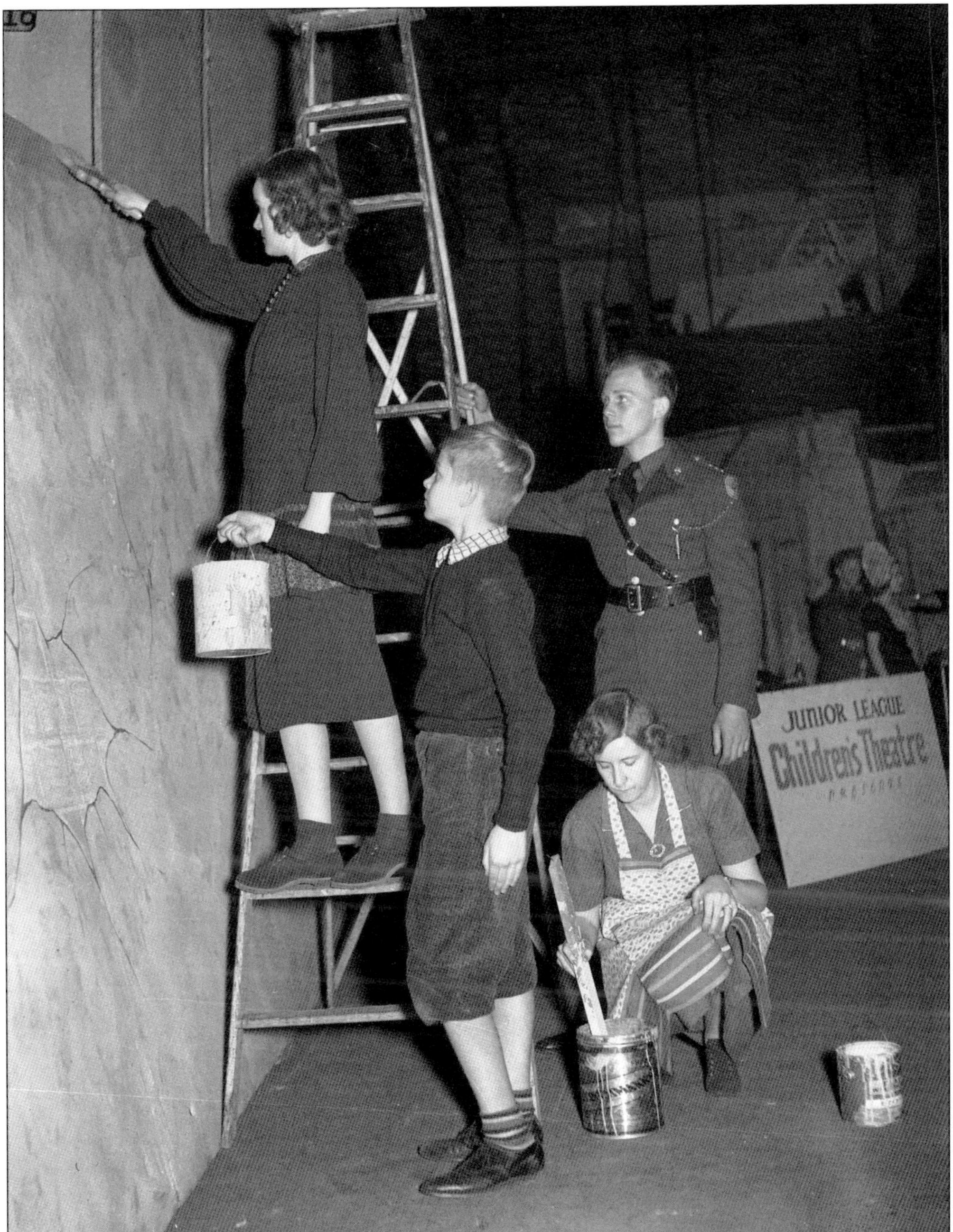

In 1931, the Children's Theatre of Nashville was started by the Junior League. The theater produced two plays in the fall of 1931. The *Aladdin* and *Alice* casts were mostly made up of children. Beginning with the second year, the children's theater created four plays a year. The building was renamed Nashville Community Playhouse. In this picture, the individuals are preparing for a Nashville presentation. The play was *Hans Brinker*, and it ran from December 15 to 18, 1937. (Courtesy of Nashville Public Library Special Collections.)

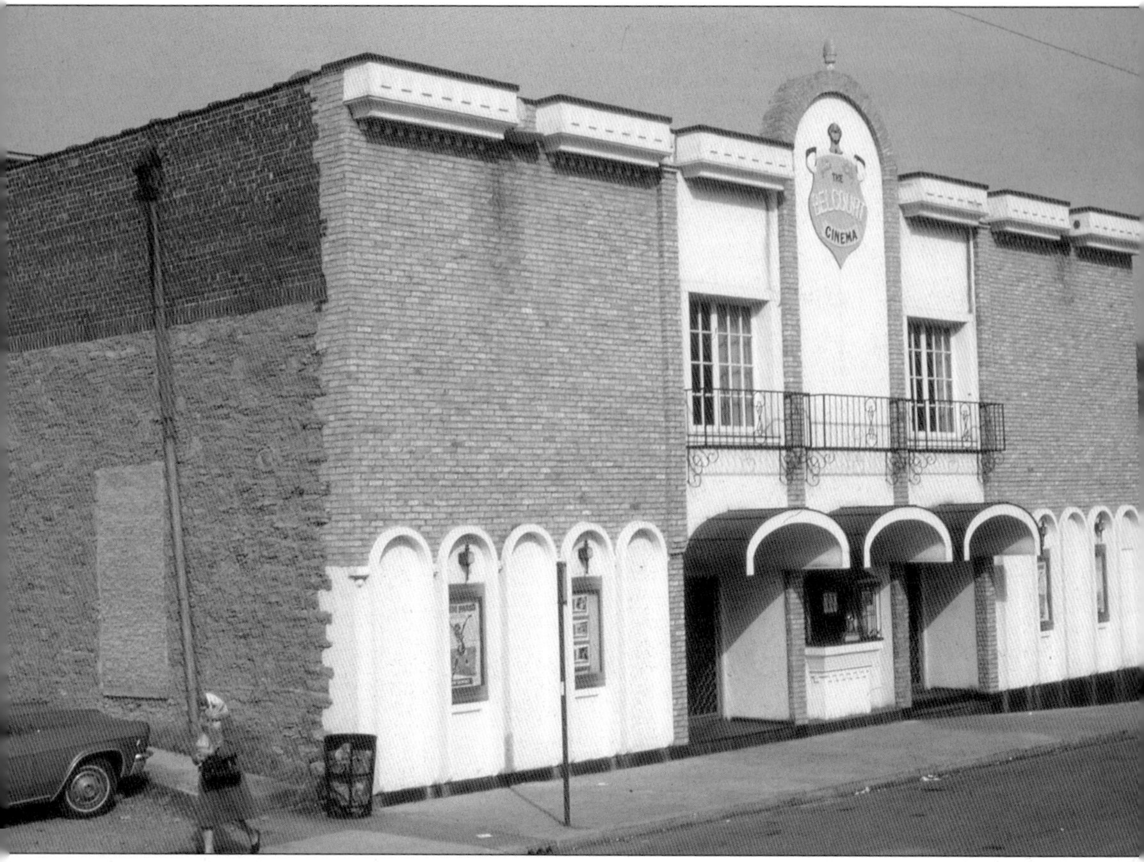

WSM begin broadcasting the *Grand Ole Opry* in 1925. The live transmission was from the National Life and Accident Building, located at Seventh Avenue and Union Street in downtown Nashville. The *Grand Ole Opry* was becoming very popular, and by 1934, the live productions were coming from the Belcourt in Hillsboro Village. In 1936, the *Grand Ole Opry* moved to a larger venue: the Dixie Tabernacle on Fatherland Street in East Nashville. Three years later, the *Grand Ole Opry* was live from War Memorial Auditorium, and in 1943, the *Grand Ole Opry* was at the Ryman Auditorium. (Courtesy of Metro Archives.)

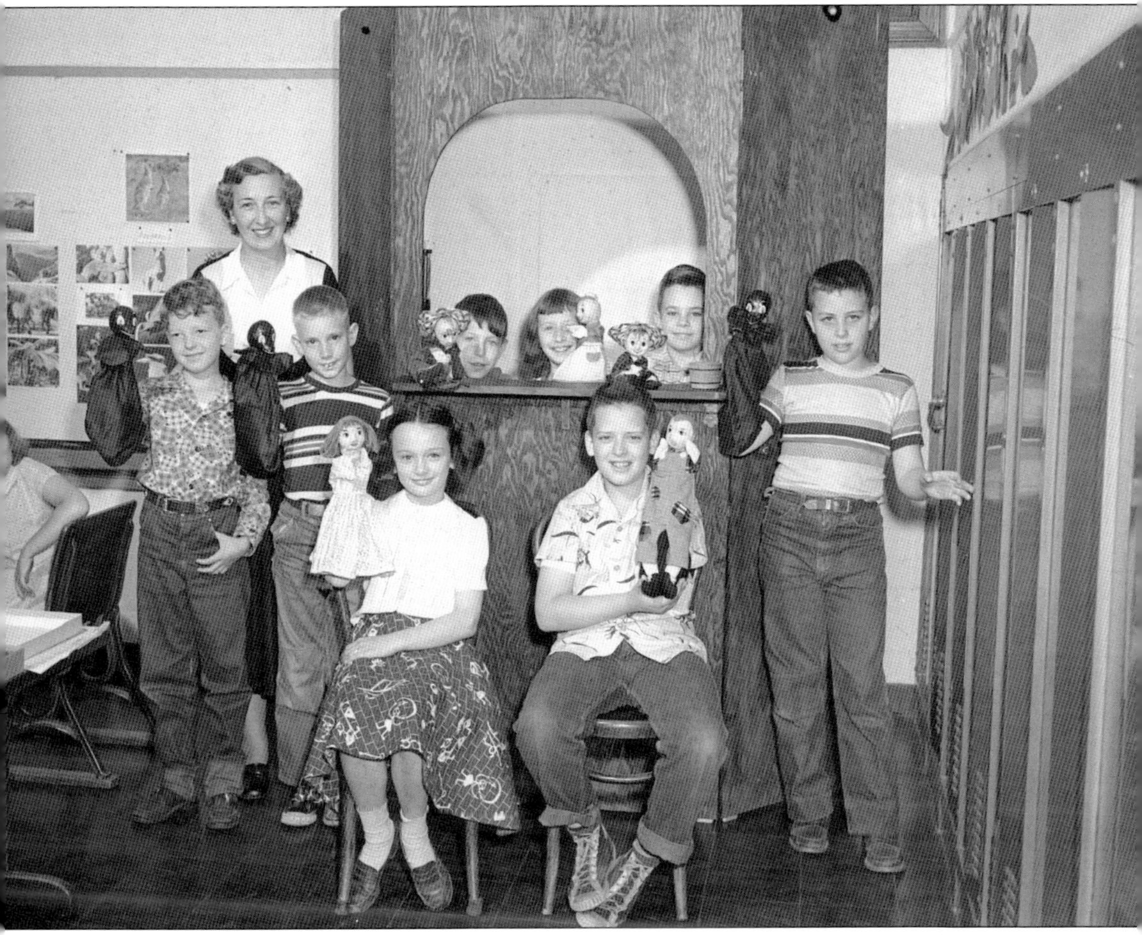

Within weeks of the Hillsboro opening, the Belmont Theatre had its grand opening. The concept of neighborhood theaters was new to Nashville. Most theaters were located in downtown Nashville, and typically, people use public transportation to get downtown. Both the Belmont and Hillsboro had parking lots for their guests. After three months, the Hillsboro was forced to close as a movie theater. (Courtesy of Nashville Public Library Special Collections.)

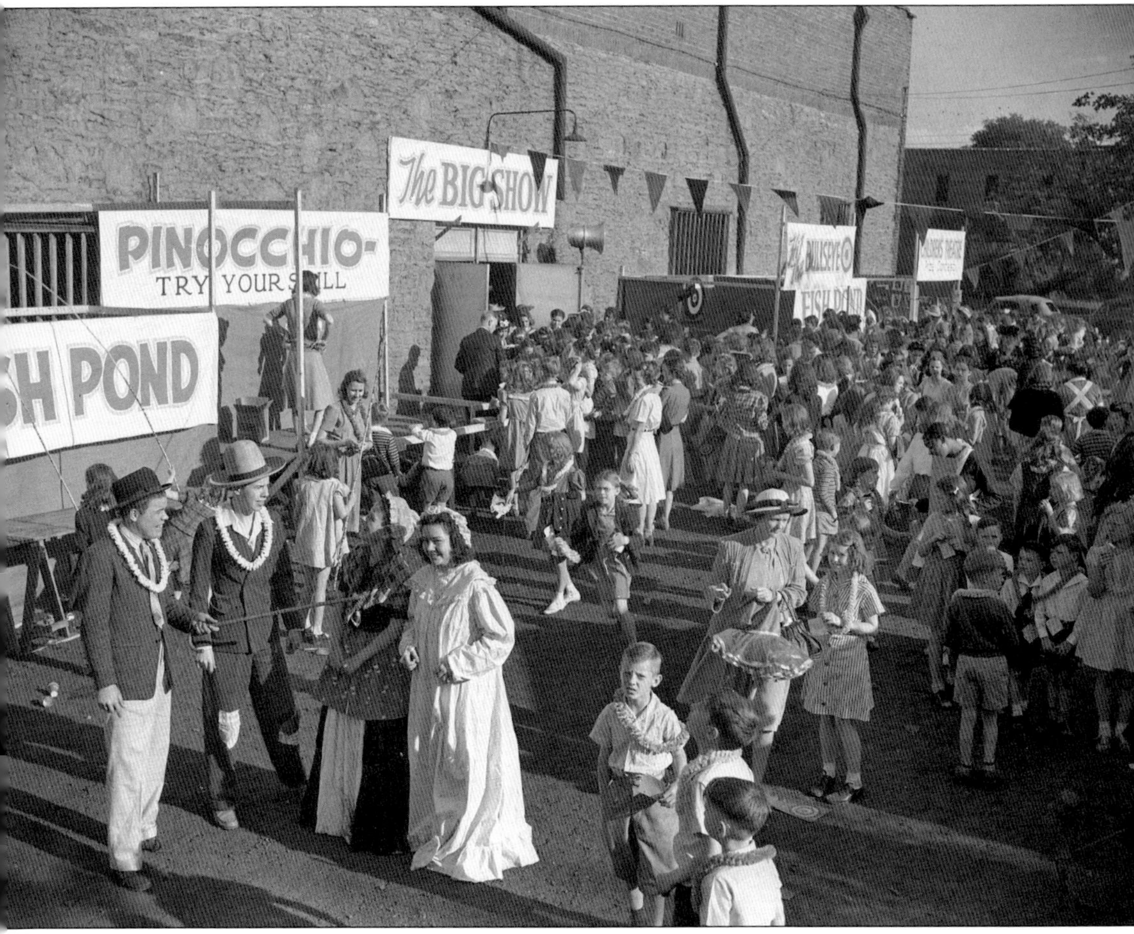

The Hillsboro may have stopped showing movies, but with a large stage, the Hillsboro provided many live performances. In the 1930s, the Hillsboro was the first place for the Children's Theatre of Nashville. From 1934 until 1936, the Hillsboro Theatre was home to a new live and local show. The *Grand Ole Opry* used the Hillsboro Theatre in the early years. That name was changed in 1937 from Hillsboro Theatre to Nashville Community Playhouse. Another production company, the New Theatre, used the Hillsboro for performances. The playhouse was used for community events, film, and theater. (Courtesy of Nashville Public Library Special Collections.)

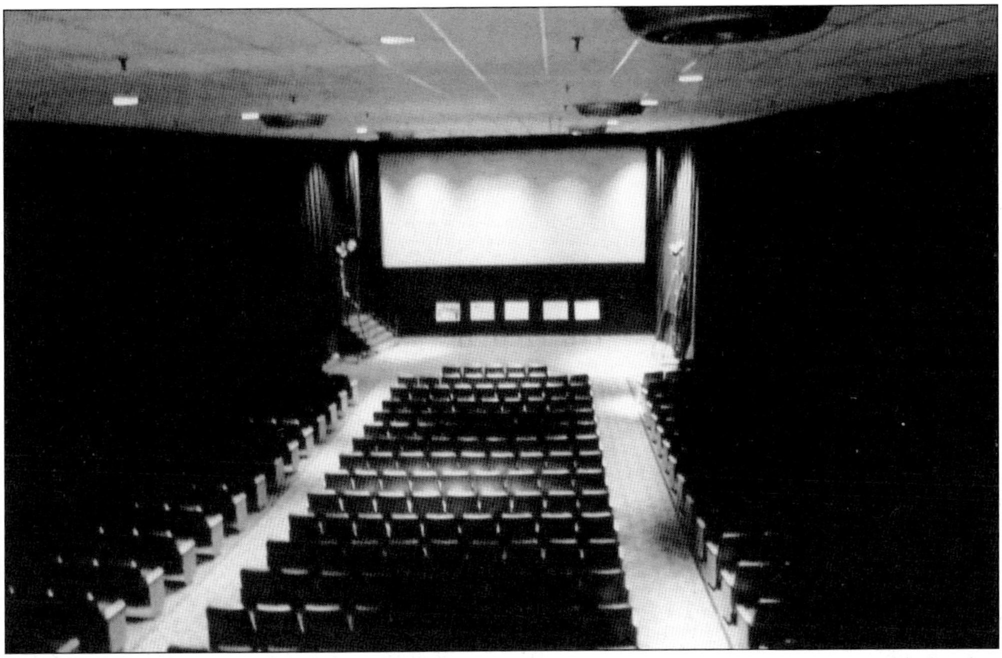

In 1966, the name was changed to Belcourt Cinema, and a second theater was added. This photograph looks inside from the seats of the smaller theater. The theater returned to showing movies. (Courtesy of Metro Archives.)

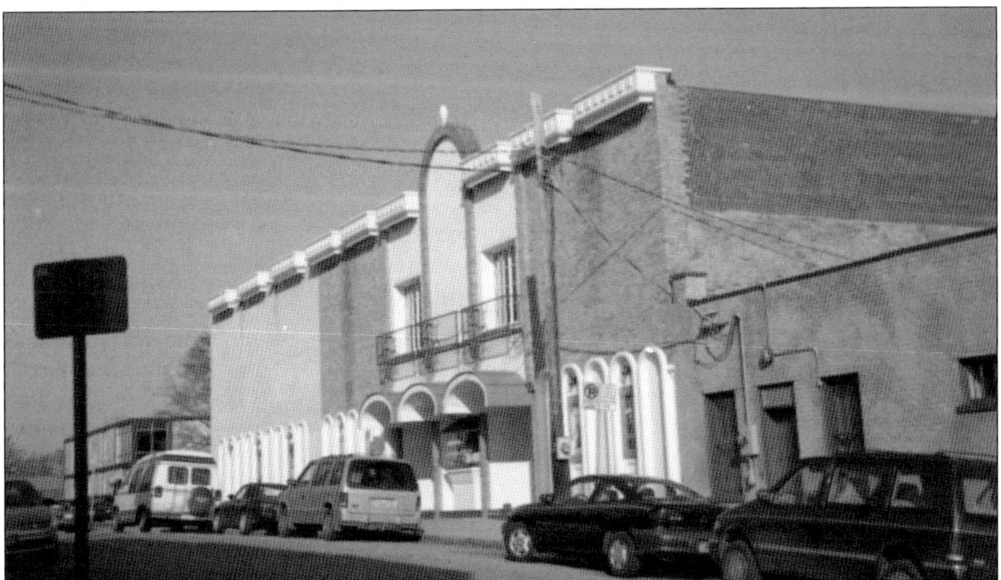

This photograph was taken in 1998 at the Belcourt Cinema. On the left side of the photograph is a building with a lighter color, indicating where a second theater was added. (Courtesy of Metro Archives.)

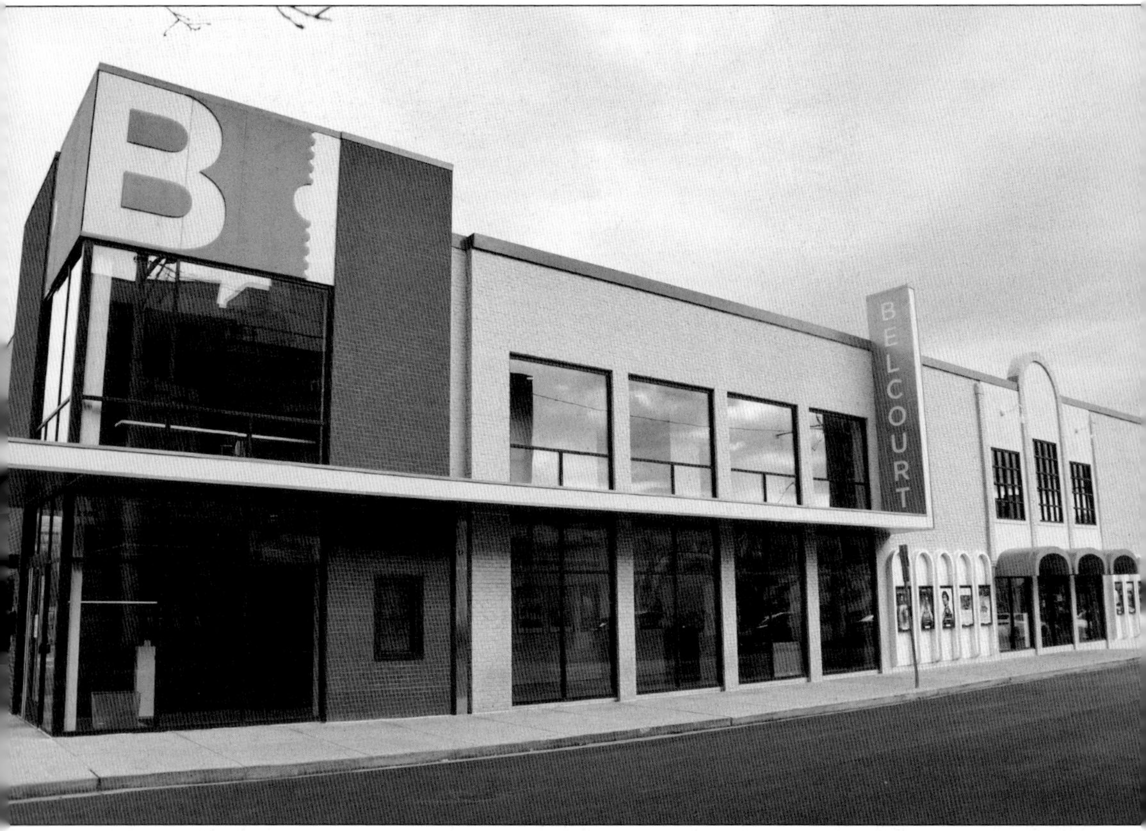

This is a current photograph. In 2015, the Belcourt closed temporarily for a major renovation project. This was the first remodel for the building in over 50 years. The project enlarged the building and improved the parking lot, and the Belcourt is now in compliance with ADA requirements. (Author's collection.)

One block away from Hillsboro Village is a park home to a large mosaic dragon. The park was originally named Sunset Park and later renamed the Fannie Mae Dees Park. (Courtesy of Metro Archives.)

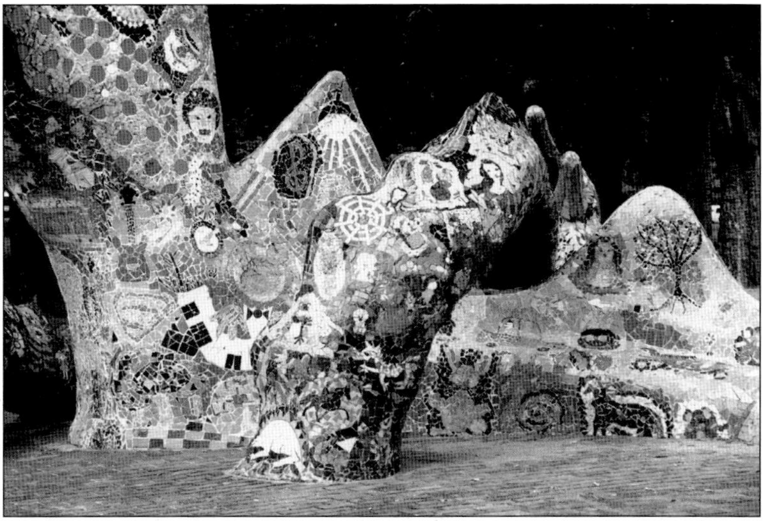

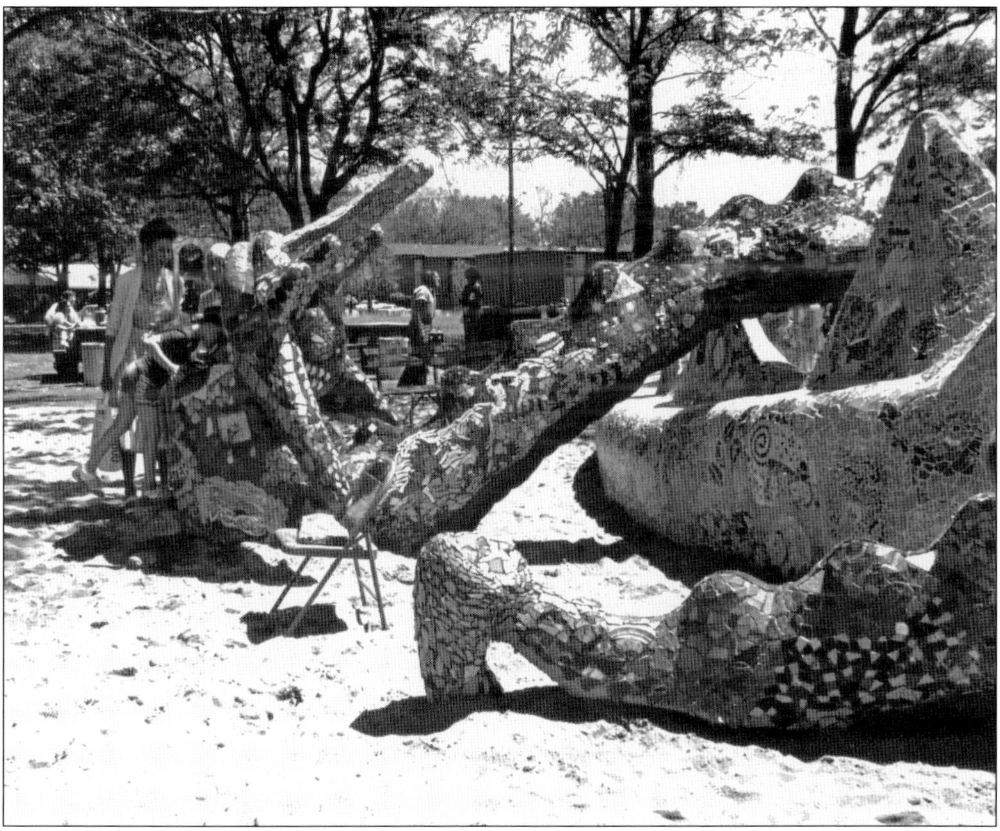

The serpent was created in 1980 as a result of community members working together. Metro Board of Parks and Recreation commissioned sculptor Pedro Silva to create artwork in Fannie Mae Dees Park. Silva had the idea to build a dragon in the park. The project was funded through a grant available for the University Center Renewal, which was to be used to reshape the neighborhoods around Vanderbilt. (Courtesy of Metro Archives.)

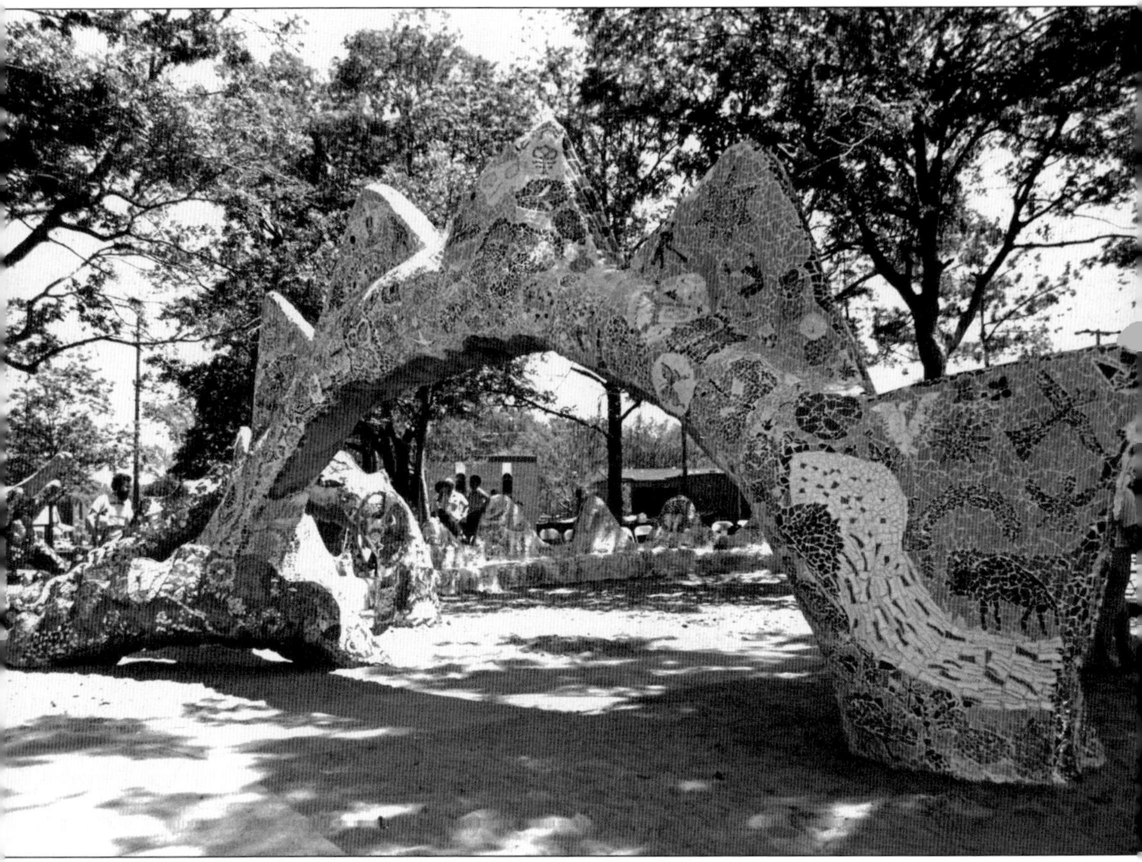

Much detail was put into creating the dragon. The sea serpent has many characters on it, including various sea creatures and a pirate. Some of the characters represent famous humans that can be quickly recognized; Dolly Parton and Minnie Pearl can be easily spotted. While creating the dragon, an estimated 1,000 volunteers came to express their creativity. Even an image of Fannie Mae Dees can be found on the sea serpent. (Courtesy of Metro Archives.)

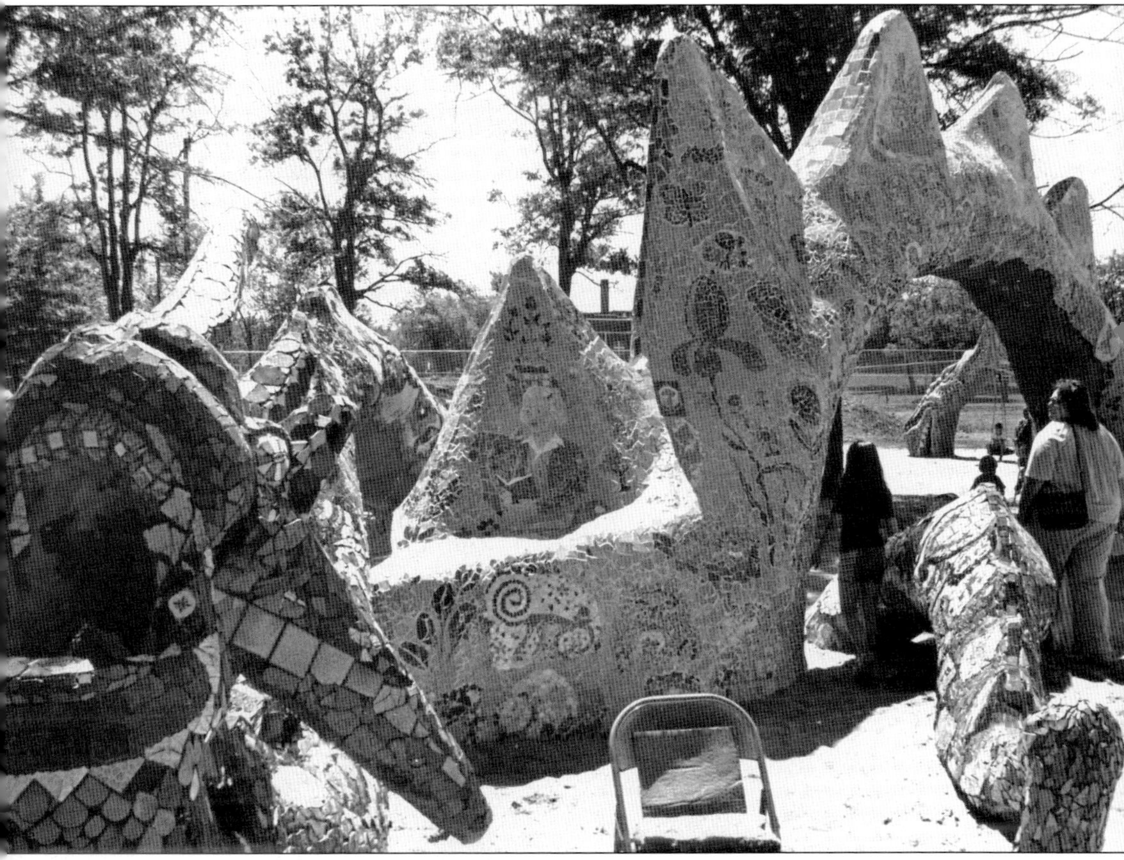

The dragon lives in the Fannie Mae Dees Park and stretches over 150 feet. The dragon is covered with tile and has many stories to share. Pedro Silva is well known for many other creations. One of his other projects is in New York City: a mosaic bench in Riverside Park that wraps 450 feet around Grant's Tomb. (Courtesy of Metro Archives.)

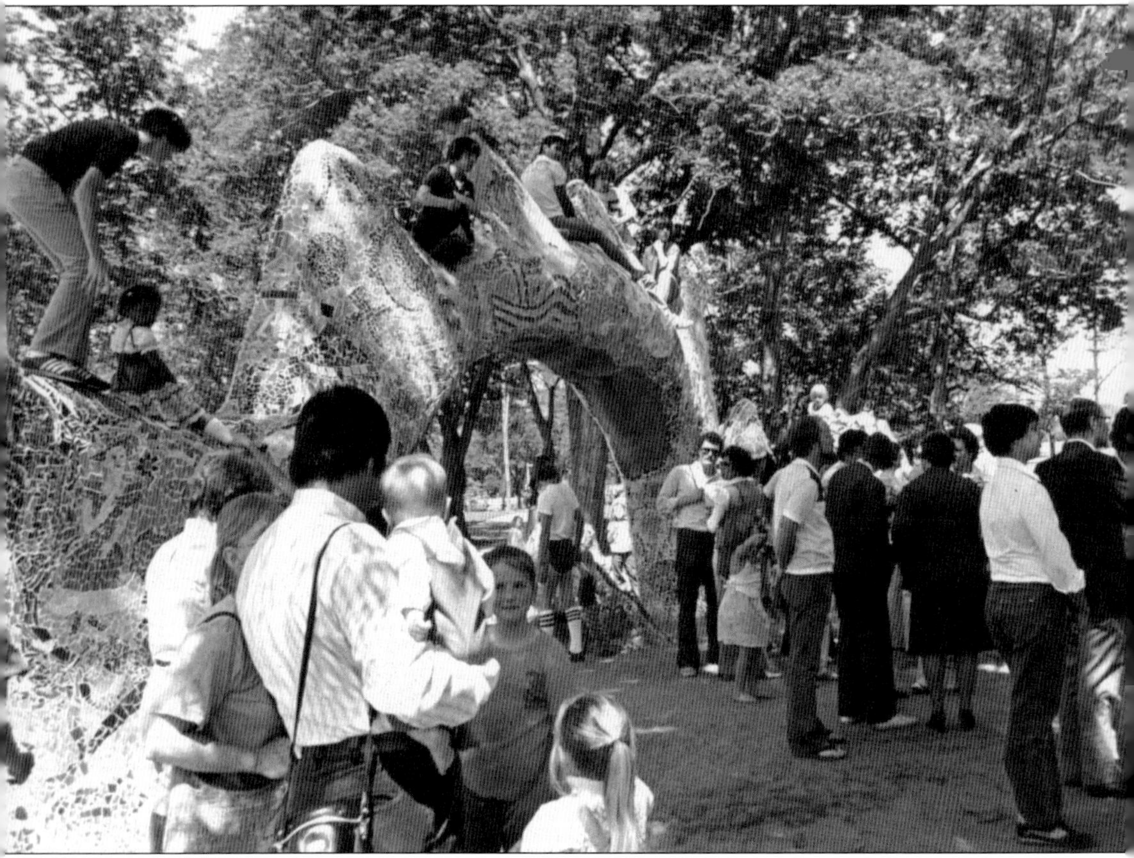

Fannie Mae Dees was a nurse employed at Vanderbilt. She and her mother lived on Capers Avenue off Twenty-First Avenue South. Their house was in the way of Vanderbilt's expansion, and Fannie Mae fought hard against that. The outside of the house was covered with signs of protest, and the front porch had a coffin with a sign about the death of a community. (Courtesy of Metro Archives.)

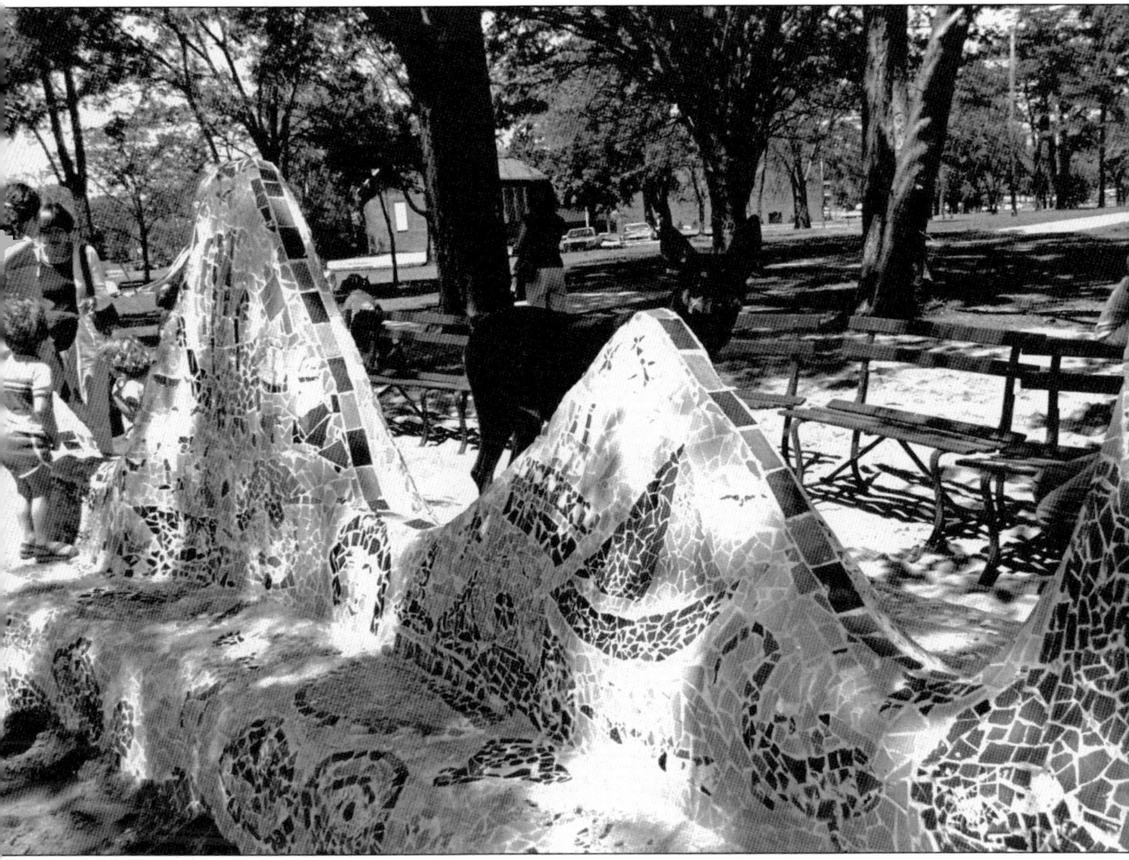

In 1965, Vanderbilt started snatching other houses around Fannie Mae Dees's home. After a 13-year battle, Dees passed away in the basement of her home. An overwhelming outpouring of the community determined to name the park in her memory. (Courtesy of Metro Archives.)

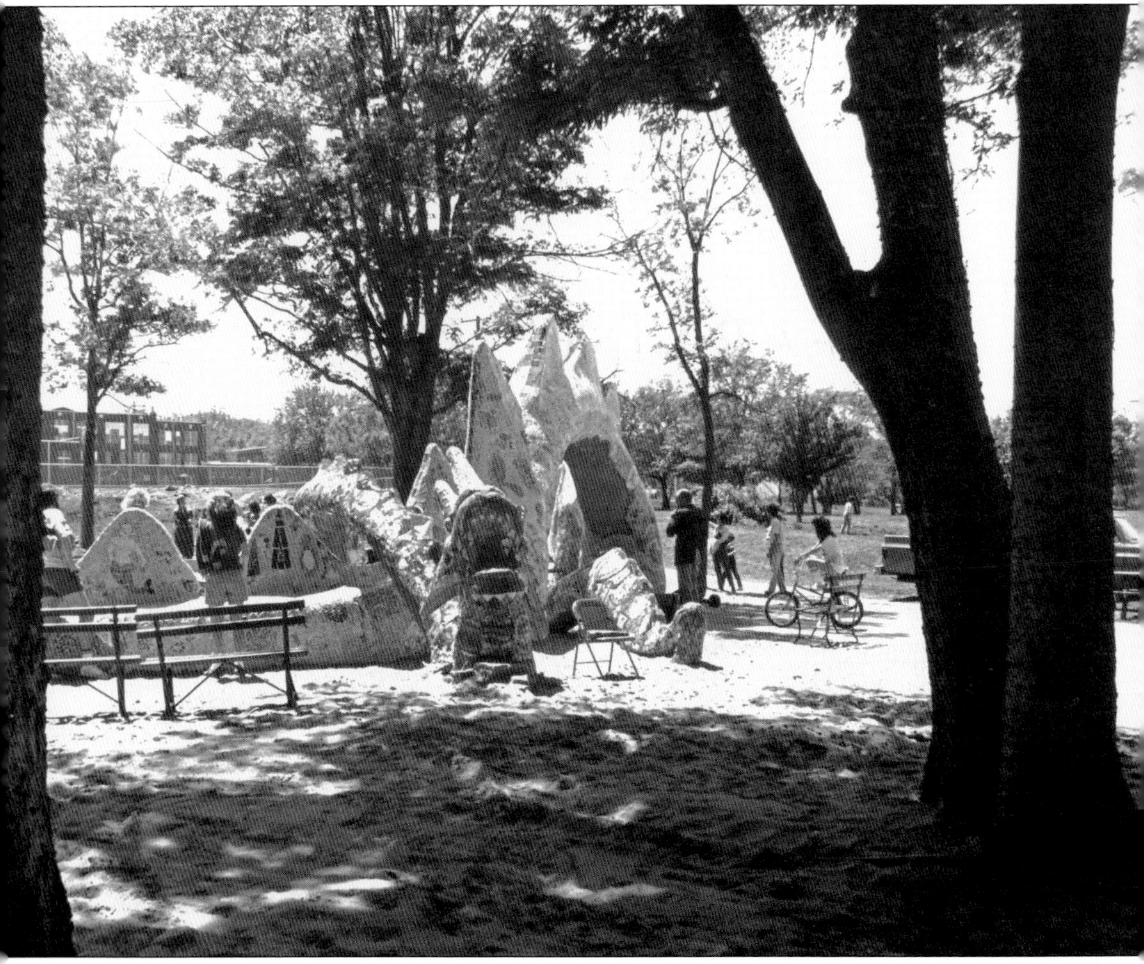

The Dragon Park is the center of a lot of family fun. There are many activities for families with children of all ages. Lily's Garden opened in 2001, and it is the first park of its kind to open in Tennessee with a playground for children with disabilities. Fannie Mae Dees Park is a perfect location for children. Both Harris Hillman School and Ronald McDonald House are very close to the Dragon Park. Fannie Mae Dees Park was nicknamed "the Dragon Park" by the local children. (Courtesy of Metro Archives.)

Four

Learning near the Village

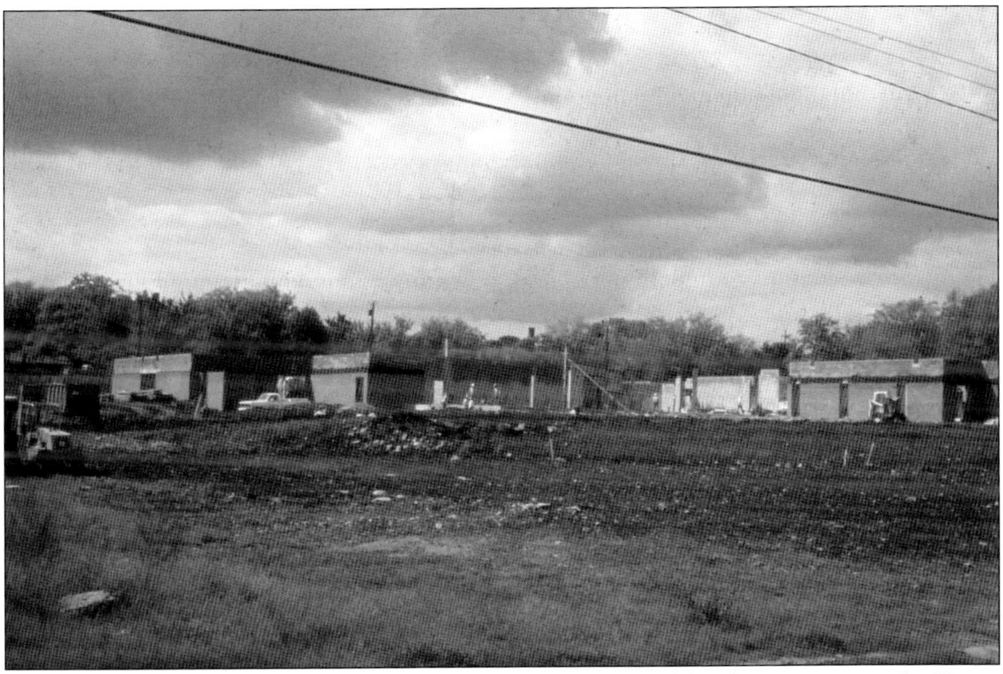

The photograph was taken in January 1974 during the ground-breaking ceremony for Harris Hillman School. In 1975, Harris Hillman opened as a school for students with special needs. The school was named for Dr. John Harris and Dr. William Hillman. Dr. Harris was the former director of Metro Nashville Schools, and Dr. Hillman was an orthopedic surgeon at Vanderbilt Hospital. A mandatory Education Act of 1973 was issued to boost the education of special-needs students. The school was opened to provide for students with crippling conditions of muscles and joints, birth defects, or serious sensory impairments. Some students were blind or deaf. The staff was all trained to work with any physical impairments a student may have. The location of Harris Hillman is ideal, as Vanderbilt Children's Hospital is close enough for any medical emergency at the school. Students from George Peabody School for Teachers were close enough to have experience teaching special-needs students. (Courtesy of Metro Archives.)

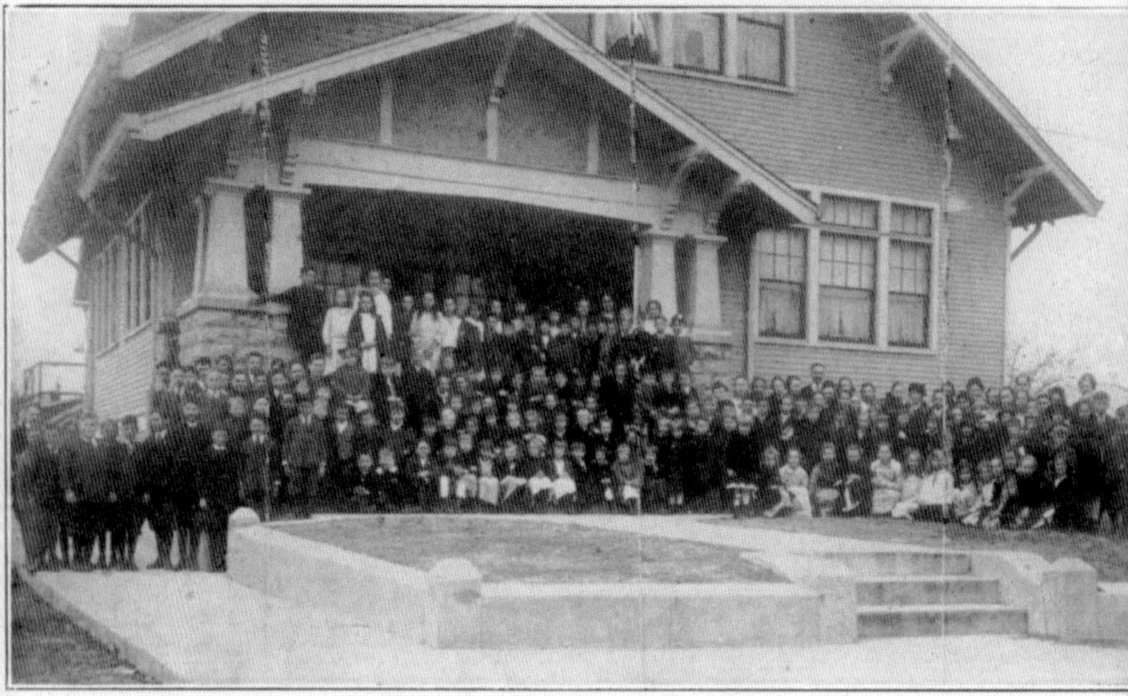

REED-HILLSBORO SCHOOL, TEACHERS AND PUPILS, SPRING, 1918.

This school, which was located in the Seventh District and led by Mrs. Charles C. Gi hairman of County Woman's Committee, did exceptional work in all war relief drives and he Junior Department, Nashville Chapter A. R. C.

Read School was located on the northwest corner of Twenty-First Avenue South and Blair Boulevard. The county school opened in 1911 and was named for John Read. After a few years, the school's name was shortened to Read School. Originally the building was a one-room shack with used furnishings from the old Watkins School. After three years, the school, with a teacher and the mothers of the 30 students, created the Improvement Club. The purpose of the organization was to assist and provide for the school. After a few years, funds were raised to construct a larger building. With the new and improved Read School, the student body grew to 200 students and 4 teachers. Other Davidson County schools considered Reed School an example of a county school. By 1928, the students were transferred to the newly built Cavert School. Four years after closing the property where Read School was located, it was sold to Standard Oil. (Courtesy of Nashville Public Library Special Collections.)

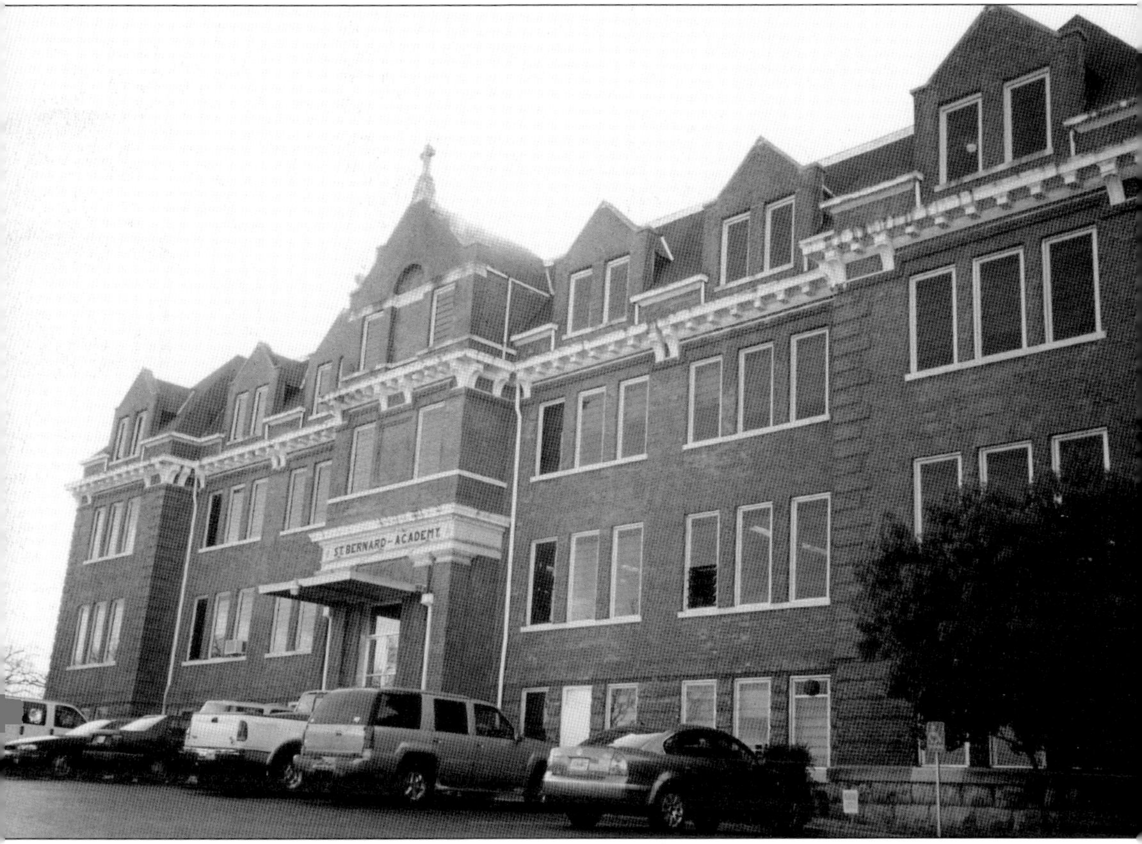

In 1866, St. Bernard's Academy opened in downtown Nashville. The school was located near the state capitol building. By 1867, the classes were from kindergarten to the eighth grade. The school moved to Twenty-First Avenue South in 1905. The building was enlarged in 1924 and offered a large chapel, cafeteria, and additional sleeping quarters for the sisters. (Courtesy of Nashville Public Library Special Collections.)

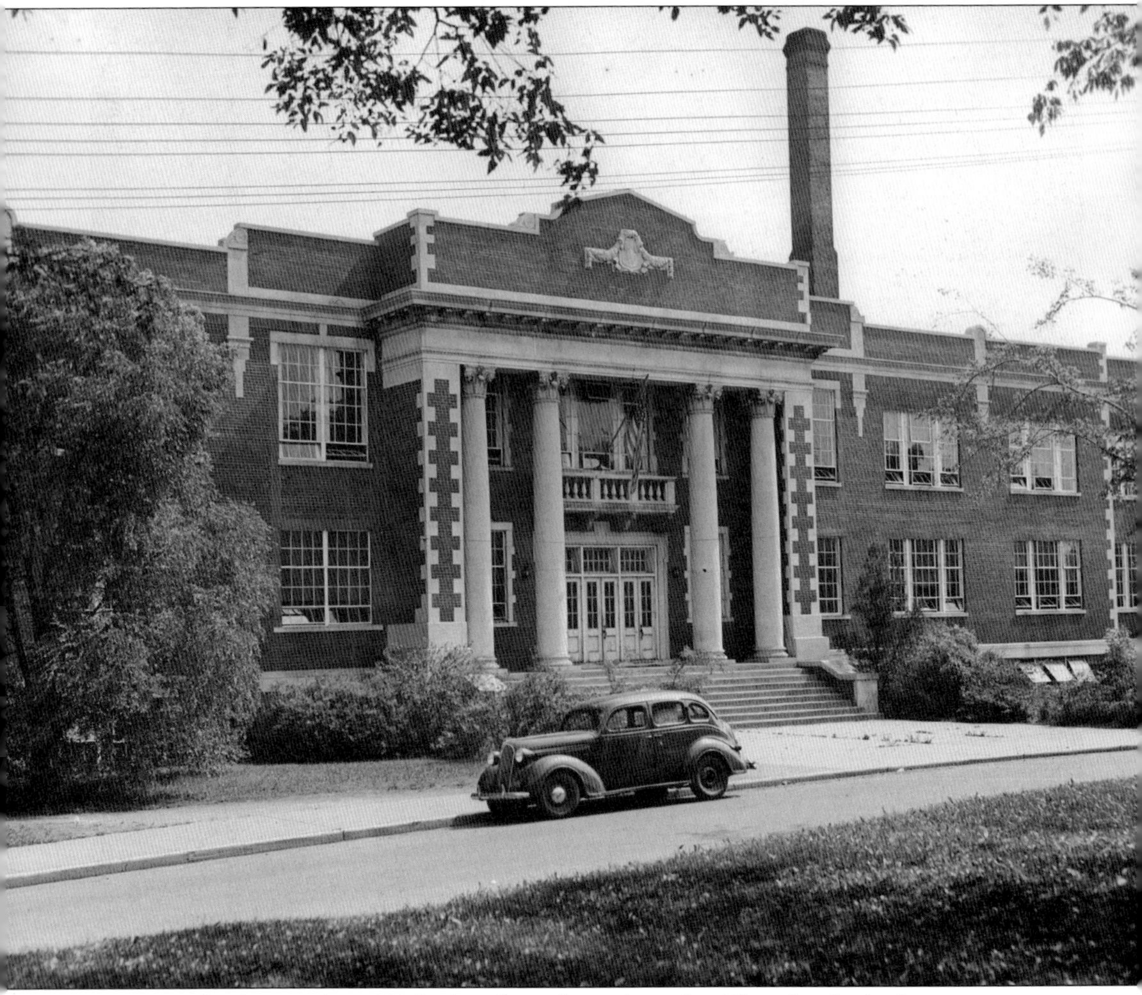

Cavert School opened in 1928 for first through ninth grades. The school is built on property once owned by a Vanderbilt dean of the School of Engineering. The school was named for Dr. Albert J. Cavert, who was superintendent of the Nashville City Schools in the late 1880s. (Courtesy of Metro Archives.)

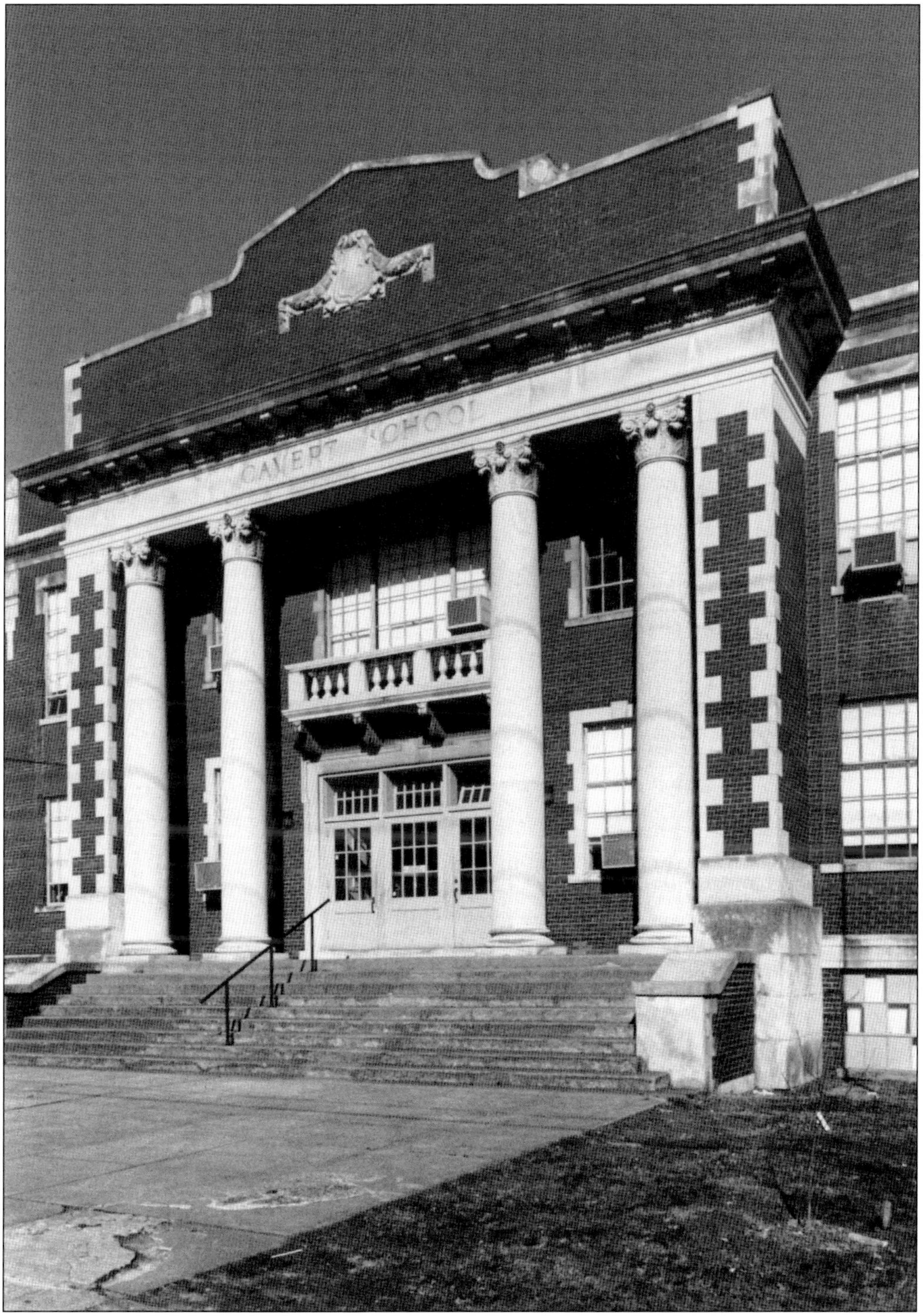

The expansion of Cavert and the construction of Eakin were a result of the New Deal. Once the Eakin building opened as an elementary school, the Cavert building became a junior high school. At one time, the Cavert building was designated to be converted into a school for special needs. (Courtesy of Nashville Public Library Special Collections.)

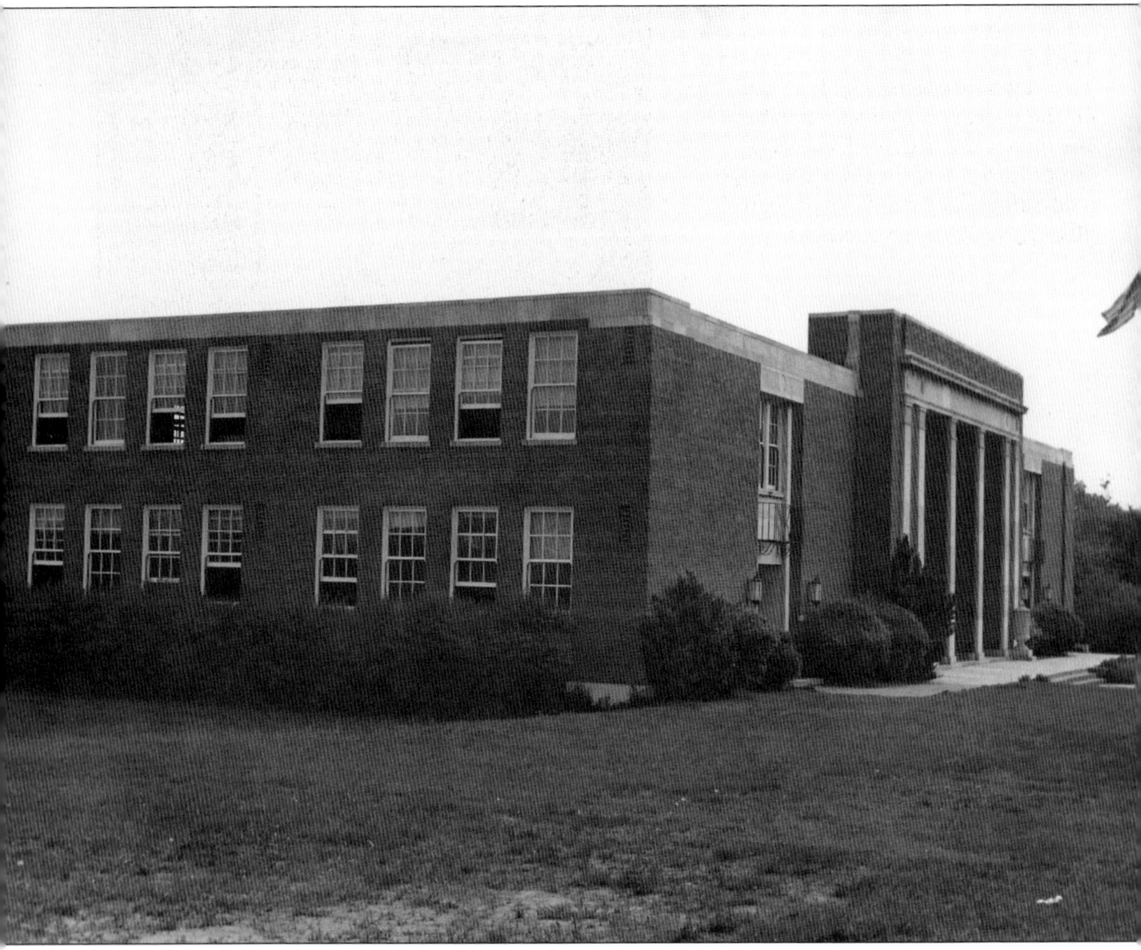

Before Eakin School opened, it was going to be named Jones School. The name changed to Eakin School in honor of Mrs. John Hill Eakin (the former Elizabeth Atchinson), the first female school board member, elected to the board in 1917. Opened in 1937 as an elementary school, Cavert became a junior high. (Courtesy of Metro Archives.)

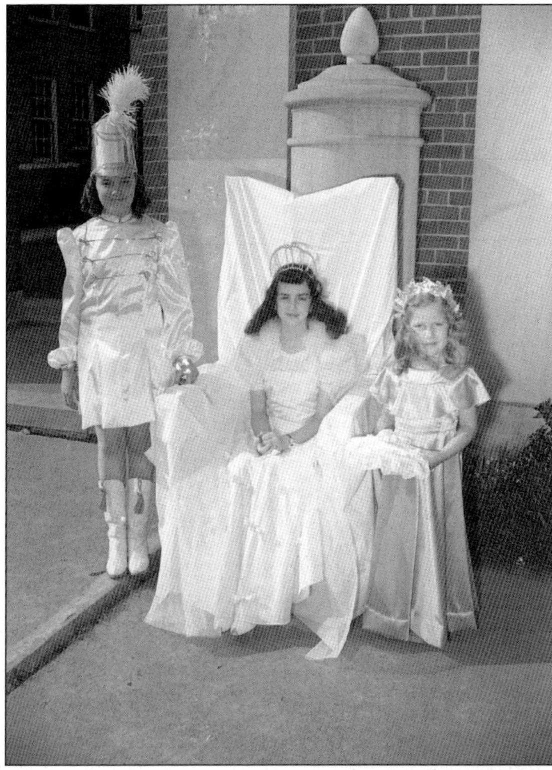

In this photograph, Eakin School is celebrating with the presentation of the May Day Queen and her court in the pageant. From left to right are Reecy Davis (Miss Democracy), Betty Ruth Methrin (May Queen), and Sally Clay Estes (Crownbearer). (Courtesy of Metro Archives.)

Pictured here is more May Day celebration from 1941, an example of how much planning went into this kind of event. There is a handmade paper chain around the chairs. Celebrating May Day in the late 1930s and early 1940s was a festive occasion. Teachers, parents, and the community also participated in the annual event. (Courtesy of Metro Archives.)

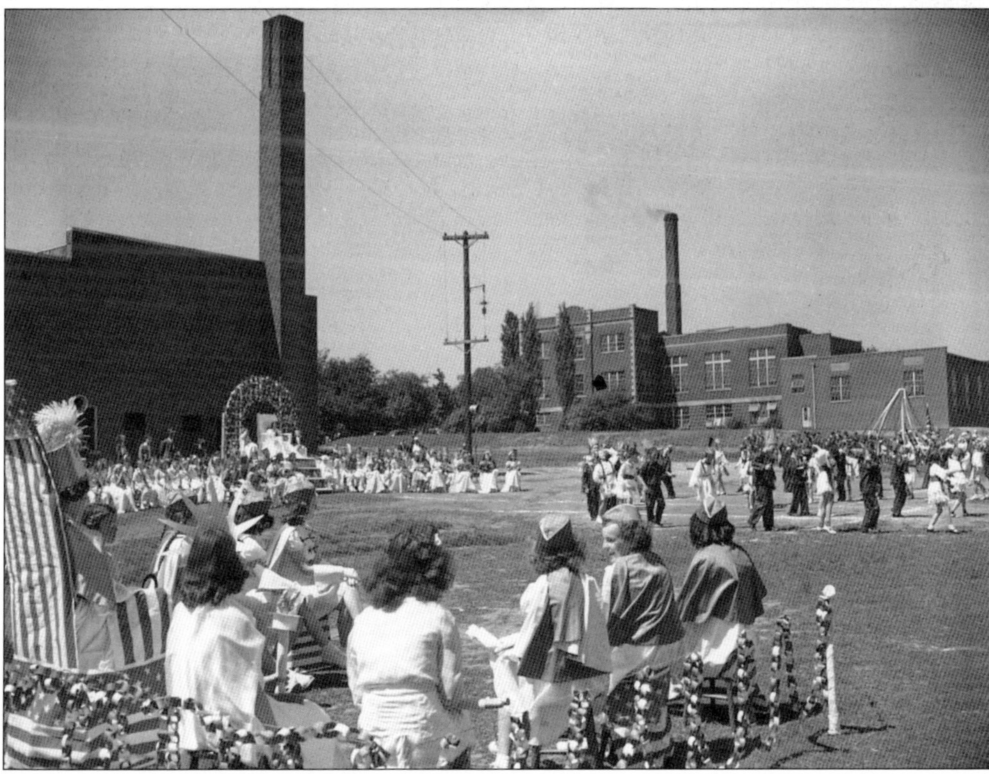

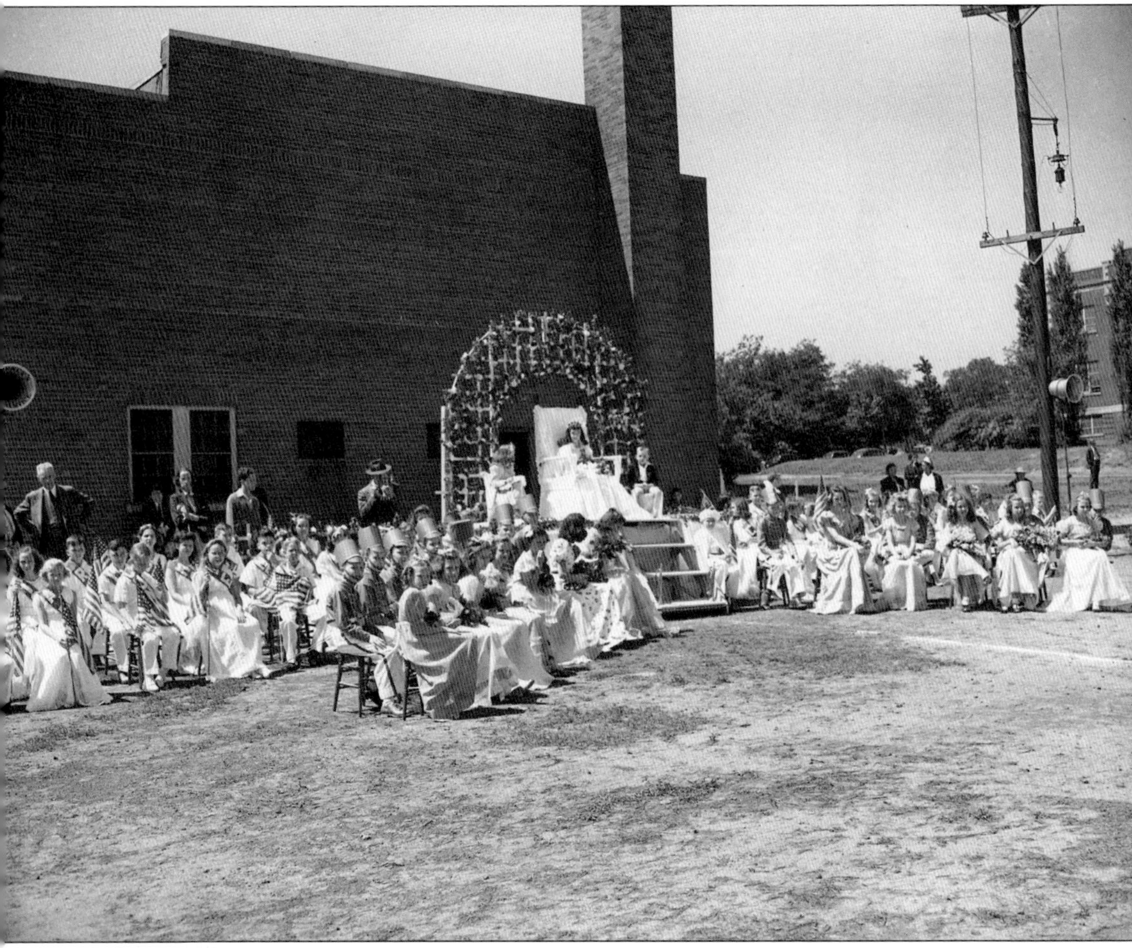

In 1941, Eakin School celebrated May Day on the ninth day of May, though May Day was typically May 1. The celebration acknowledges the halfway point from spring to summer. The historic holiday dates back to ancient times and was celebrated by different countries and cultures. (Courtesy of Metro Archives.)

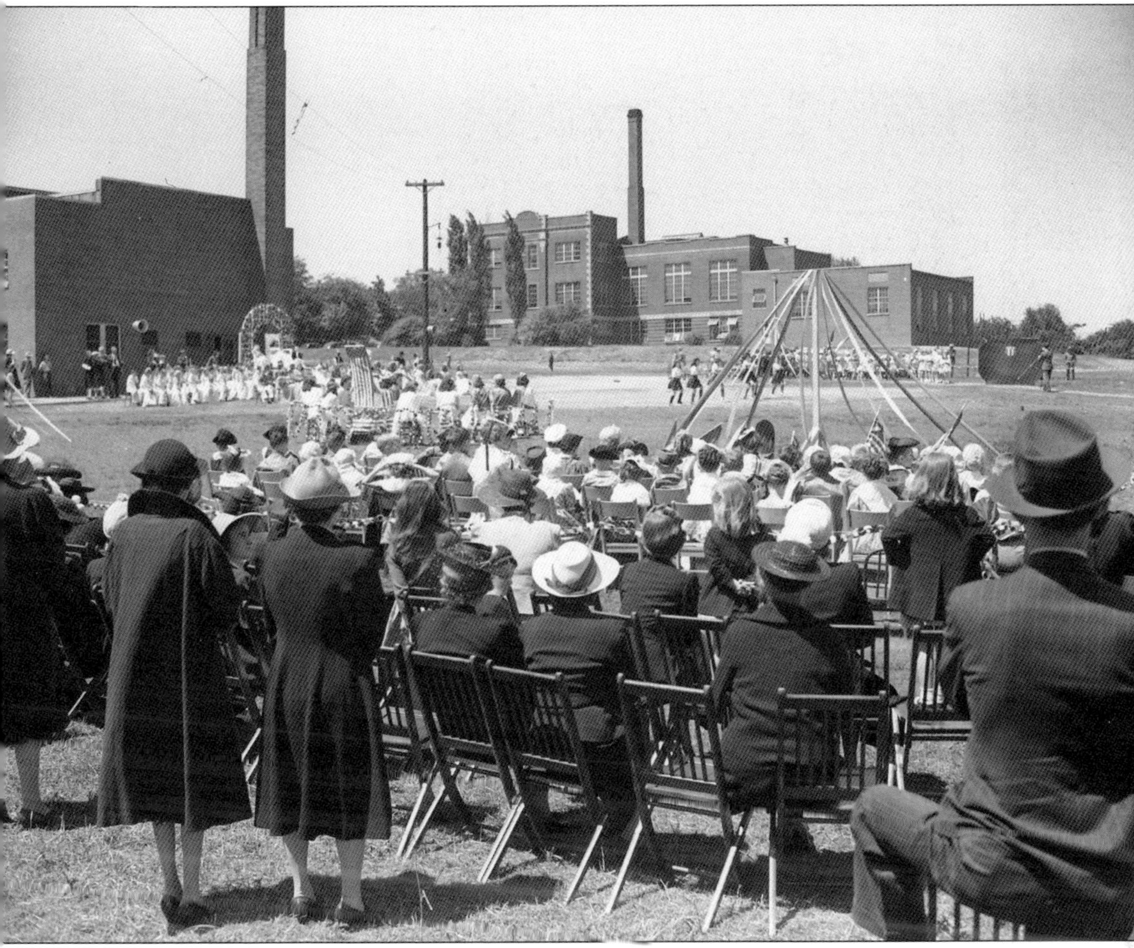

The maypole was an important part of celebrating May Day. The school used a large pole like the flagpole. Adults would attach colorful ribbons to the pole, and the students would hold the ribbons and dance around the pole. (Courtesy of Metro Archives.)

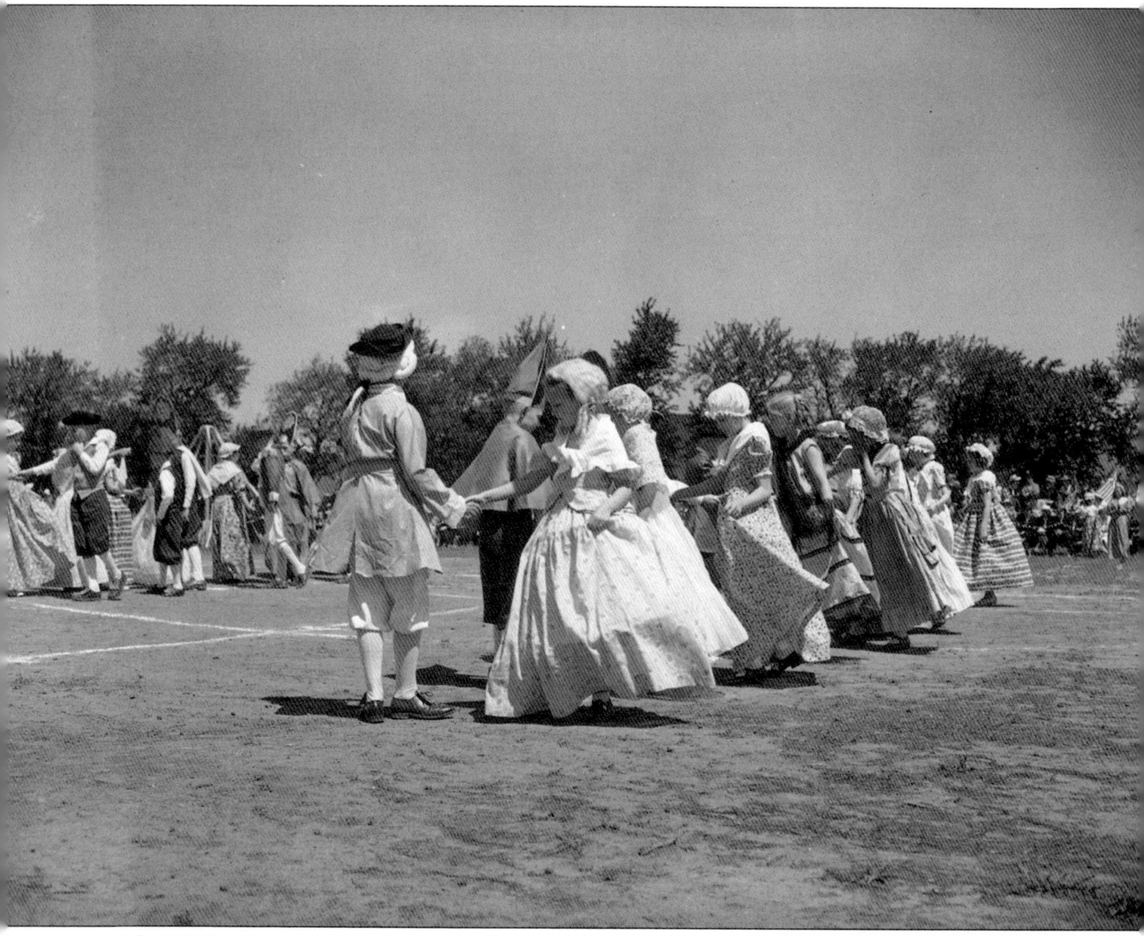

In the 1940s, the students enjoyed celebrating May Day. The students would have brought flowers to school. All the kids would have come to school dressed in festive clothes. May Day celebrations would be an all-day party with dancing and music. By the late 1950s, May Day was beginning to fade. In 1958, President Eisenhower attempted to bring interest back to celebrating May Day. Maybe after World War II, the phrase "May Day" had a meaning other than to celebrate. (Courtesy of Metro Archives.)

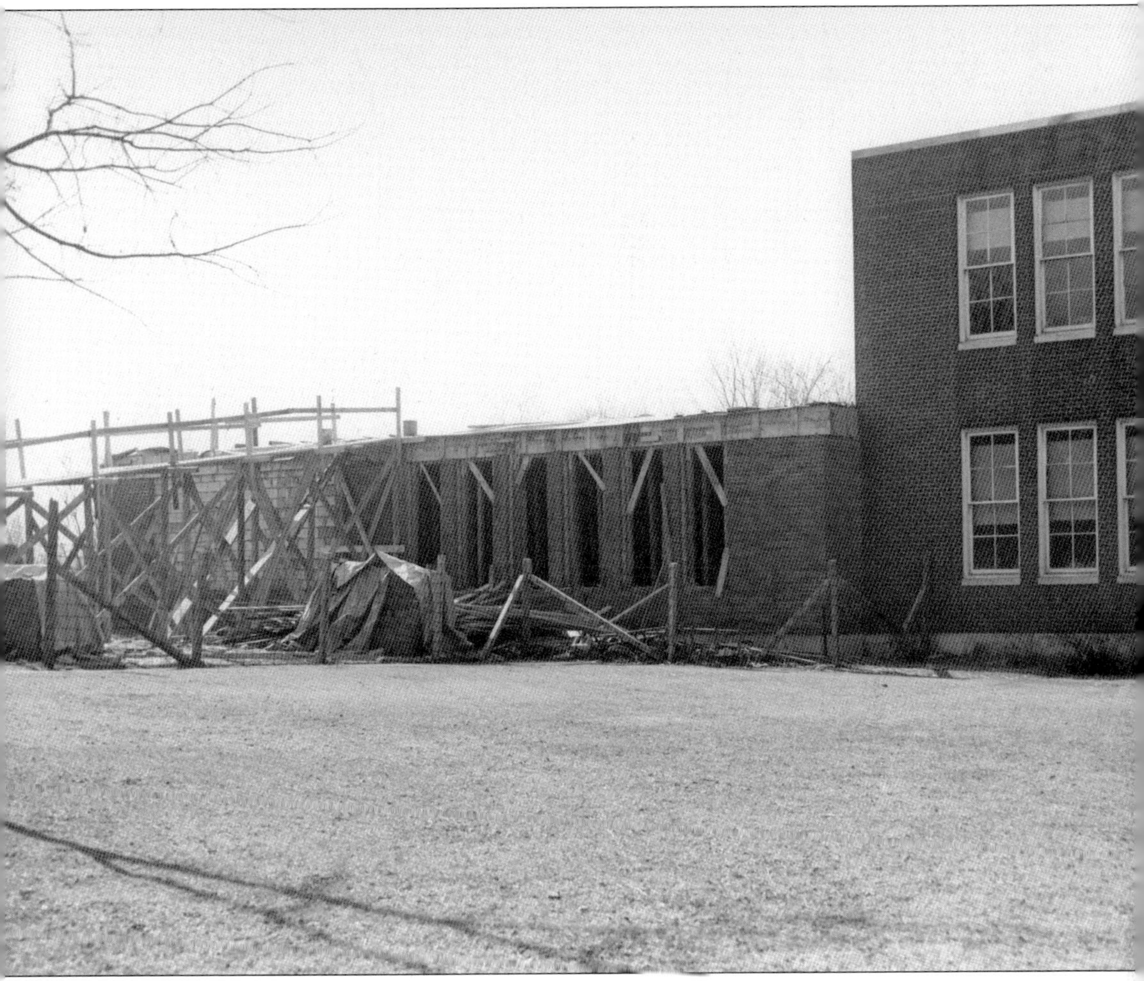

Eakin has experienced several expansions through the years. In this photograph, four rooms were added to the school, and more rooms were added years later. (Courtesy of Metro Archives.)

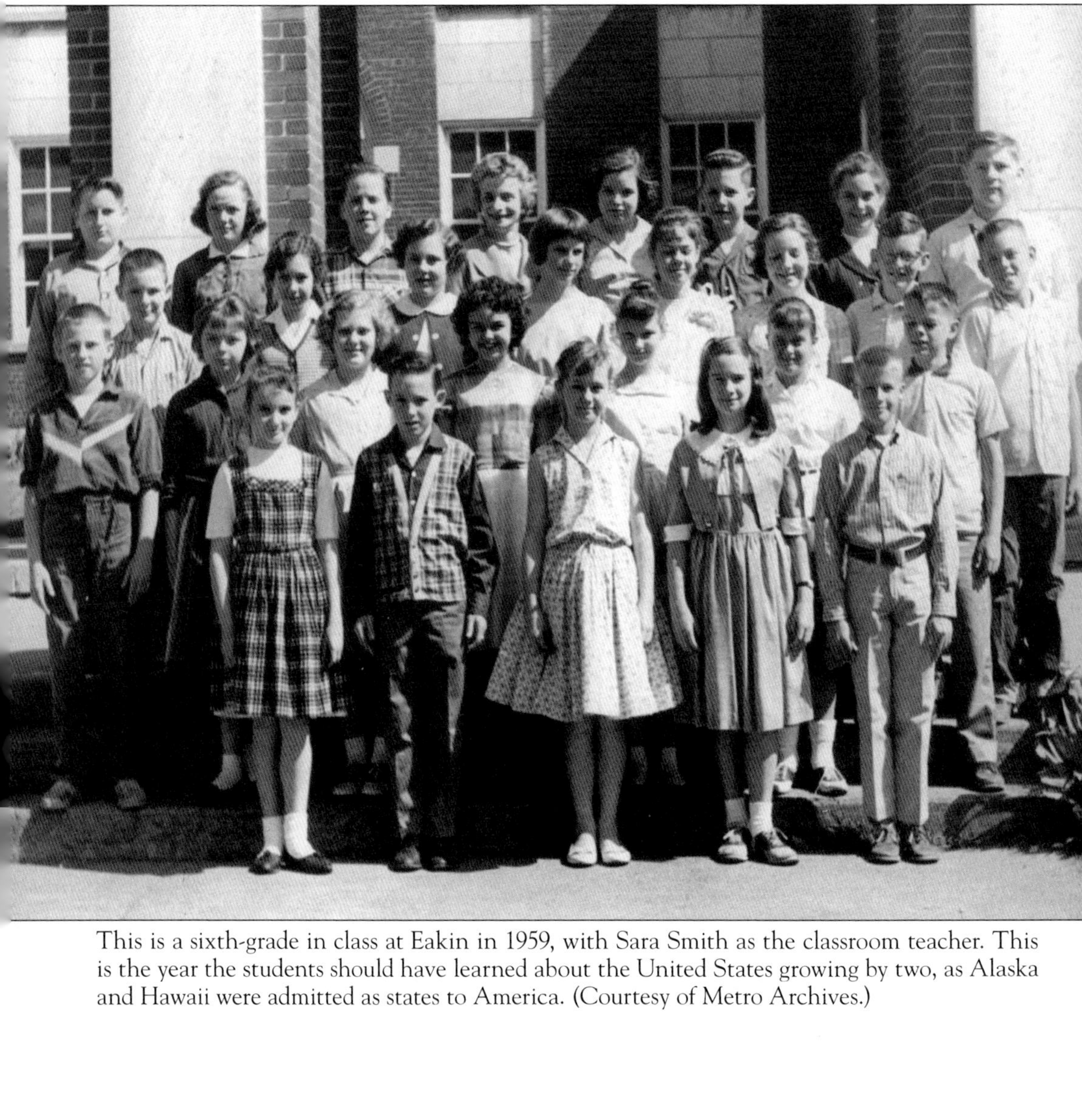

This is a sixth-grade in class at Eakin in 1959, with Sara Smith as the classroom teacher. This is the year the students should have learned about the United States growing by two, as Alaska and Hawaii were admitted as states to America. (Courtesy of Metro Archives.)

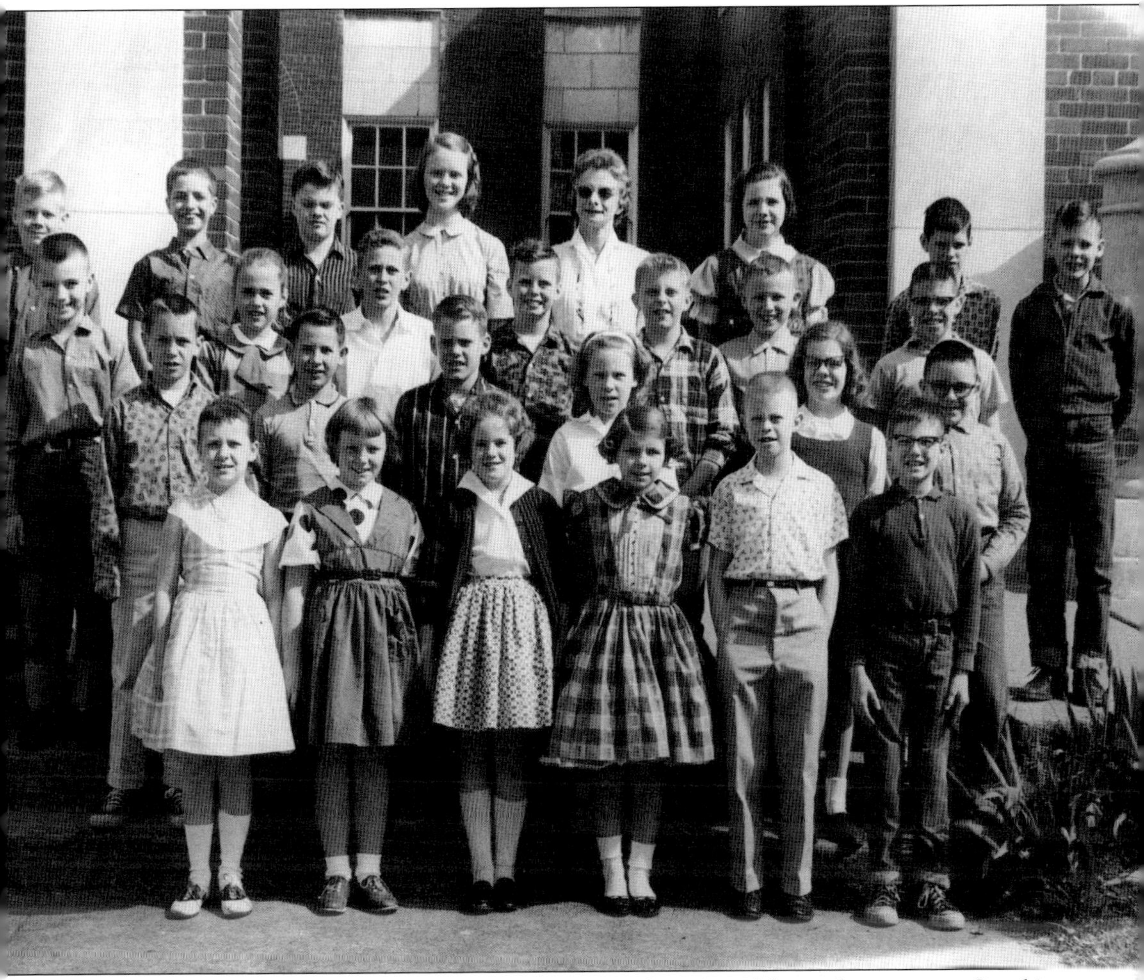

Pictured is a classroom of Sara Smith sometime in the early 1960s. If the students were in Smith's class in 1963, they would have learned about Nashville City and Davidson County becoming Metro as one government. (Courtesy of Metro Archives.)

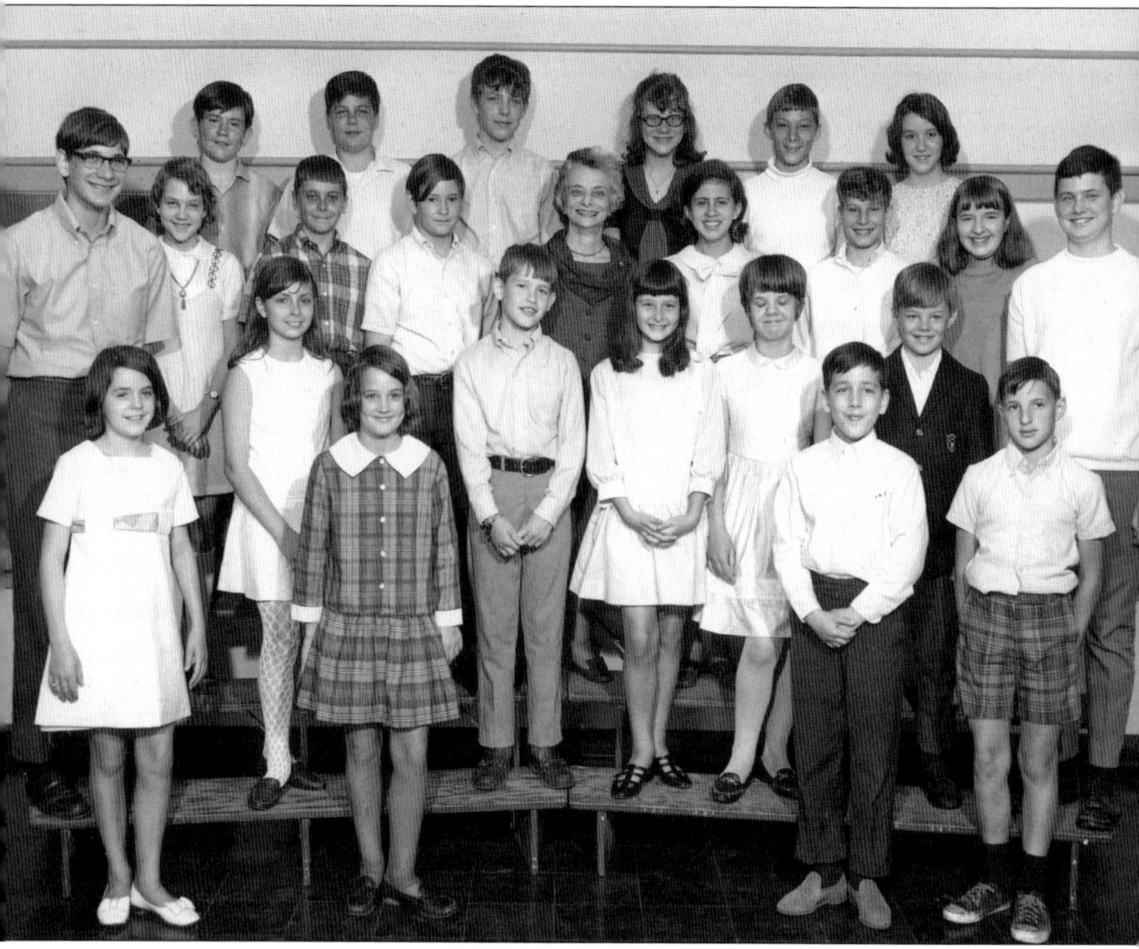

This classroom photograph was taken sometime during the 1960s. The Vietnam War and the civil rights movement were both in the news. (Courtesy of Metro Archives.)

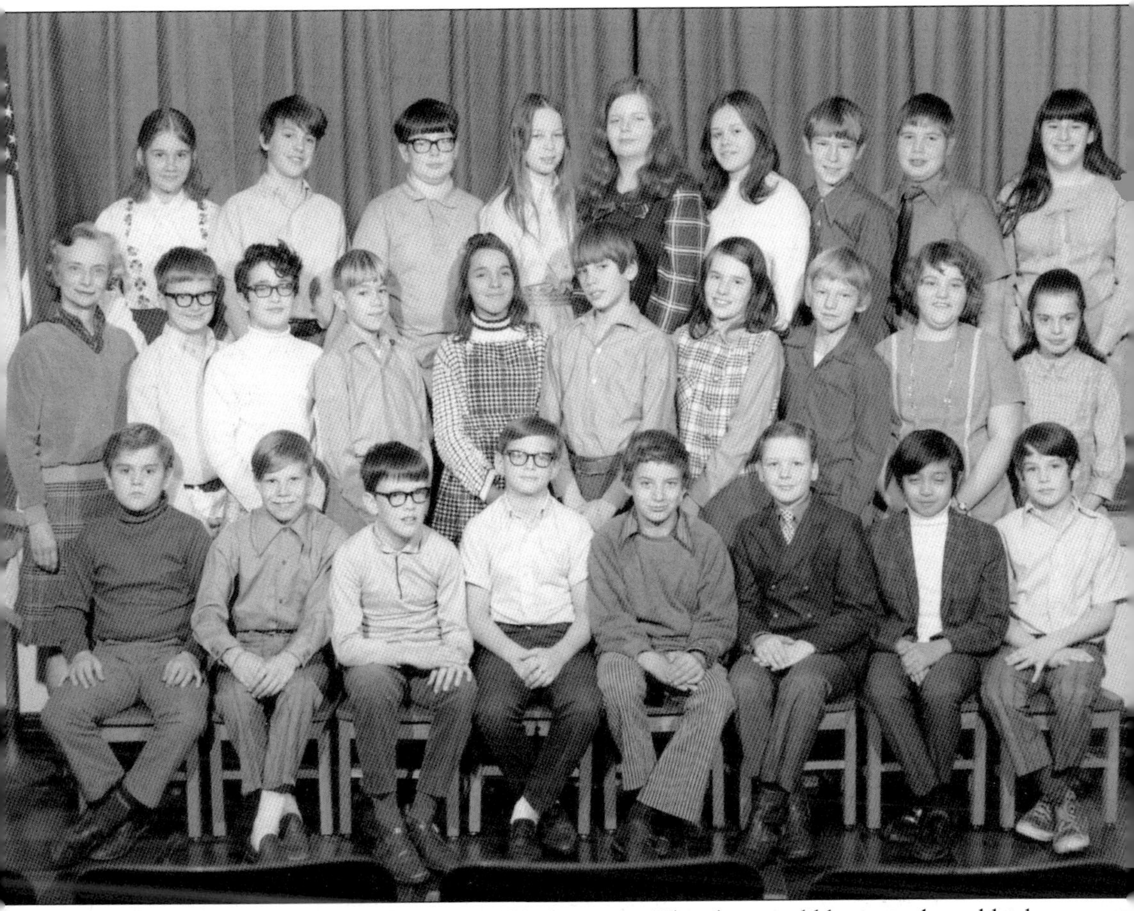

This photograph is of Sara Smith's 1969–1970 classroom. The class would have graduated high school in 1976, the same year America celebrated its 200th birthday (Courtesy of Metro Archives.)

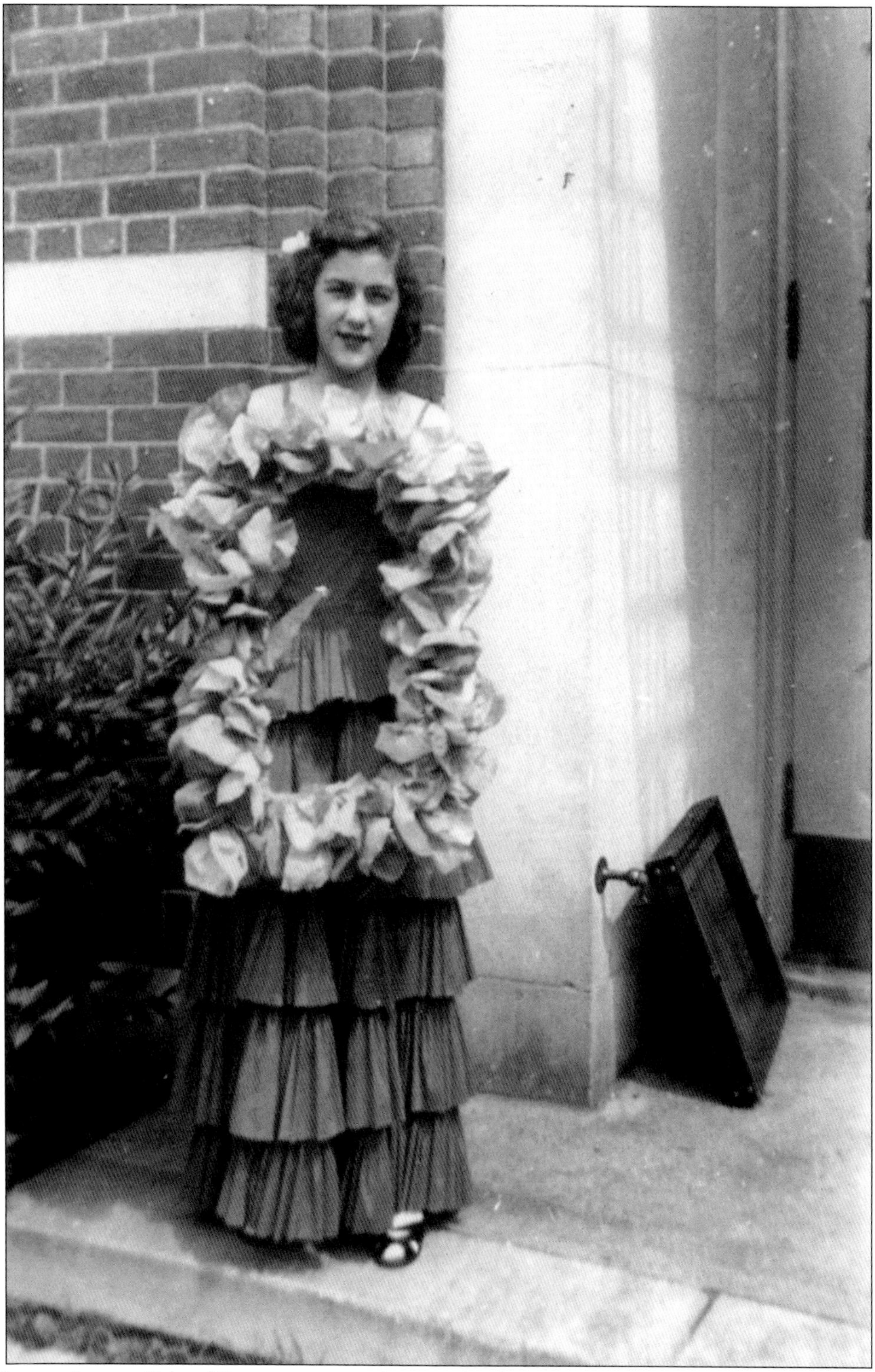

The teachers at Eakin Elementary joined in on the festivities on May Day. Pictured is Sarah Smith, who taught at Eakin for several years. (Courtesy of Metro Archives.)

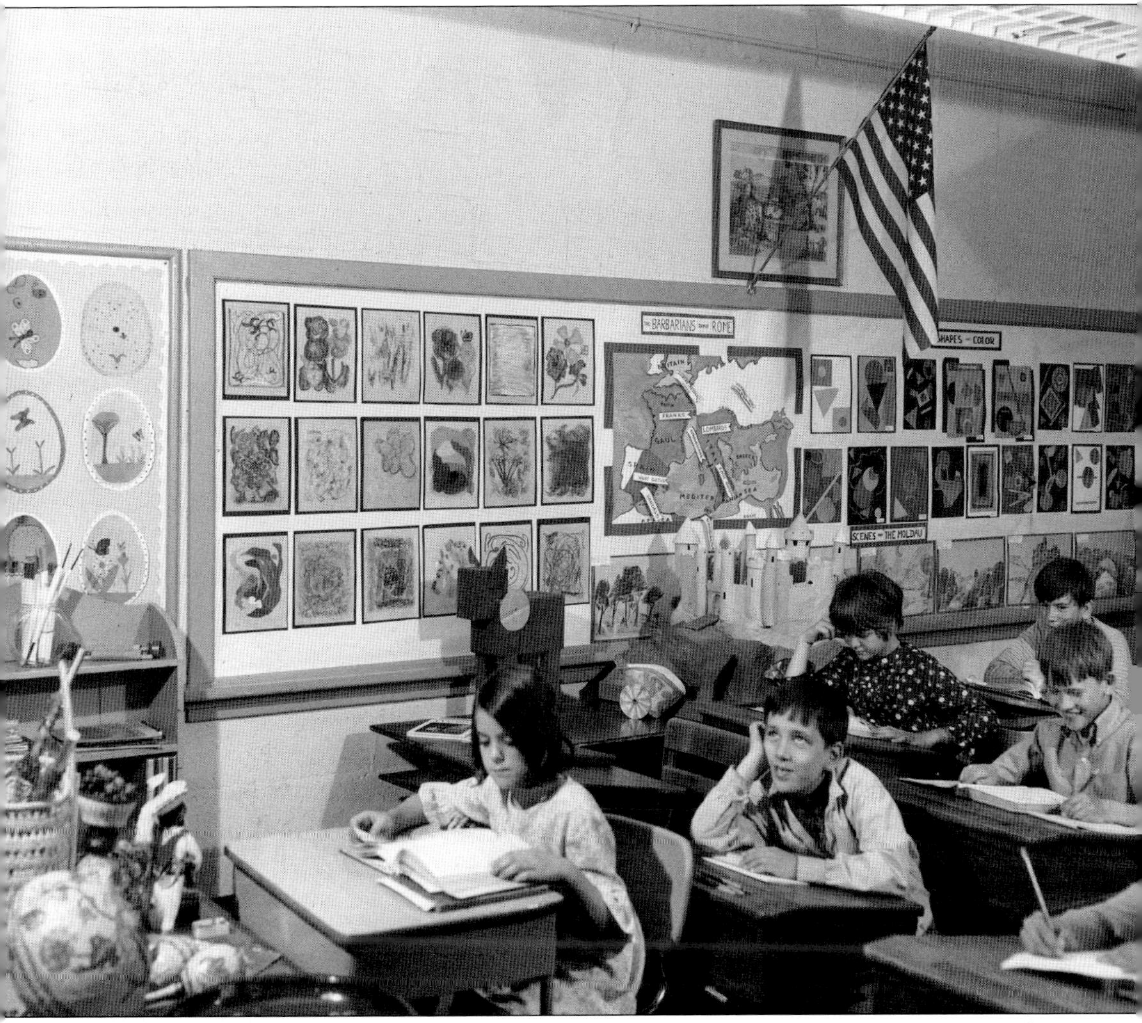

This photograph of Sarah Smith's classroom was taken in the late 1960s. From the poster on the wall, it appears the class may have been studying the invasion of the Roman Empire. The castle is a creative addition to the classroom. (Courtesy of Metro Archives.)

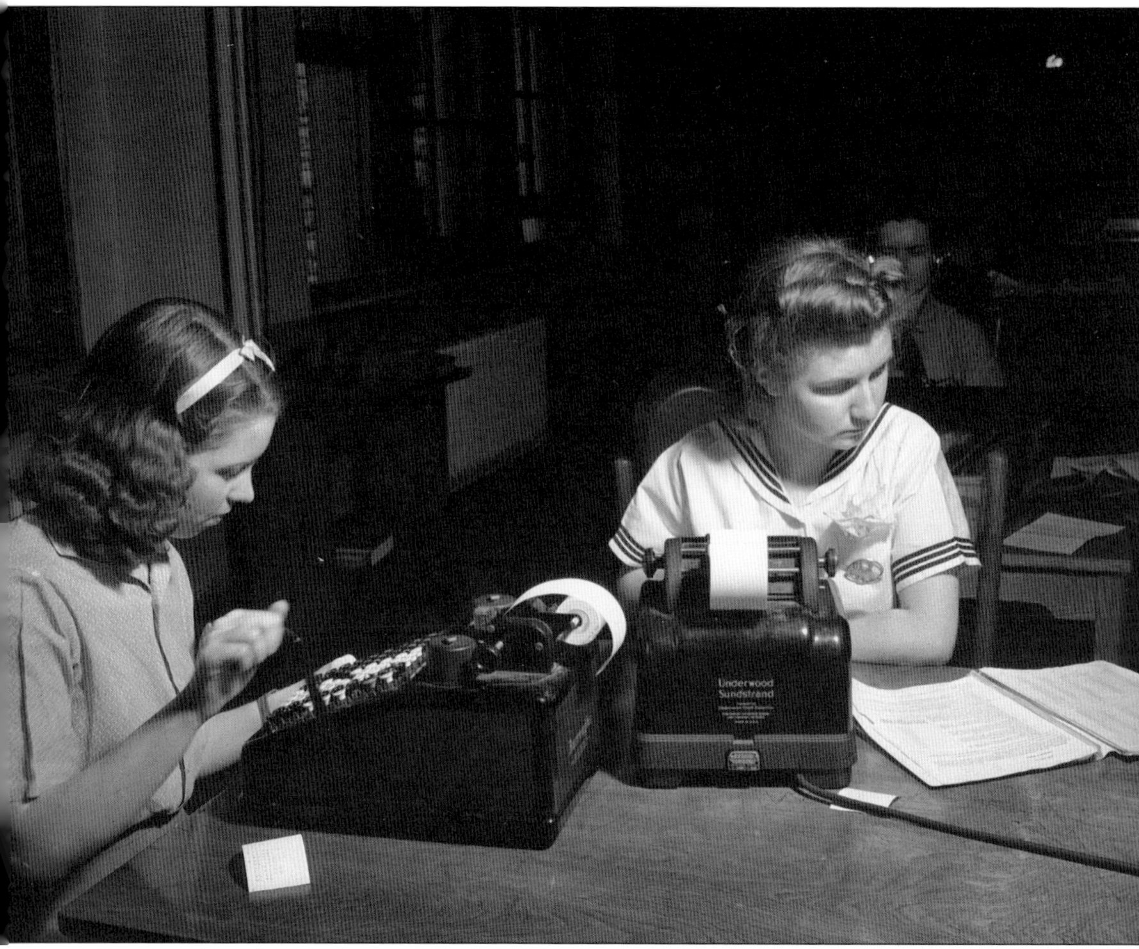

In 1941, the Eakin students are studying democratic principles. In 1941, the Nashville Public School System had a planned program on democracy and defense. Not only were the students taught the fundamentals of their form of government, but they also learned about preserving it. (Courtesy of Metro Archives.)

Five

Higher Education

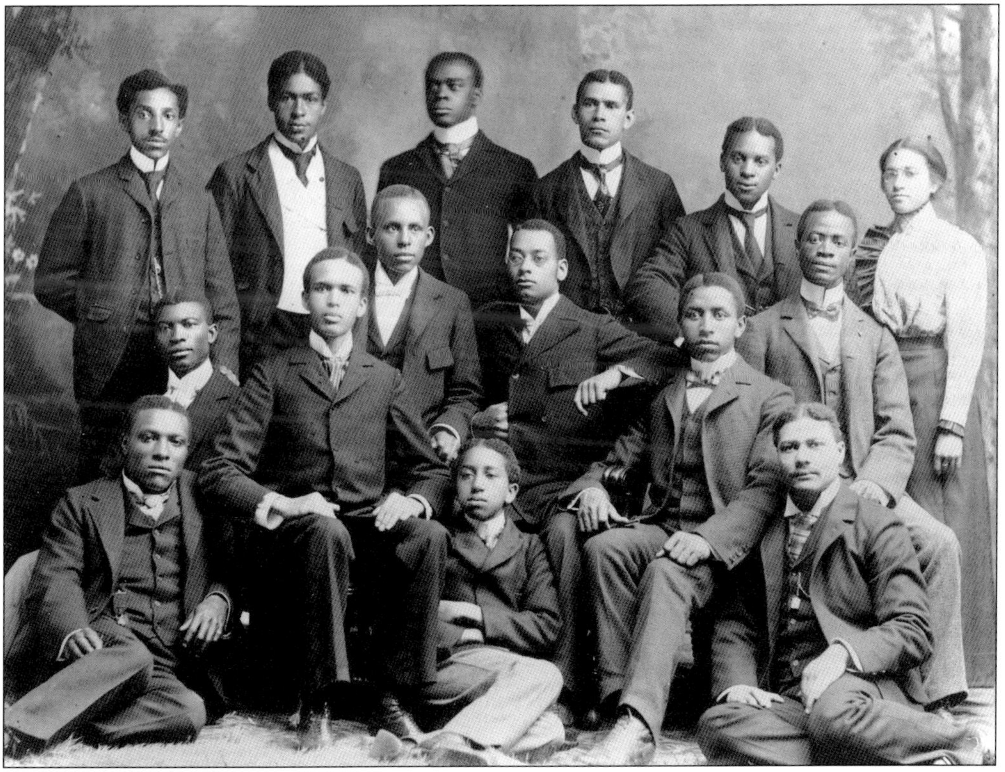

This photograph was taken in 1899 in an academic class at Roger Williams University. In 1866, Massachusetts Baptist minister Daniel W. Phillips arrived in Nashville. The purpose of Phillips coming to Nashville was to start a school for black preachers. Before a campus could be built, classes were taught from Phillips's basement. He approached other abolitionists across the country and, within two years, raised money to fund a building. Originally, the school was named the Nashville Normal and Theological Institute. (Courtesy of Library of Congress.)

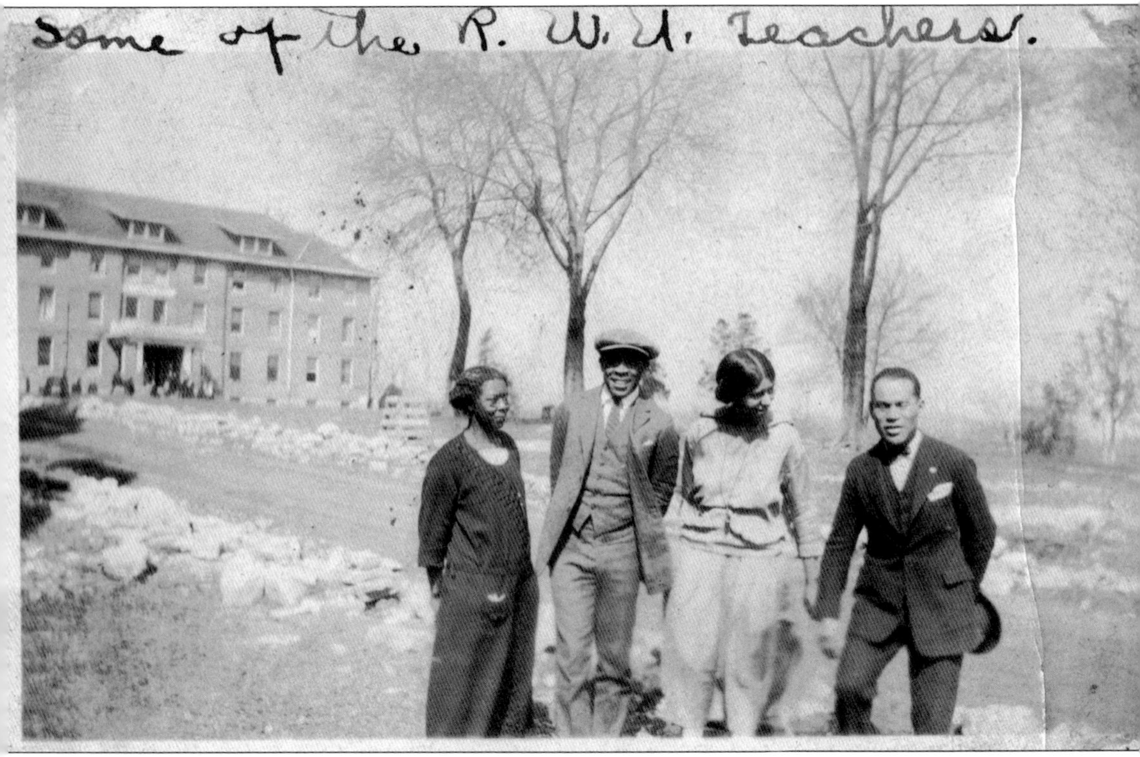

A few of the teachers from Roger Williams University are in this photograph. Thirty thousand dollars had been raised by Nashville Normal and Theologist Institute to purchase property near Vanderbilt University. (Courtesy of Tennessee State Library & Archives.)

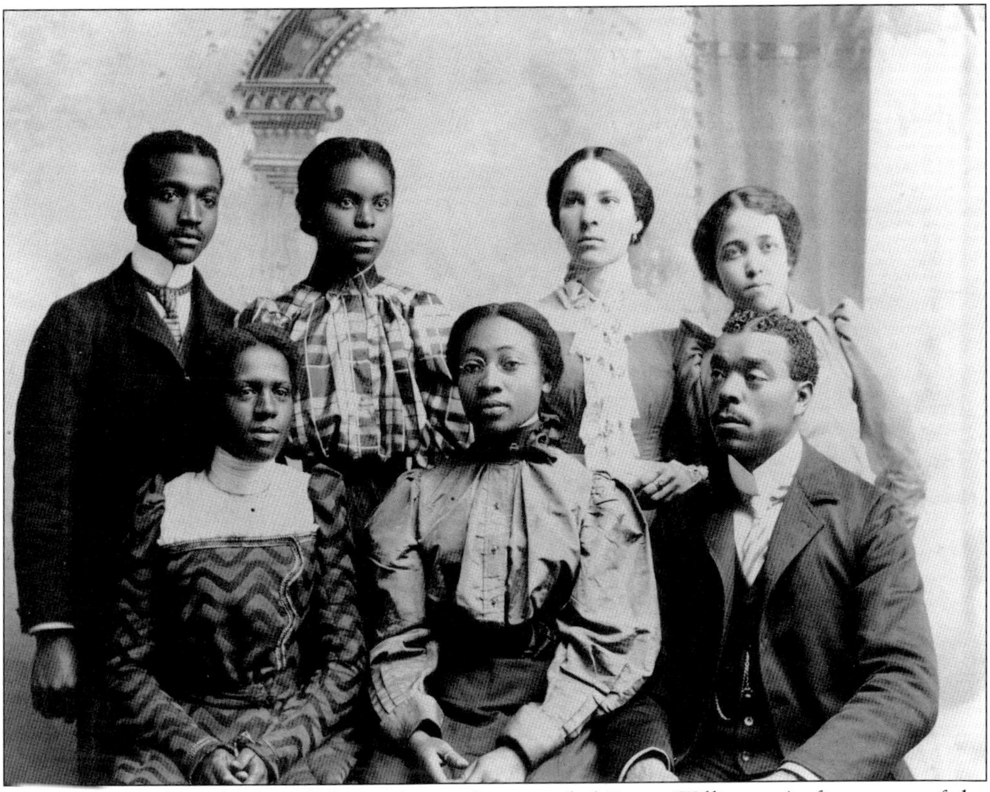

This photograph is of a few of the students who attended Roger Williams. At first, most of the adult students were extremely uneducated. Any students who could prove they had accomplished a fourth-grade education were accepted. (Courtesy of Library of Congress.)

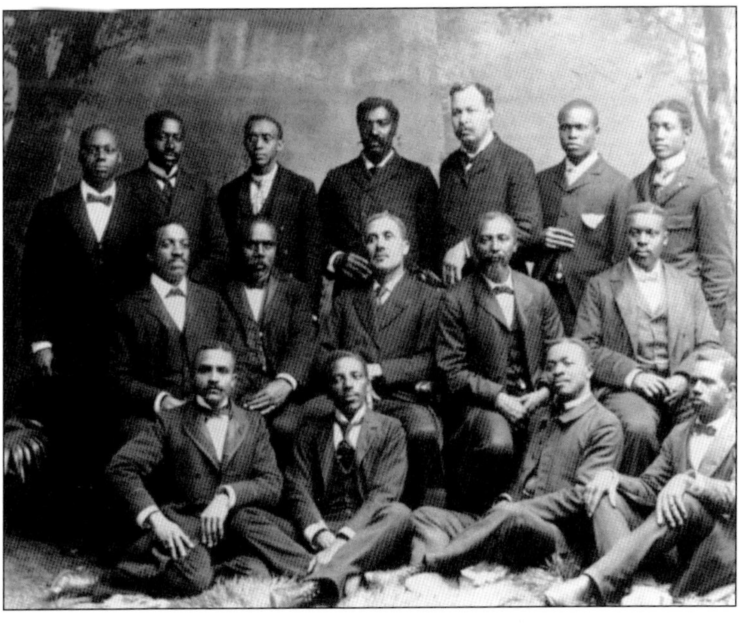

This photograph shows more of Roger Williams University. The students seen here were studying to be ministers. (Courtesy of Library of Congress.)

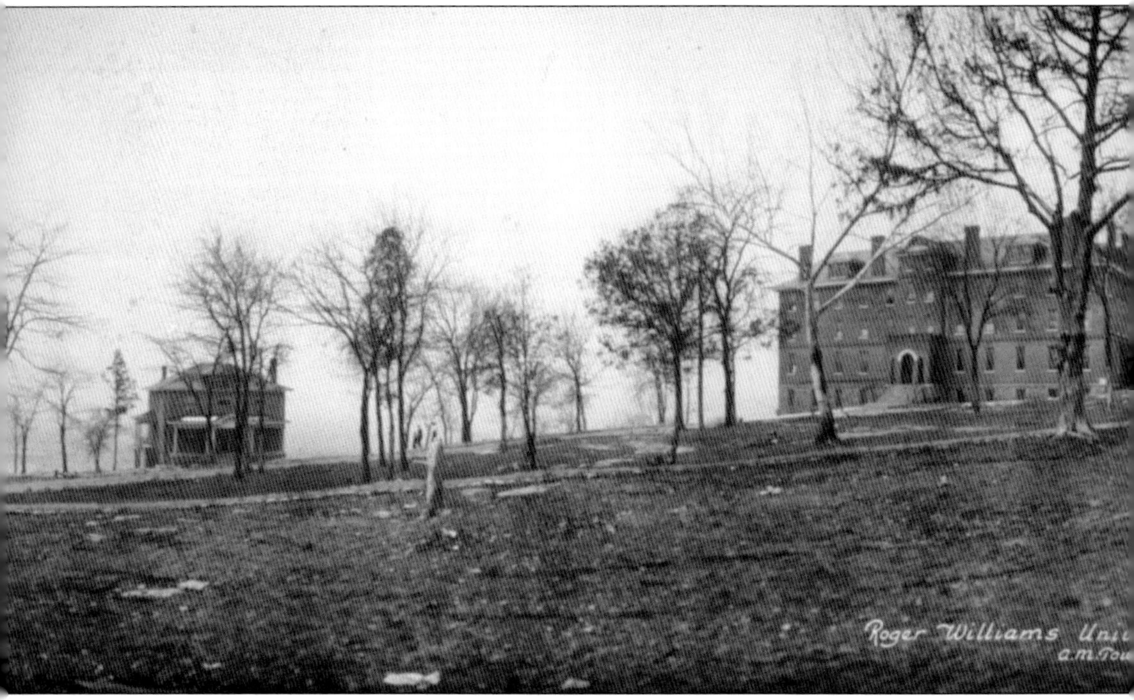

The campus was a farm once owned by William H. Gordan. Roger Williams was located on Twenty-First Avenue South across from Vanderbilt and stretched from Edgehill Avenue to Belcourt Avenue. The Gordans' former home was renamed Centennial Hall. A floor and two wings were

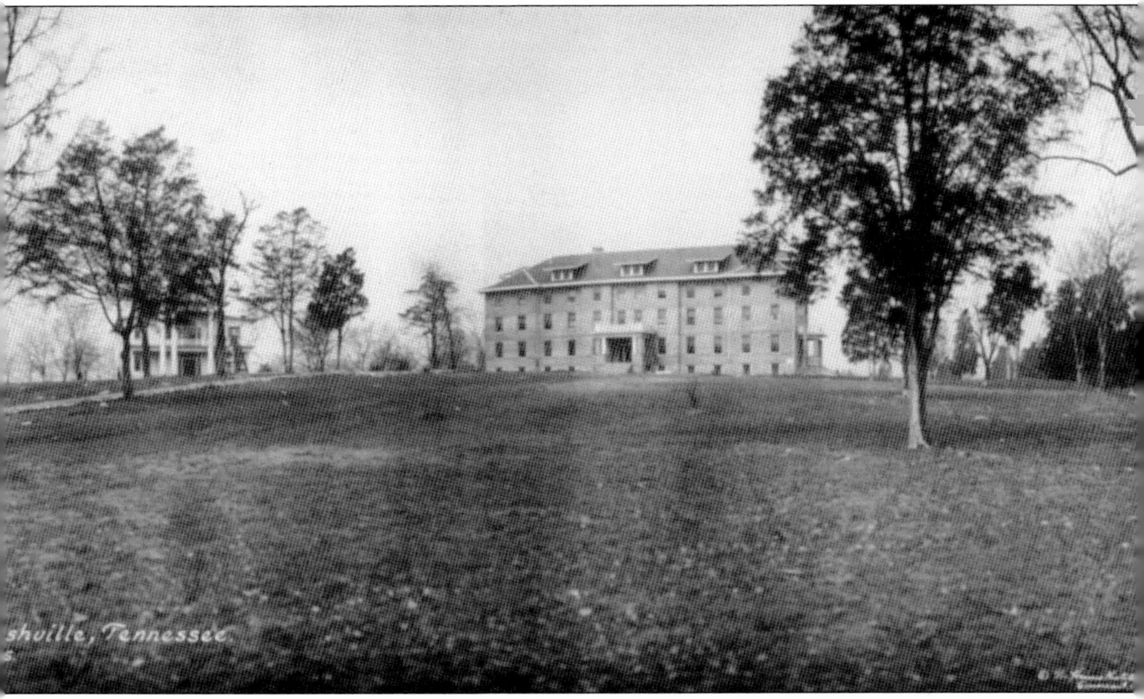

added to the building. Centennial Hall was the main structure on the grounds and housed the science library dormitories. By 1886, Roger Williams was one of first African American universities to offer a master's degree. (Courtesy of Library of Congress.)

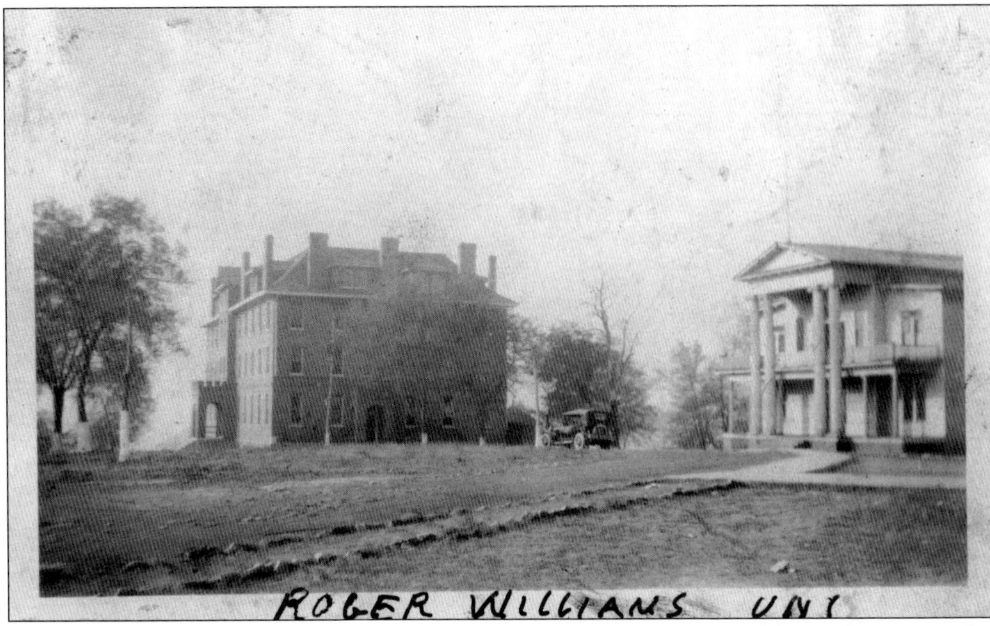

The campus and buildings at Roger Williams were victims of gunshots and fires. Three years after the last fire, Roger Williams relocated to Whites Creek Pike on the east side of the Cumberland River. In 1922, Roger Williams suffered another hard blow. The student body had diminished to 159, and the faculty was down to 12 teachers. Financially, Rogers Williams would not survive, and by the end of 1929, Roger Williams was closing the Nashville campus. The school merged with Howe Institute (Lemoyne Owen College), and the students and teachers moved to Memphis. American Bible College is now located on the Whites Creek Pike site that was once occupied by Roger Williams. The property on the east side of Twenty-First Avenue South stretched to today's Belcourt Avenue. Much of the land became home to George Peabody College for Teachers. (Courtesy of Tennessee State Library & Archives.)

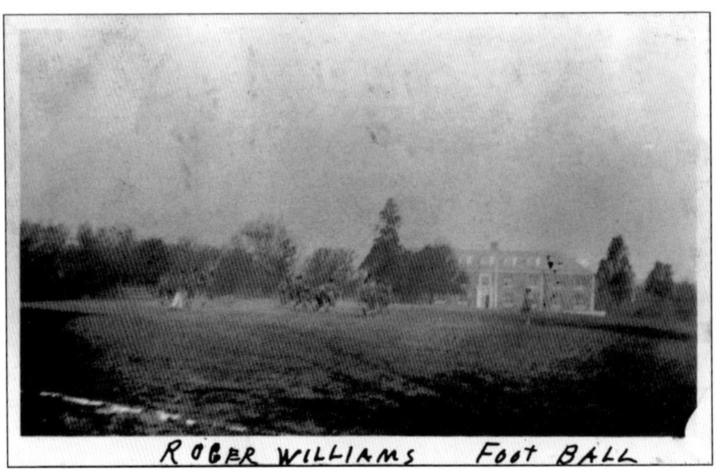

This is a photograph of a group at Roger Williams playing football. The campus grounds look very isolated. (Courtesy of Tennessee State Library & Archives.)

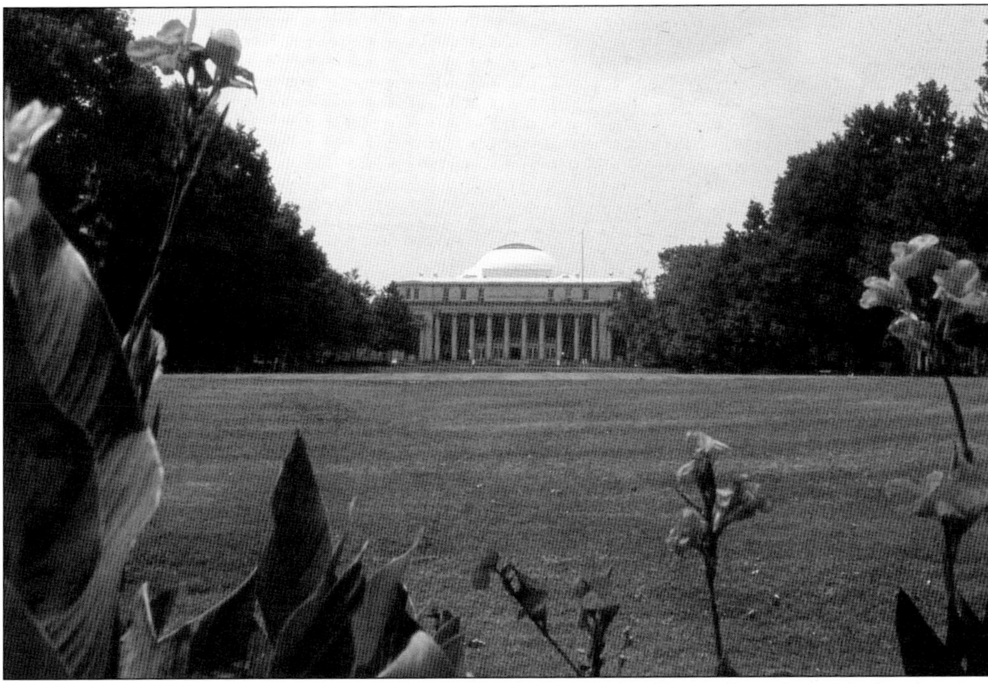

The Peabody campus was spectacular in the springtime. Nashville's earliest form of schooling was in 1784 at Davidson Academy. For over 200 years, Davidson Academy had seen different names before becoming George Peabody College for Teachers. After Davidson Academy, the school was renamed Cumberland College. Another name was the University of Nashville. By 1909, the school was named George Peabody College for Teachers. Within five years of the last renaming, the school was moved to the former Roger Williams site near Hillsboro Village. (Courtesy of Metro Archives.)

This photograph is of a gathering of students and the public in 1962 on the lawn at the Social Religious Building. The Social Religious Building is the most recognized building on Peabody's campus. The dome on the building was imitated from Thomas Jefferson's Monticello. The building is now known as the Wyatt Center. (Courtesy of Tennessee State Library & Archives.)

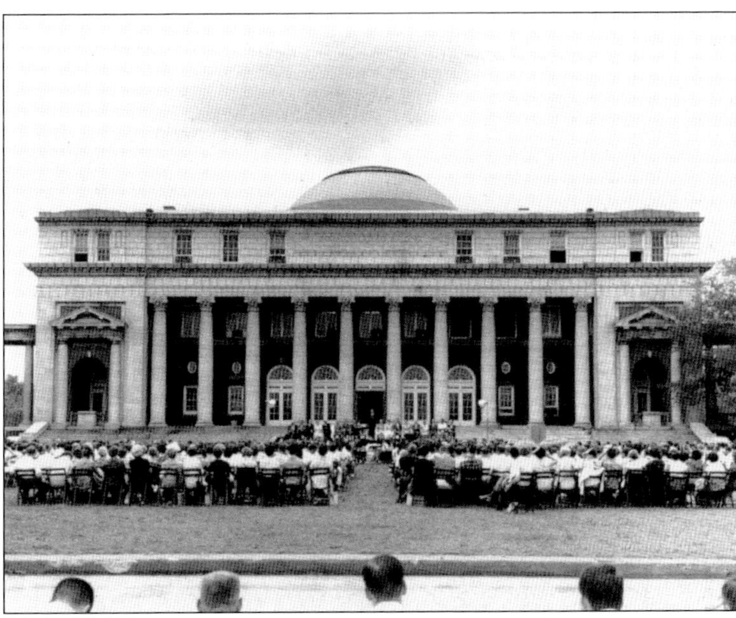

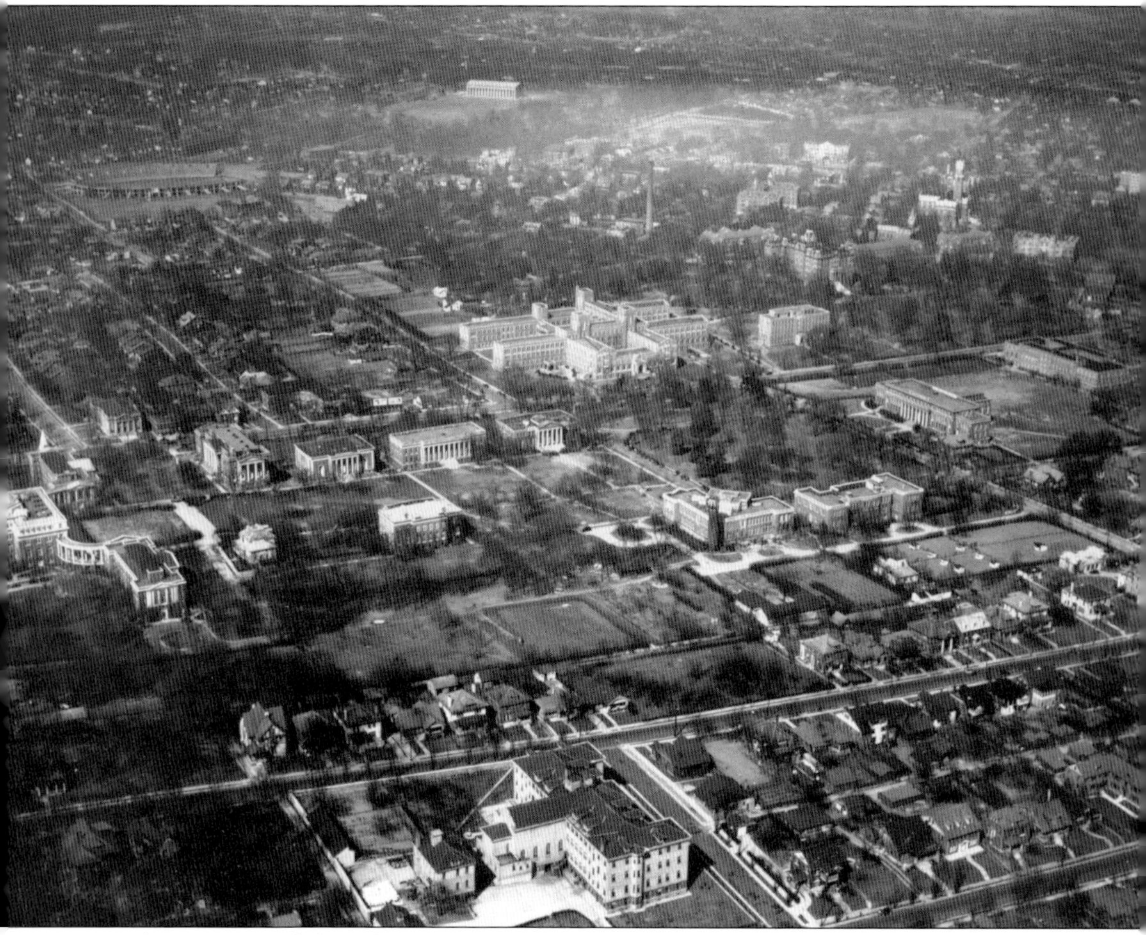

In this 1930s aerial shot of George Peabody College for Teachers, all of the building's entrances are to the center of the grounds. The campus grew to 22 buildings and was on almost 50 acres of property. The design of the campus was inspired by Thomas Jefferson's design for the University of Virginia's Academical Village. The Wyatt Center is probably the most recognized building at Peabody; the domed-shaped rooftop was copied from Thomas Jefferson's Monticello. Bruce Payne transferred from the University of Virginia and moved to Nashville to oversee the start of Peabody. Payne eventually became president of Peabody. In 1979, Peabody merged with Vanderbilt. The Parthenon in Centennial Park is visible in the top center of the photograph. (Courtesy of Metro Archives.)

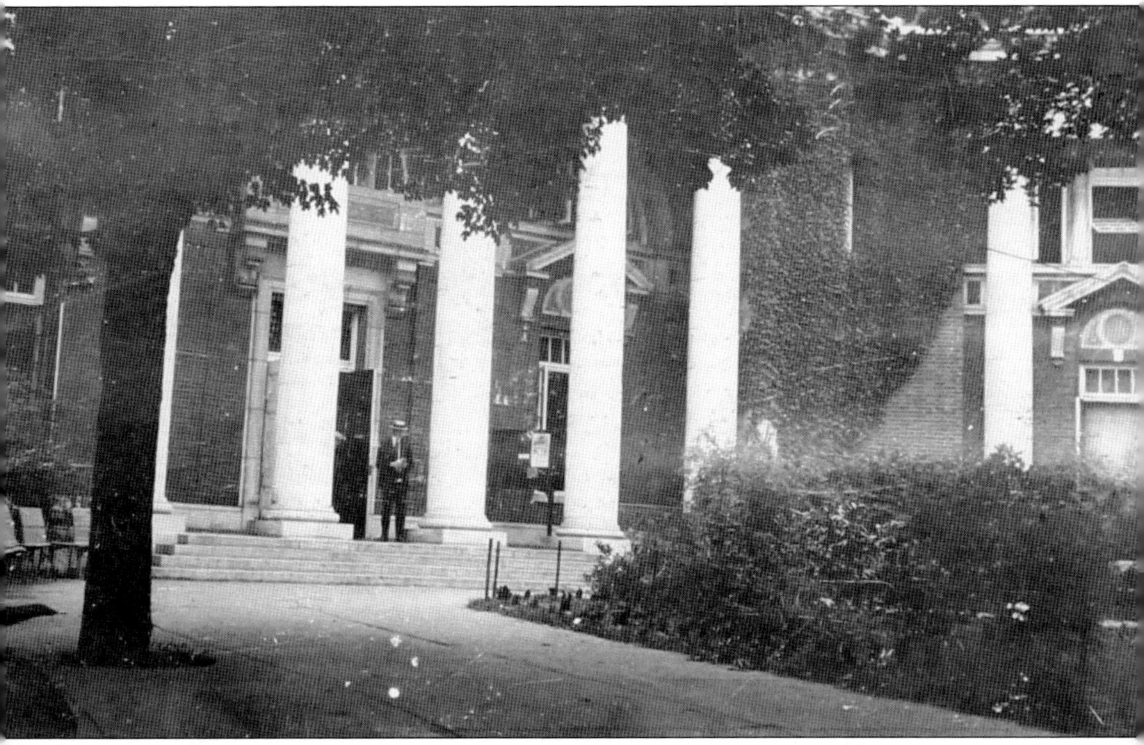

The Mayborn Building at Peabody was first known as the Manual Training Building. It was erected in 1914 and is considered the oldest building on the Peabody campus. (Courtesy of Metro Archives.)

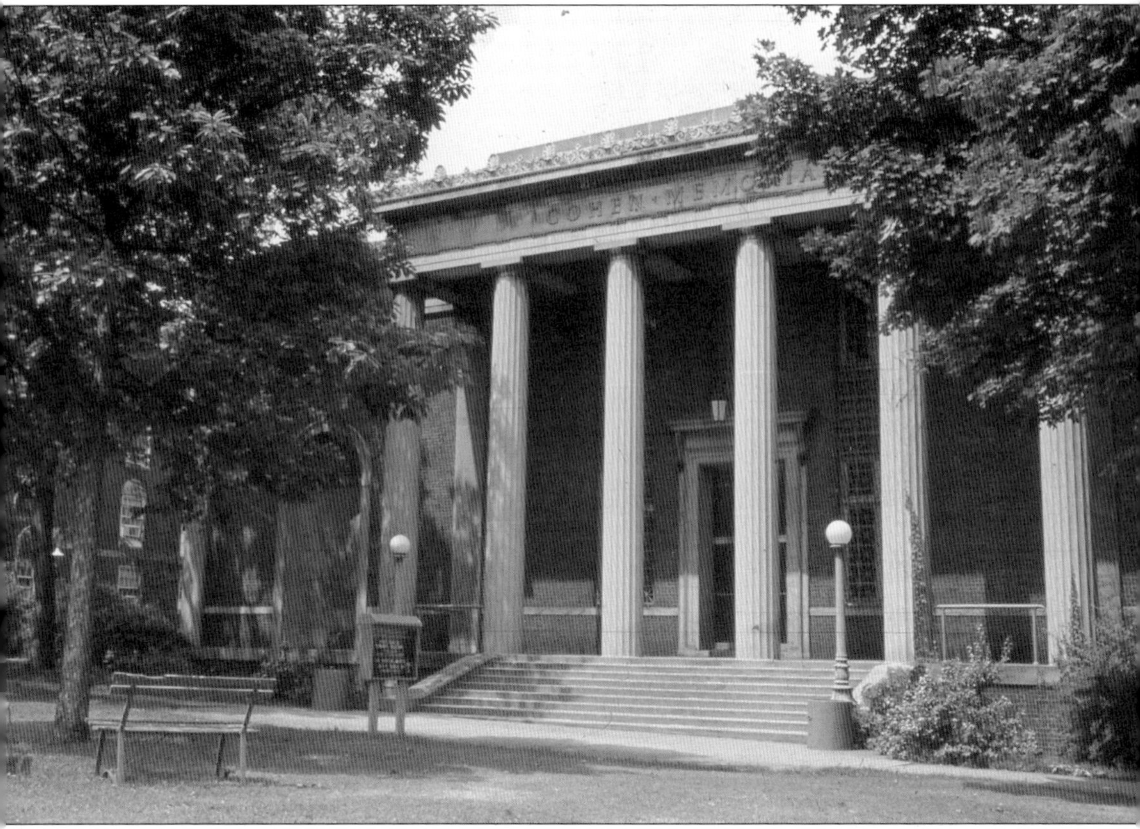

The Cohen Memorial Hall was built in 1926, a donation from George Etta Brinkley Cohen, the widow of Meyer Cohen. The gift became the art department at Peabody. Until her passing, George Etta Cohen lived in a small apartment in the building on the third floor looking over the lawn. (Courtesy of Metro Archives.)

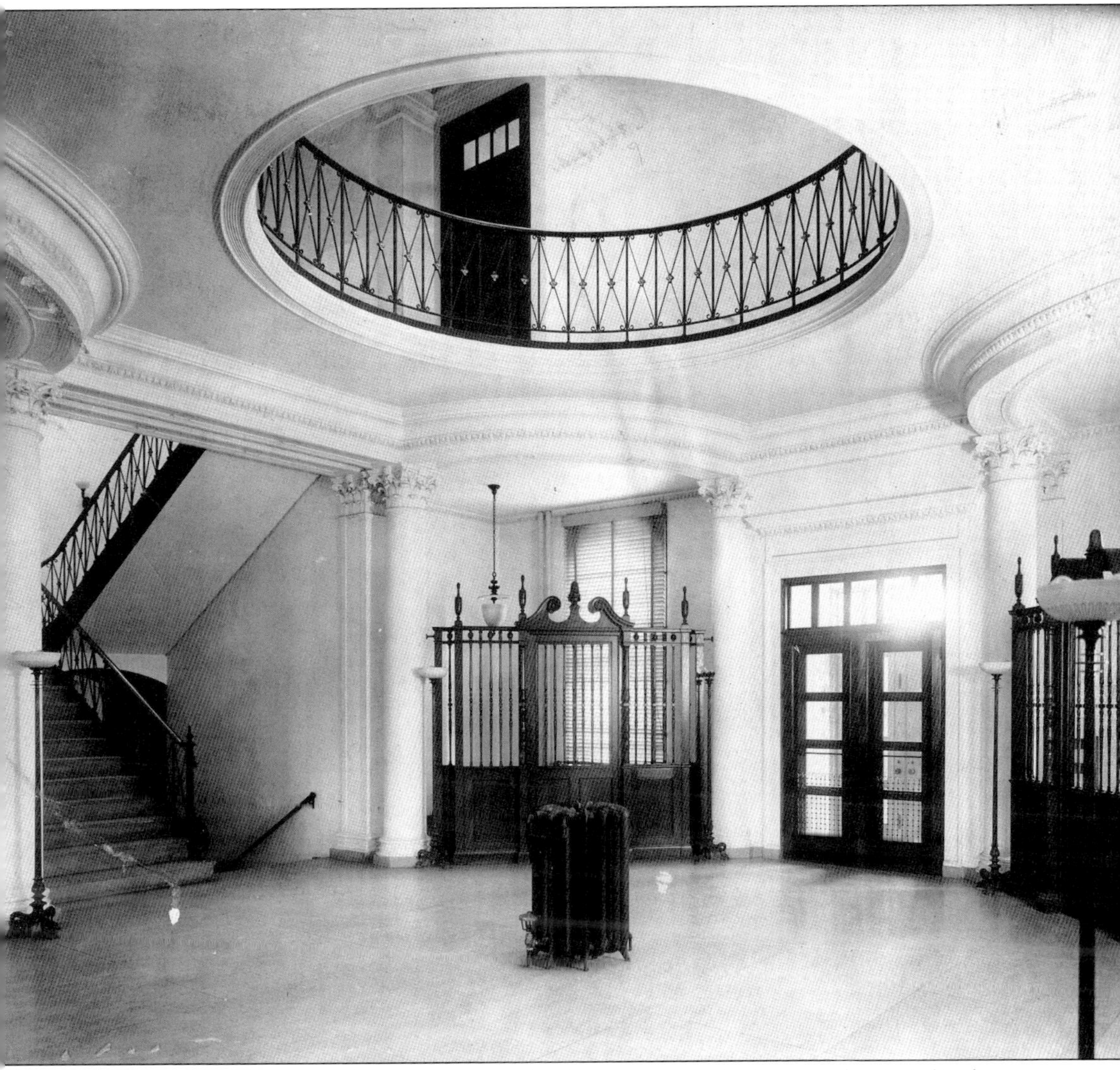

This picture was taken in 1917 and appears to be from inside the hallway at the Social Religious Building on the Peabody campus. The name of the Social Religious Building was changed to the Wyatt Center in 2000. (Courtesy of Metro Archives.)

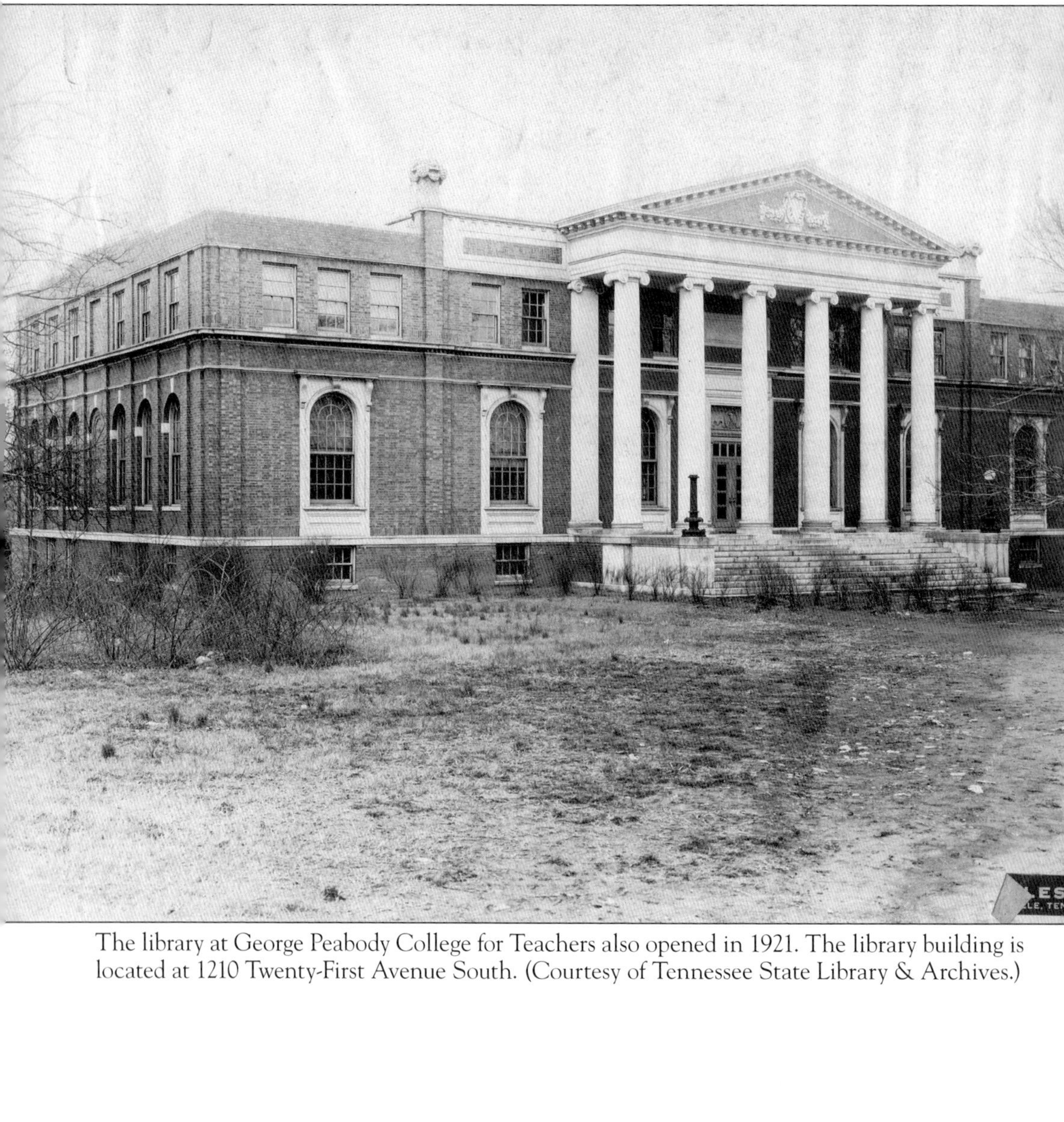

The library at George Peabody College for Teachers also opened in 1921. The library building is located at 1210 Twenty-First Avenue South. (Courtesy of Tennessee State Library & Archives.)

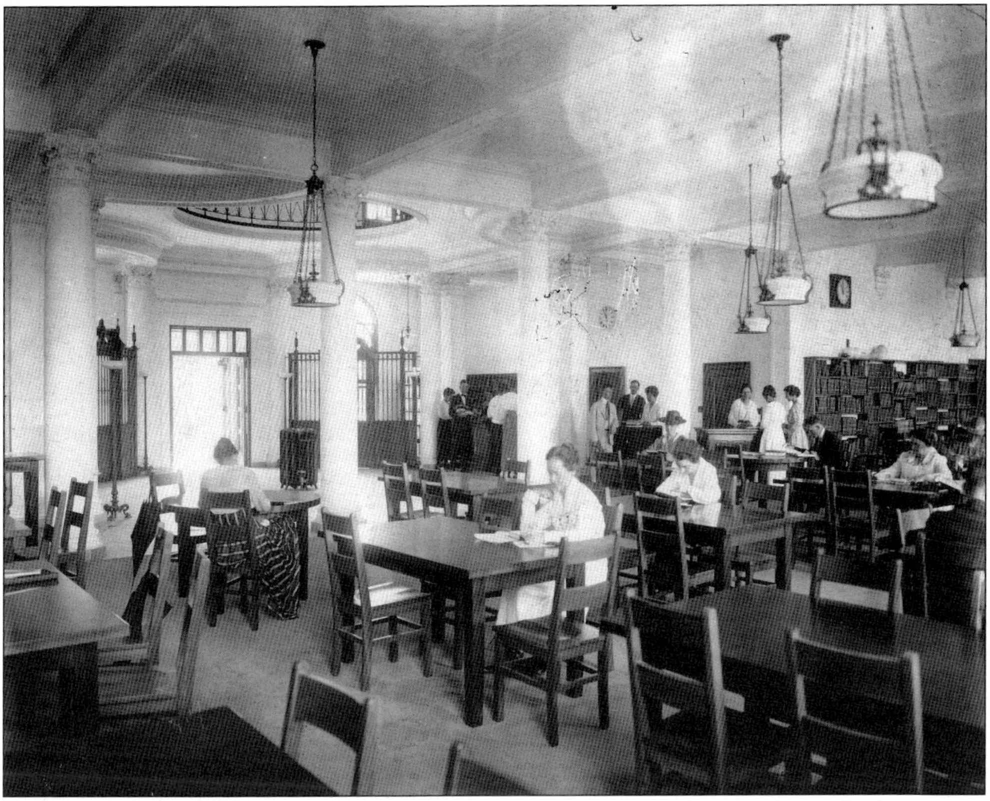

This 1917 photograph was taken inside the Social Religious Building on the Peabody campus. The rotunda is visible in the background. (Courtesy of Metro Archives.)

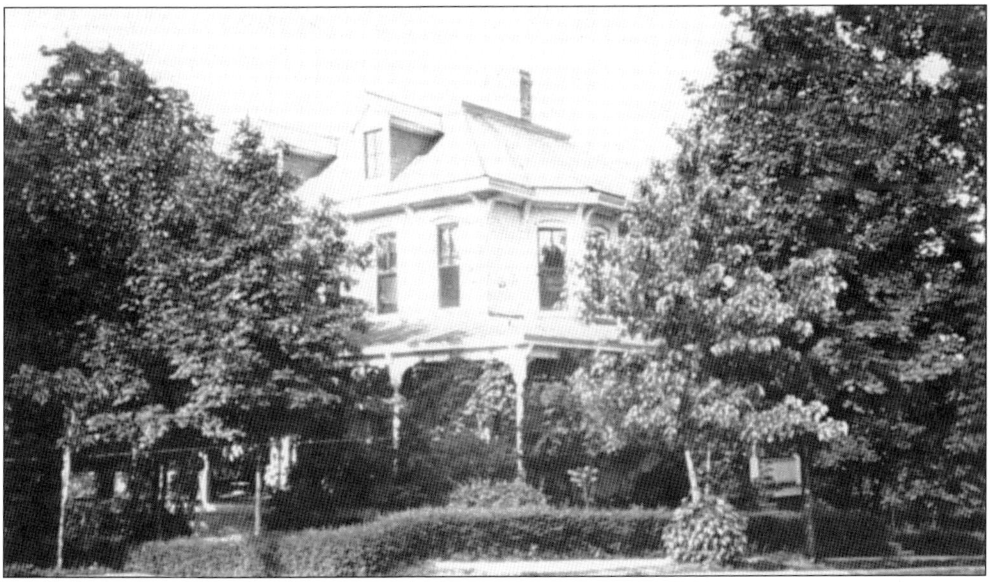

The Peabody College Administration Building was erected in 1925. In 1965, twenty-two of the buildings on the George Peabody College for Teachers campus was nominated to be included in the National Register of Historic Places. (Courtesy of Metro Archives.)

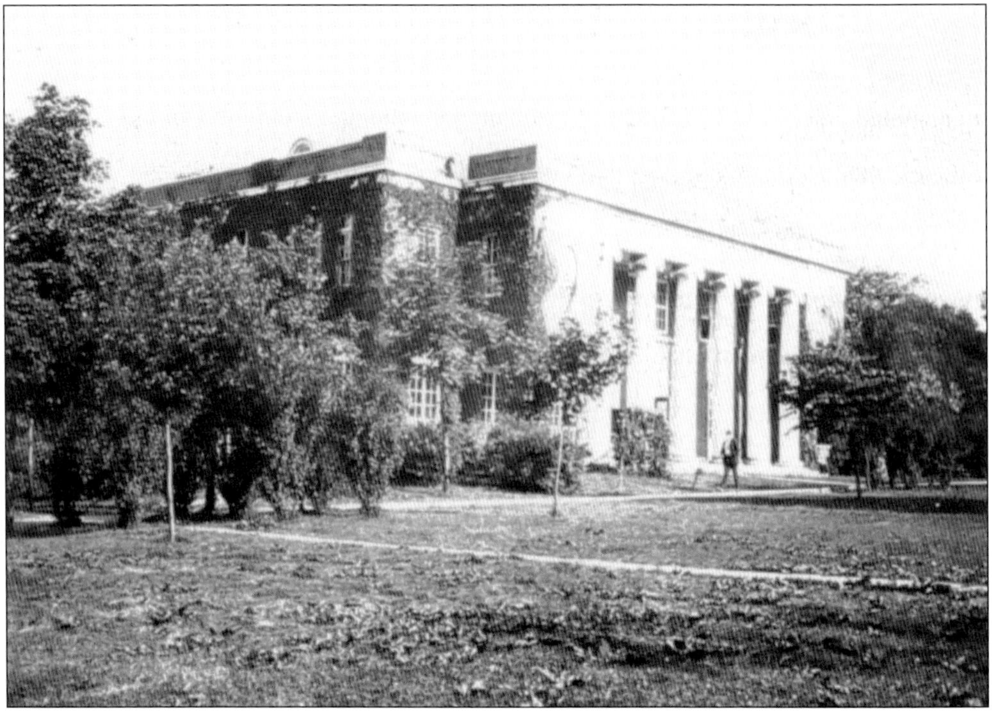

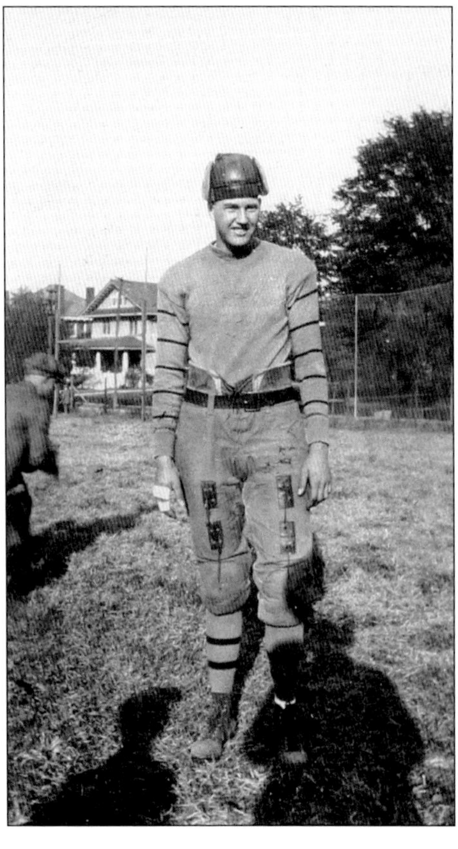

The Peabody Demonstration School was started in 1915 as a summer school observation program for students becoming teachers and school administrators. From 1915 to 1921, the demonstration school used the basement of the Jesup Building at Peabody. The Peabody Demonstration School building was ready in 1921. (Courtesy of Tennessee State Library & Archives.)

This is a member of the 1921 Peabody football team. The first classes of Peabody Demonstration School were in 1915, but the school did not have a football team for three years. During the fall of 1934, the school completed the season with a 9-0 record. During the nine games, none of the opposing teams scored any points. (Courtesy of Tennessee State Library & Archives.)

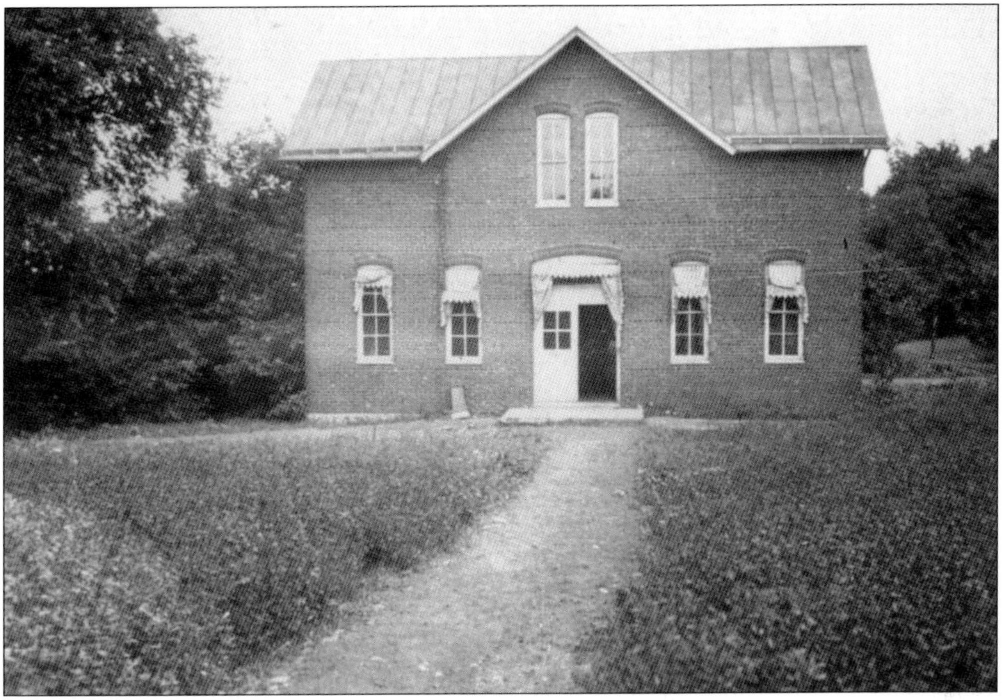

George Peabody College for Teachers Bookstore opened in 1921 on campus. The bookstore closed after George Peabody College for Teachers merged with Vanderbilt. (Courtesy of Tennessee State Library & Archives.)

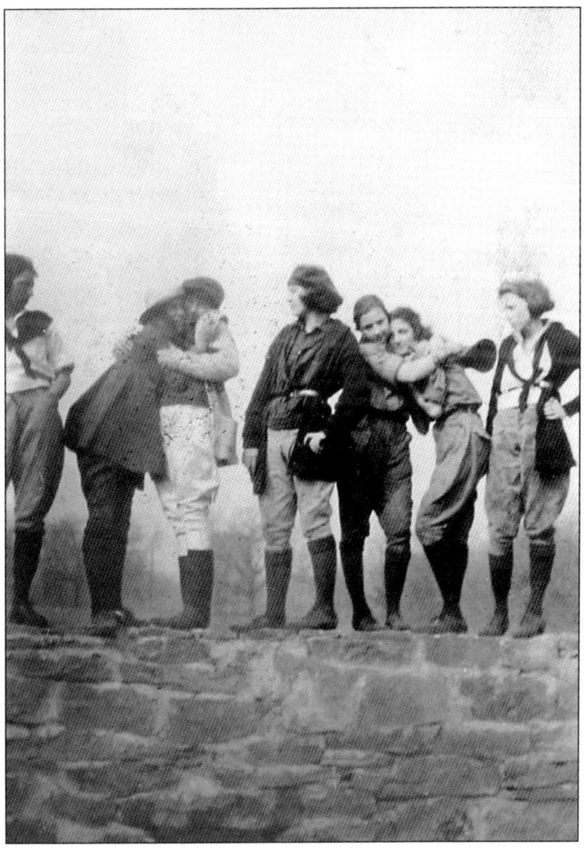

This is the Peabody Demonstration School girls' basketball team for the 1920–1921 season. During the 1920s, the girls' team won several city championships and placed second in state tournaments. The girls actually won a state championship in 1927. (Courtesy of Tennessee State Library & Archives.)

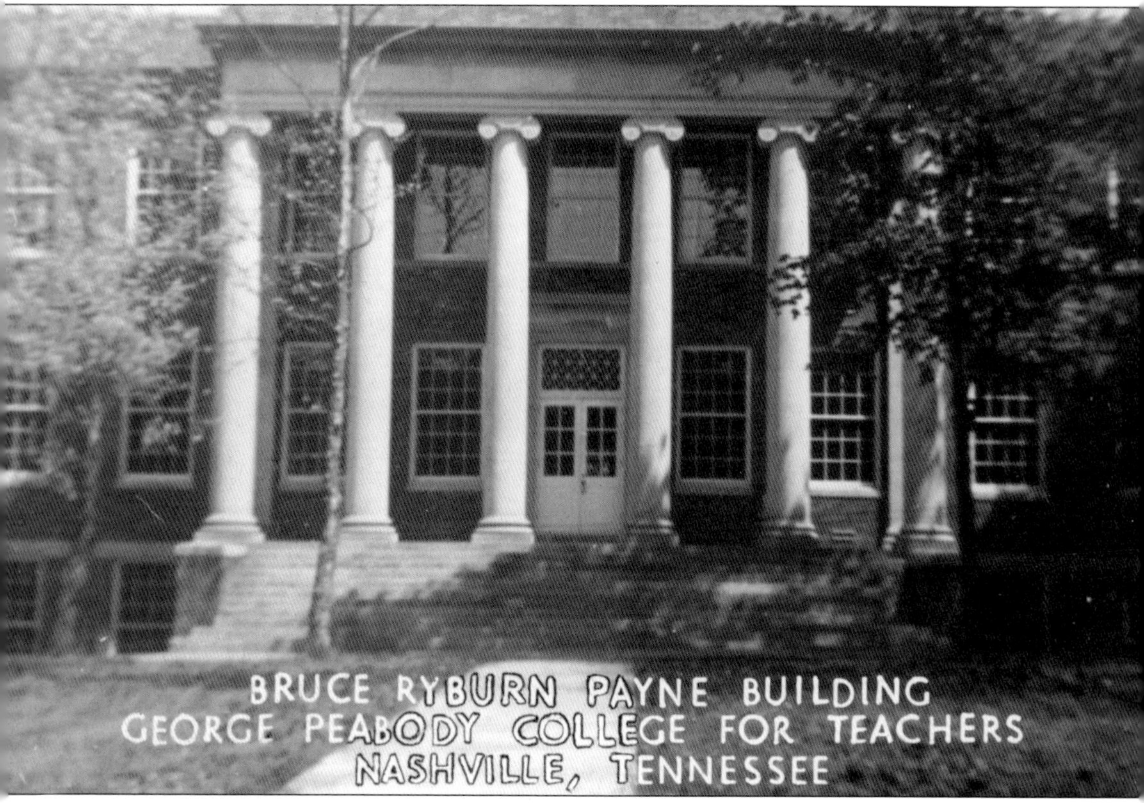

This is a postcard for the Bruce Ryburn Payne Building. Payne was the president of George Peabody College for Teachers from 1911 to 1937. He was also the mastermind of creating the grounds. The entrances to all the buildings face the center of the campus. Walking through the campus was like taking a walk in a spacious park. (Courtesy of Tennessee State Library & Archives.)

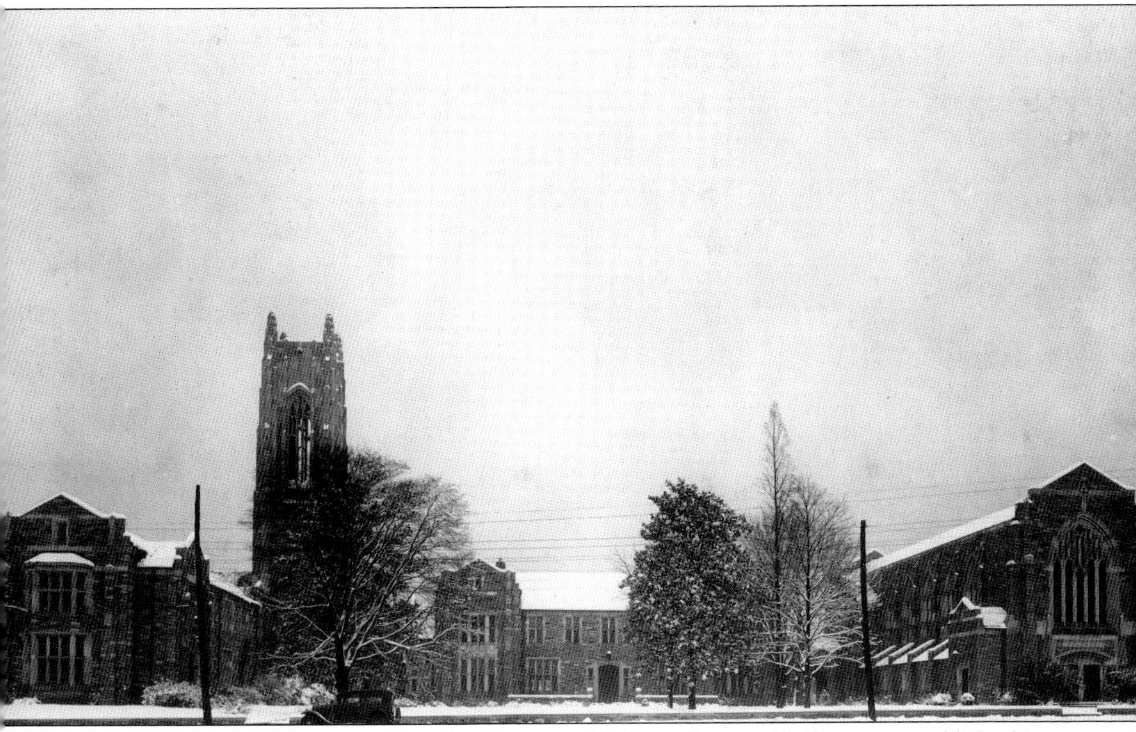

Originally known as Scarritt College for Christian Workers, Scarritt College was established in Kansas City, Missouri, in 1892. In 1923, the college moved to Nashville to be close to George Peabody College for Teachers. Peabody's strong reputation for teaching techniques influenced Scarritt College's move to Nashville. Scarritt College's purpose was to train women missionaries. The school closed in 1988, and the campus reopened in 1989 as Scarritt Bennett Center. Scarritt Bennett was named in honor of Dr. Nathan Scarritt and Belle Harris Bennett. The two were founders of the original Scarritt Bible and Training School in Kansas City. (Courtesy of Scarritt Bennett Archives.)

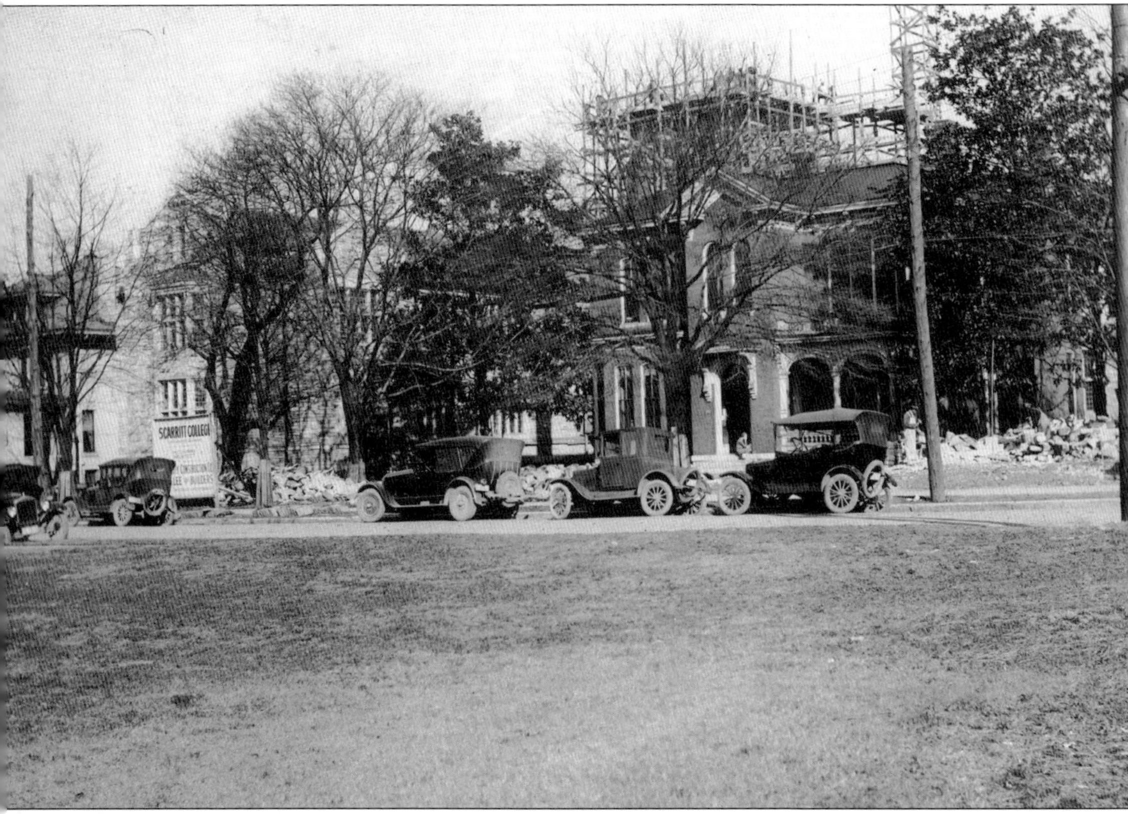

Seen here in the 1920s, the houses around Grand Avenue and Nineteenth Avenue South were part of the Hayes-Rokeby subdivision. The homes were just a couple of blocks away from the trolley system. The residents were within walking distance of Hillsboro Village. The sign in the picture appears to be the notice of construction of Scarritt College. The scaffolding could be the tower at Scarritt Hall being built. (Courtesy of Scarritt Bennett Archives.)

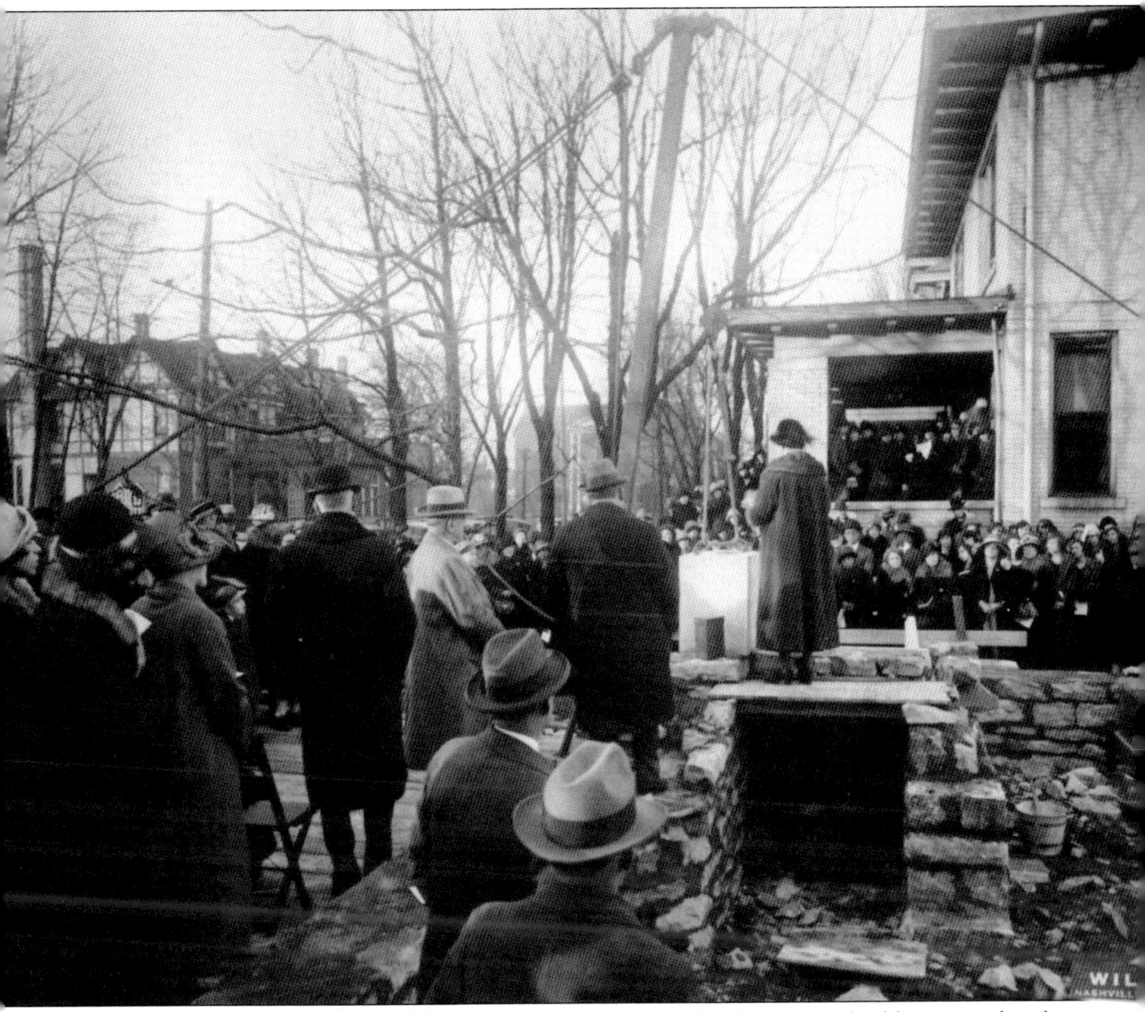

In 1927, the cornerstone was laid for the Susie Gray Dining Hall, the first building completed. The total cost of building the early phase of Scarritt Bennett was around $625,000. Most of the funding came from the Women's Board of Foreign Missions of the Methodist Episcopal Church, South. (Courtesy of Scarritt Bennett Archives.)

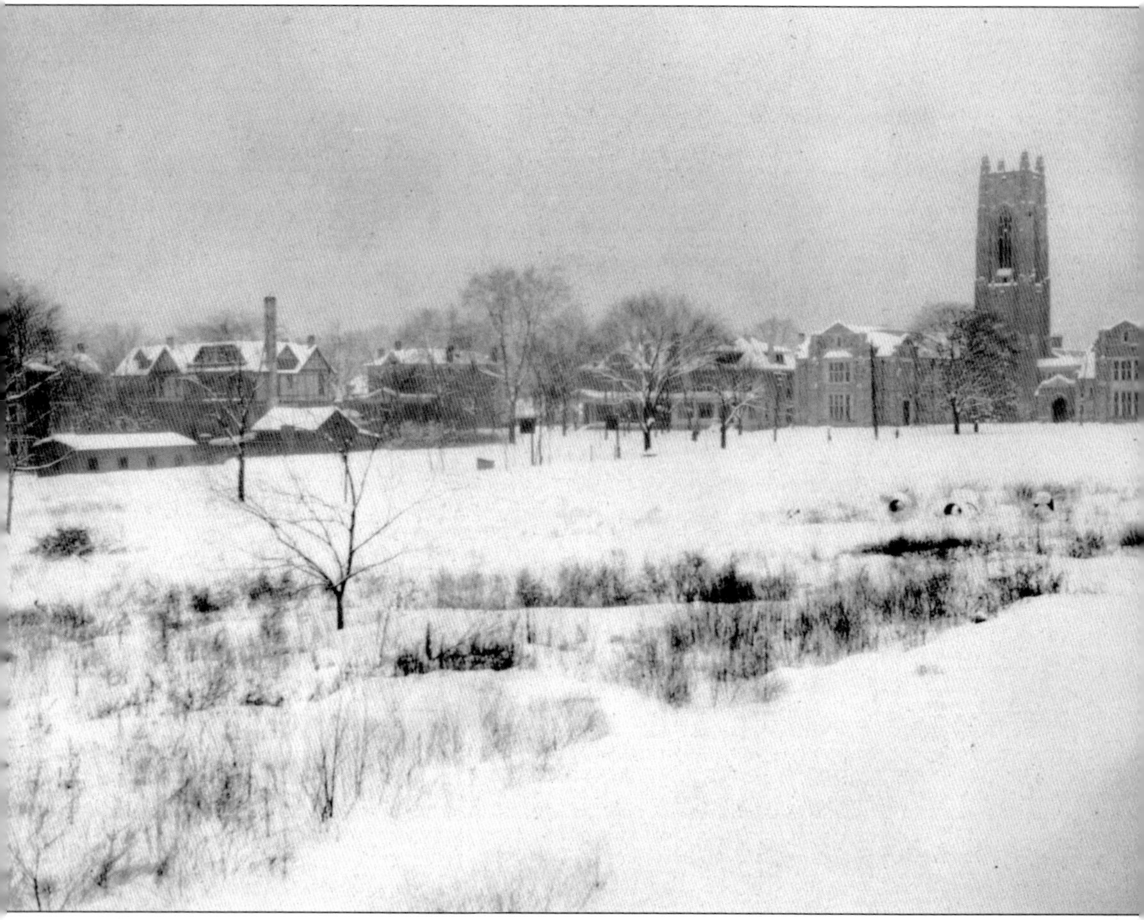

The architect who built Scarritt Bennett was Henry Hibbs. In 1929, Hibbs was awarded the American Institute of Architects Gold Medal for the early buildings. Hibbs was also the architect for buildings on the Vanderbilt, Fisk, and Peabody campuses. (Courtesy of Tennessee State Library & Archives.)

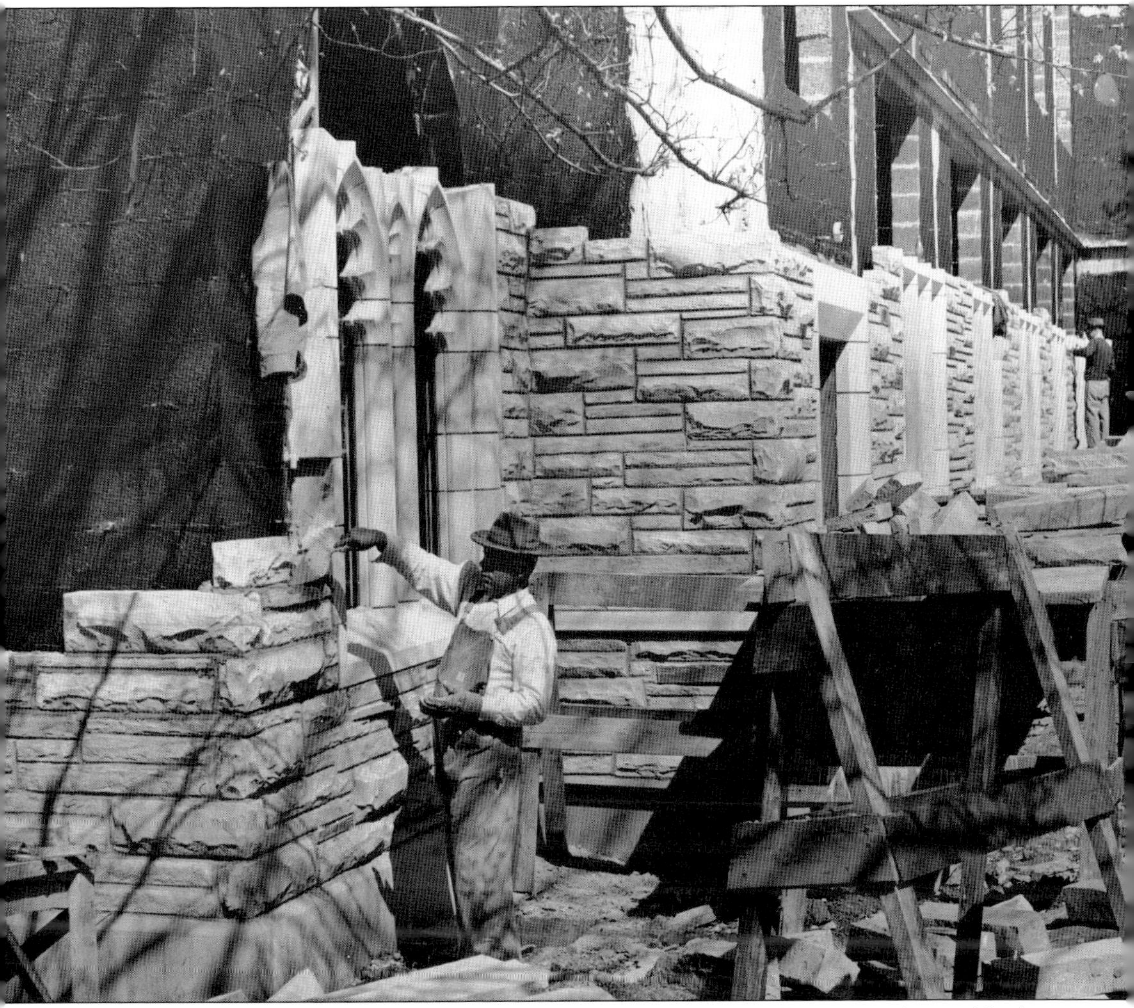

Much of the architectural design at Scarritt Bennett was created in Collegiate Gothic and built of Crab Orchard stone quarried from East Tennessee. The breathtaking campus was part of the Rokeby farm site. The property was acquired by Edgar Jones, a banker who lived in nearby Glen Oak, and he donated the land for the building of Scarritt Bennett. (Courtesy of Tennessee State Library & Archives.)

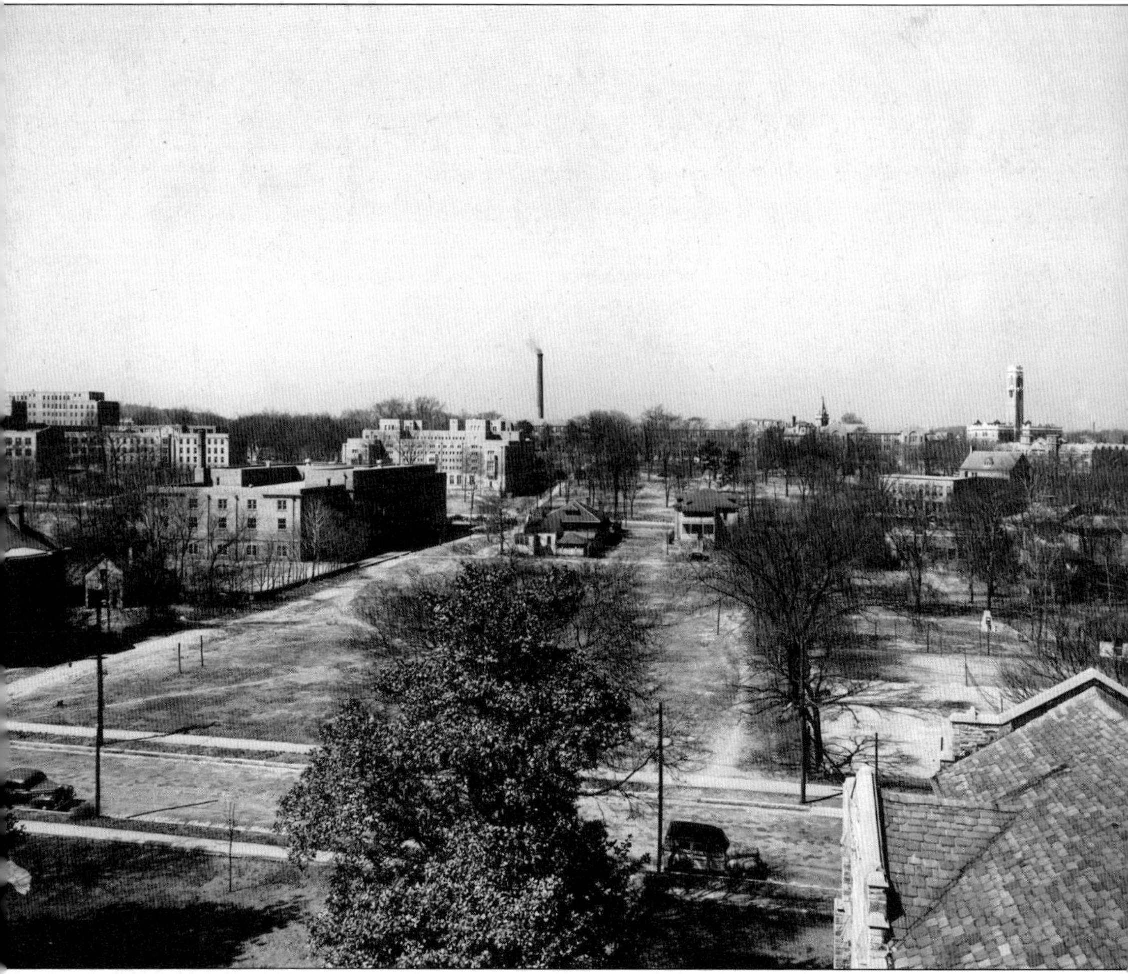

The view from the tower at Scarritt Bennett looks over Twenty-First Avenue South. On the right side of the picture is Vanderbilt's Kirkland Hall, with the tall tower, as well as other buildings on Vanderbilt's campus. (Courtesy of Tennessee State Library & Archives.)

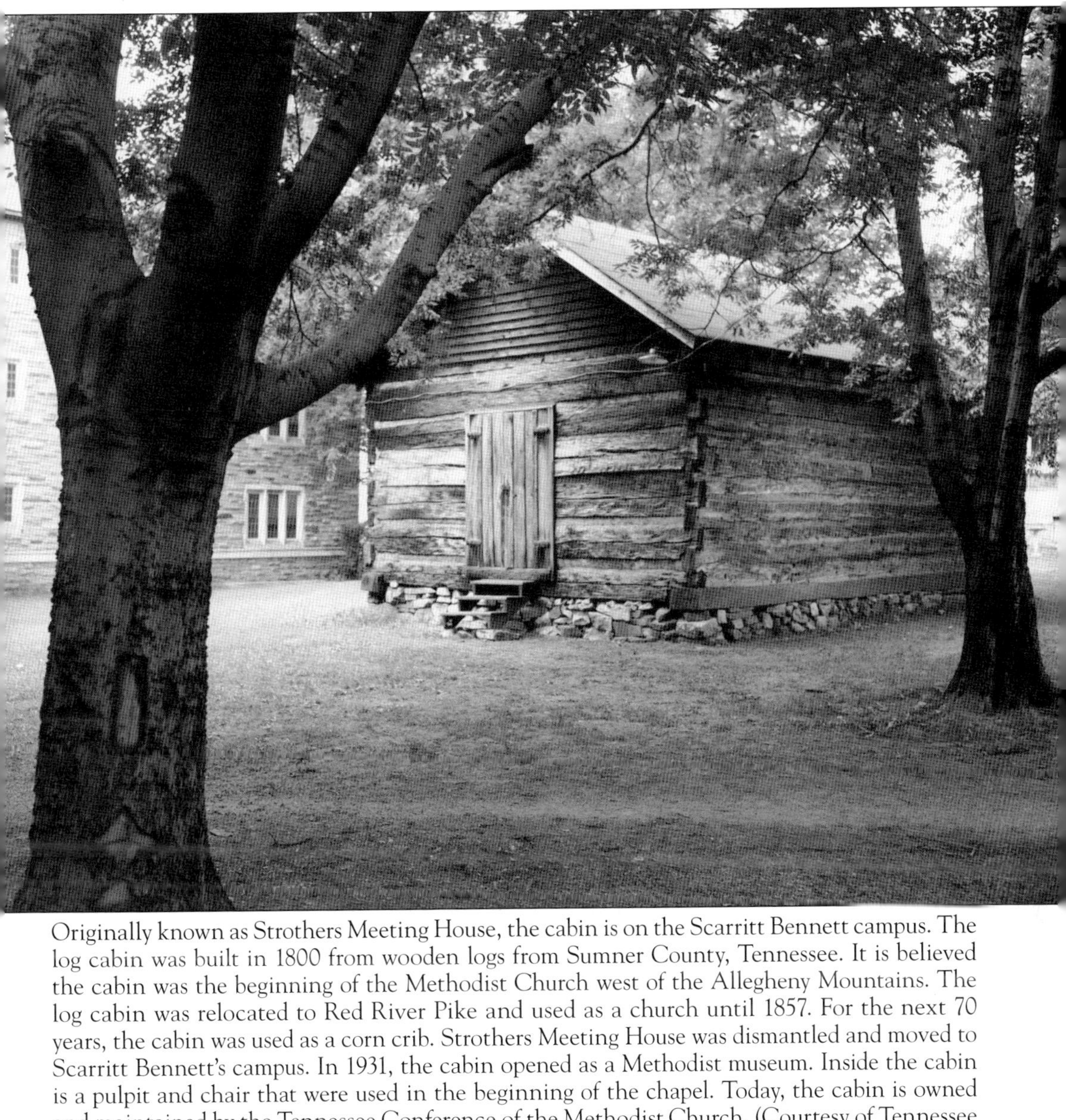

Originally known as Strothers Meeting House, the cabin is on the Scarritt Bennett campus. The log cabin was built in 1800 from wooden logs from Sumner County, Tennessee. It is believed the cabin was the beginning of the Methodist Church west of the Allegheny Mountains. The log cabin was relocated to Red River Pike and used as a church until 1857. For the next 70 years, the cabin was used as a corn crib. Strothers Meeting House was dismantled and moved to Scarritt Bennett's campus. In 1931, the cabin opened as a Methodist museum. Inside the cabin is a pulpit and chair that were used in the beginning of the chapel. Today, the cabin is owned and maintained by the Tennessee Conference of the Methodist Church. (Courtesy of Tennessee State Library & Archives.)

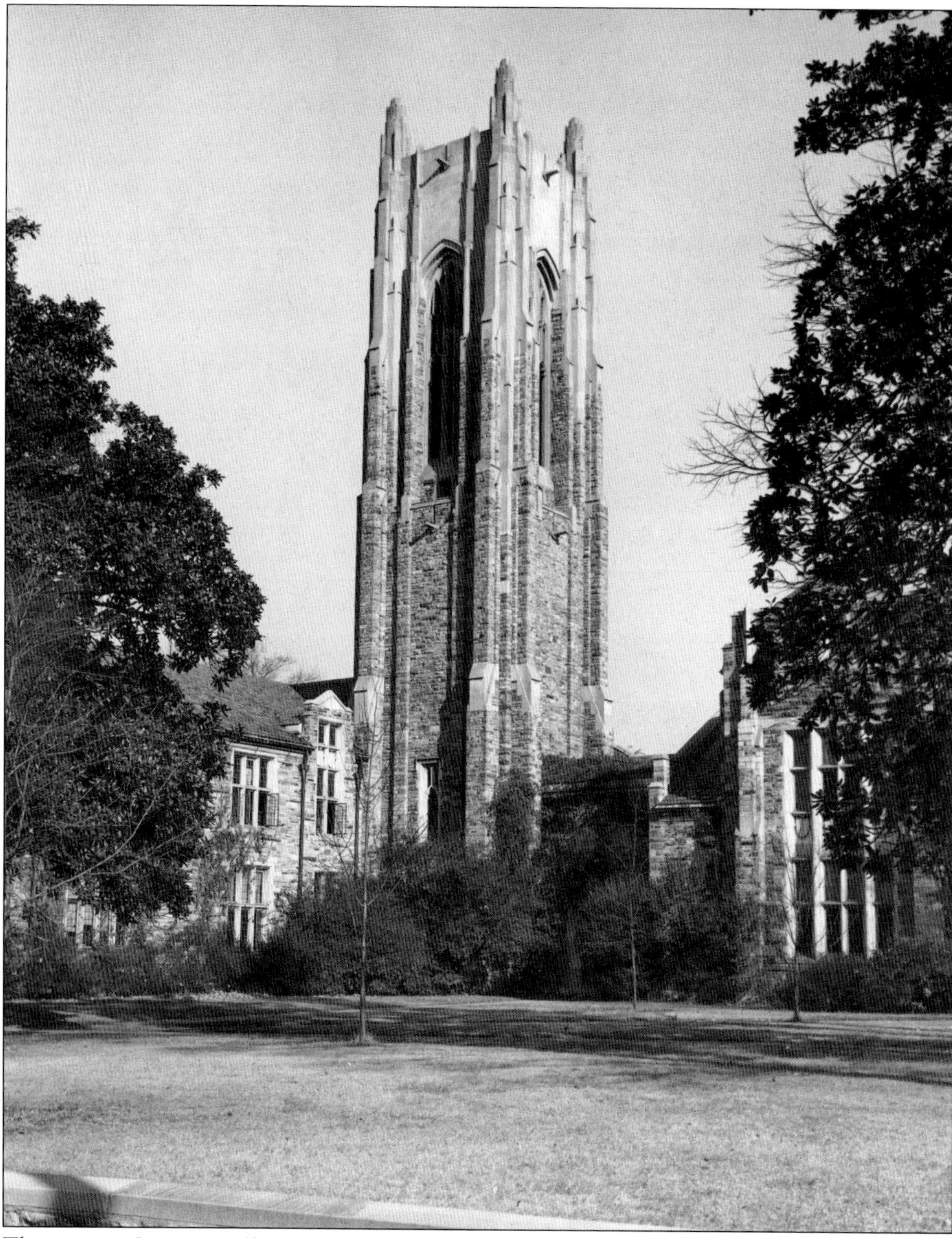

The tower at Scarritt Hall may be the most recognized building on the Scarritt Bennett campus. It is also the tallest building at 115 feet. At the time of completion, it was the tallest building in Nashville. (Courtesy of Scarritt Bennett Archives.)

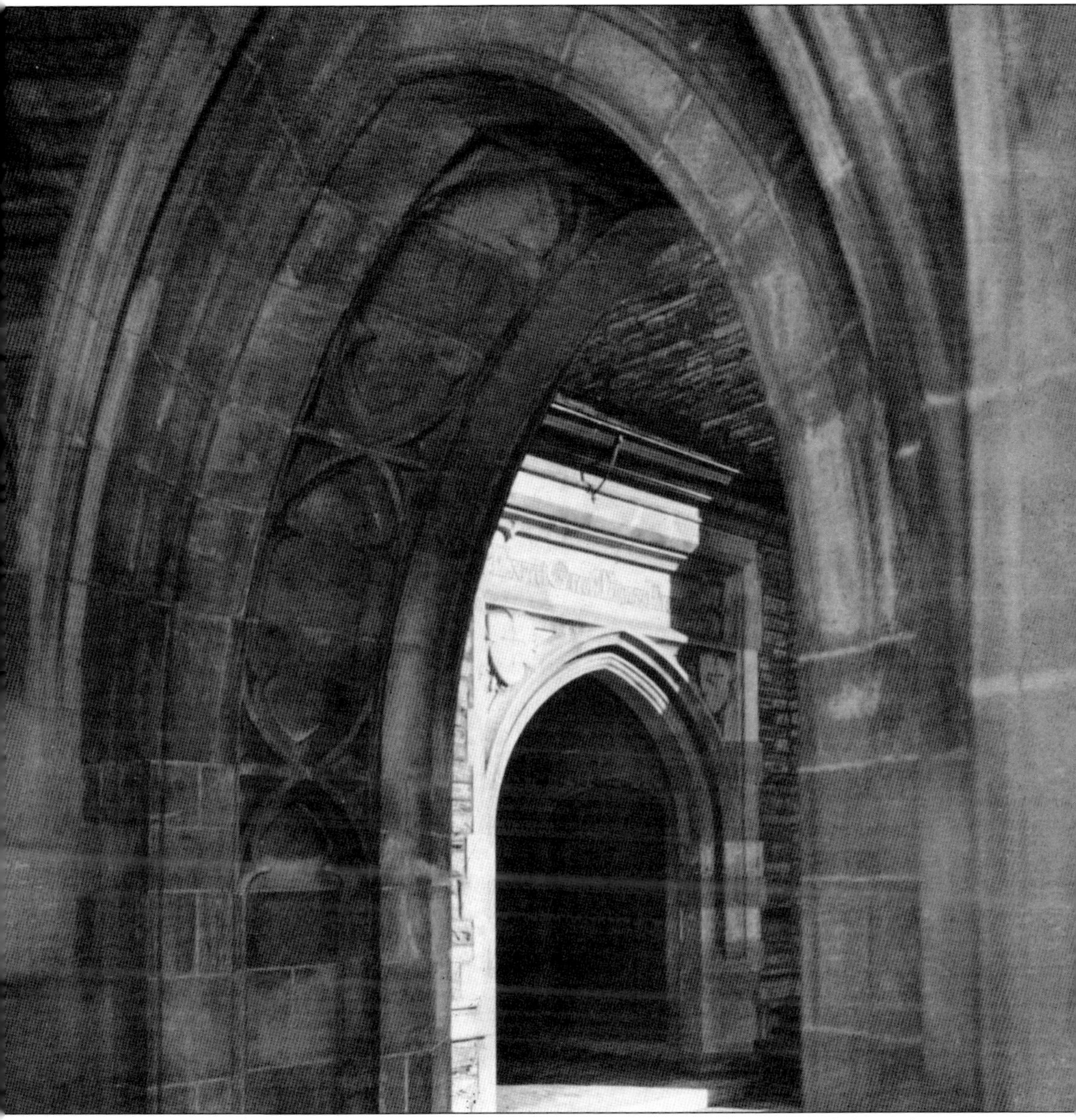

The details inside the tower walls are breathtaking. The stonework is elegant, and the ceilings are pointed arches. While inside, the walls could remind a visitor of Gothic catacombs. (Courtesy of Scarritt Bennett Archives.)

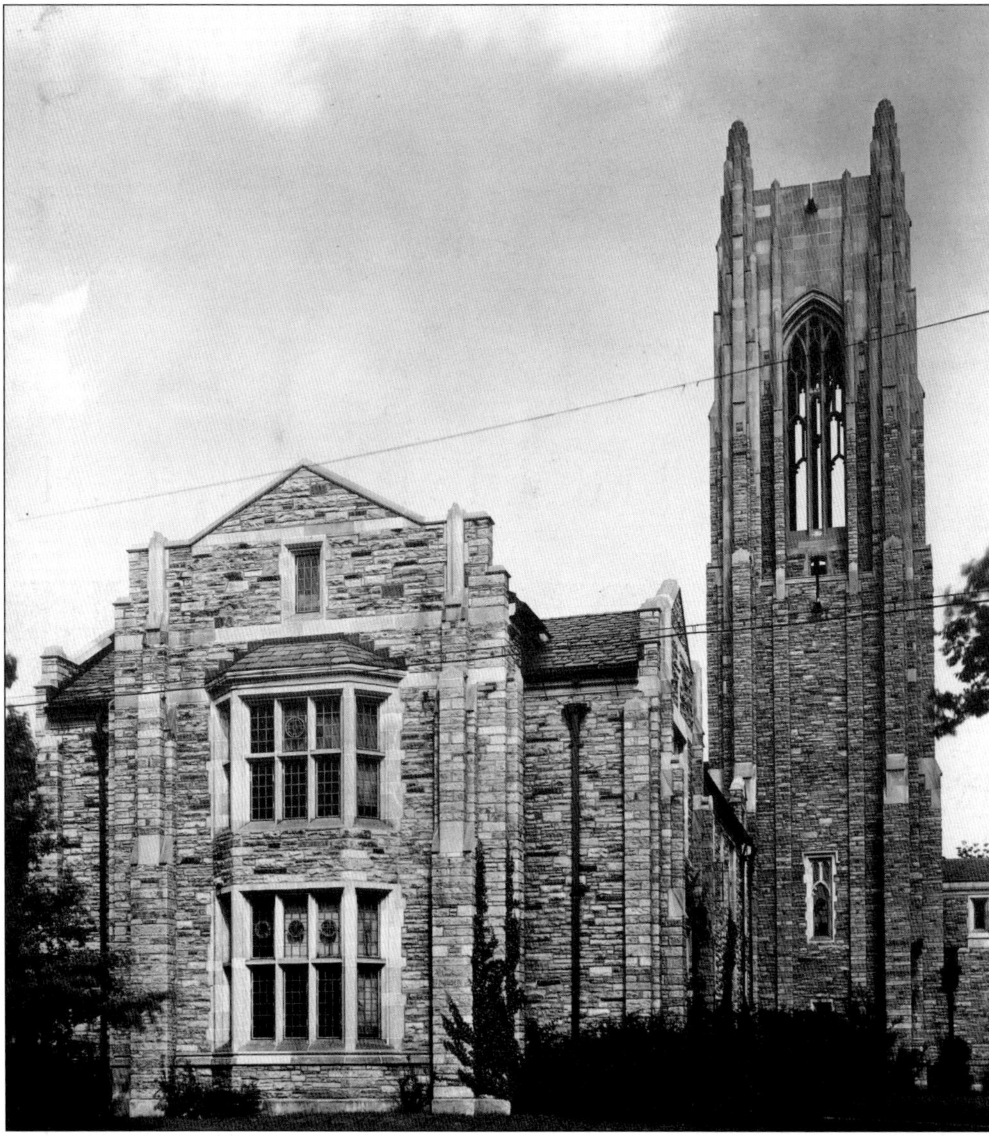

In this picture are Scarritt Hall and the Scarritt Bennett tower. Not pictured is the Wightman Chapel, which was also on the Scarritt Bennett campus and featured in a PBS documentary. The first floor of Scarritt Hall was once used for administration offices. The second floor is the International Room. Inside the center of the tower is the Room of Remembrance. (Courtesy of Scarritt Bennett Archives.)

Six

Upper Room and the Methodist Church

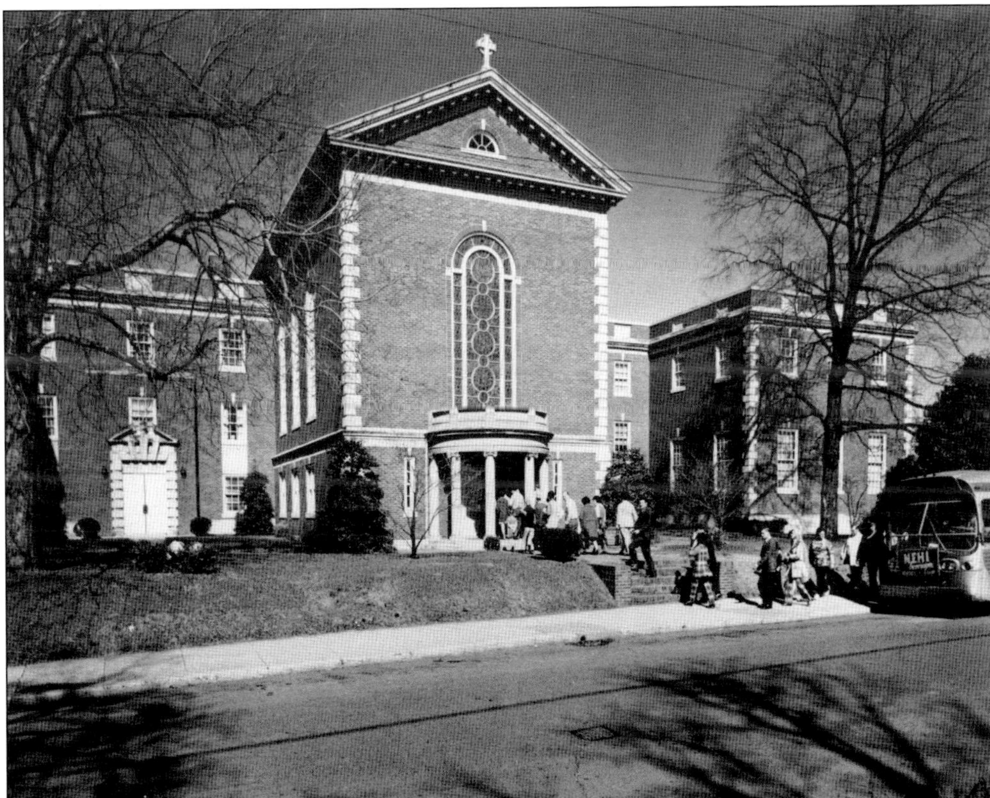

The beginning of the Upper Room goes back to after Great Depression. A Sunday school teacher in Texas and her pastor created a newsletter with a brief inspirational reading. In 1934, Dr. Grover Emmons started publishing a devotional publication. He had heard a minister mention the Upper Room in a sermon. Against the advice of others, he ordered 100,000 copies of the *Upper Room* to be printed. The weekly publication sold out very quickly, and by 1938, the publication was issuing a million copies a week. (Courtesy of Tennessee State Library & Archives.)

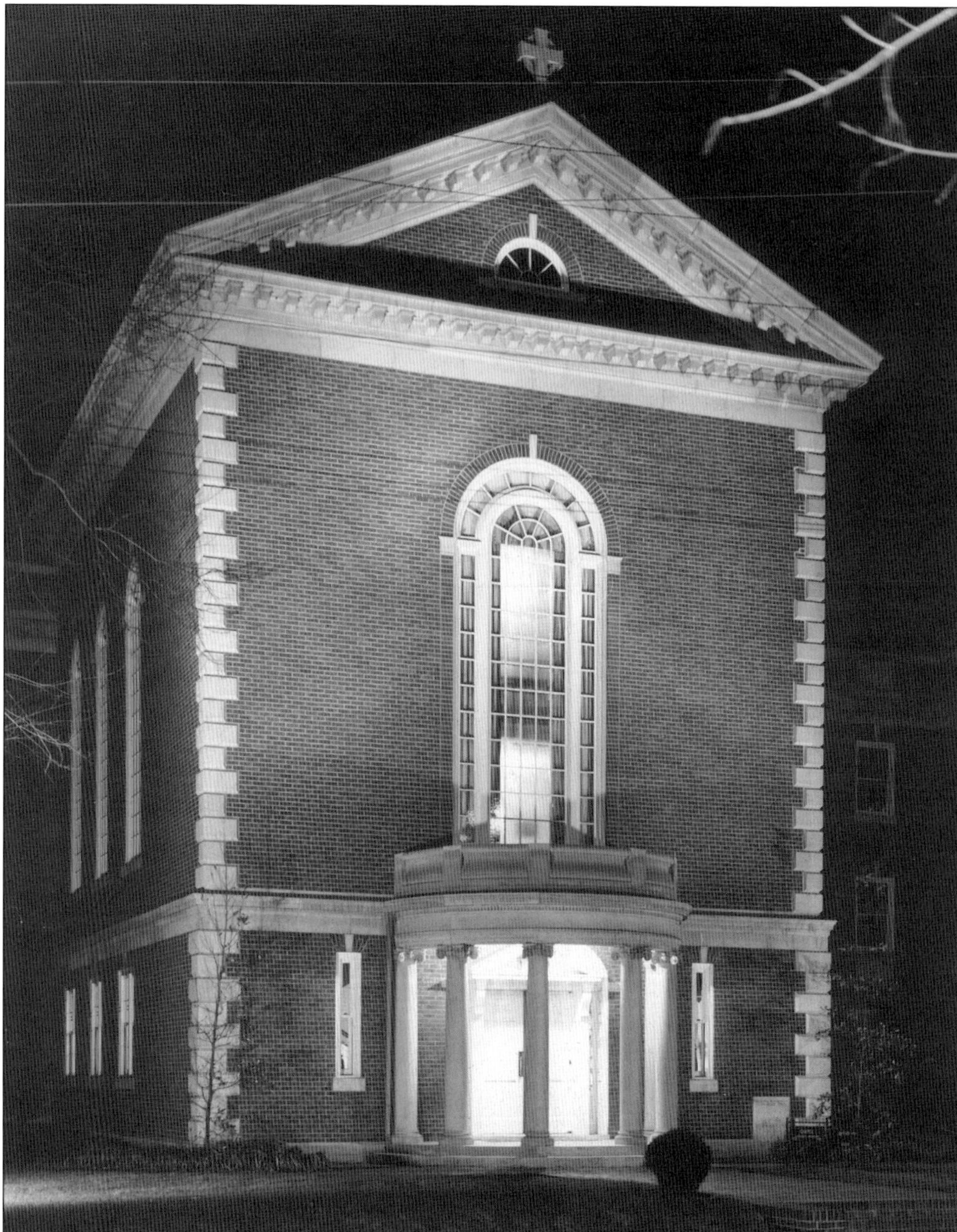

This is a photograph of the Upper Room at night. The publication named the *Upper Room* was printed in Nashville by the Southern Methodist Publishing House. A 1938 *Time* magazine article mentions the publication; collectively, almost 10 million copies had been sold. At one time, the *Upper Room* devotional publication was printed in 40 different languages and reached out to 75 countries. (Courtesy of Tennessee State Library & Archives.)

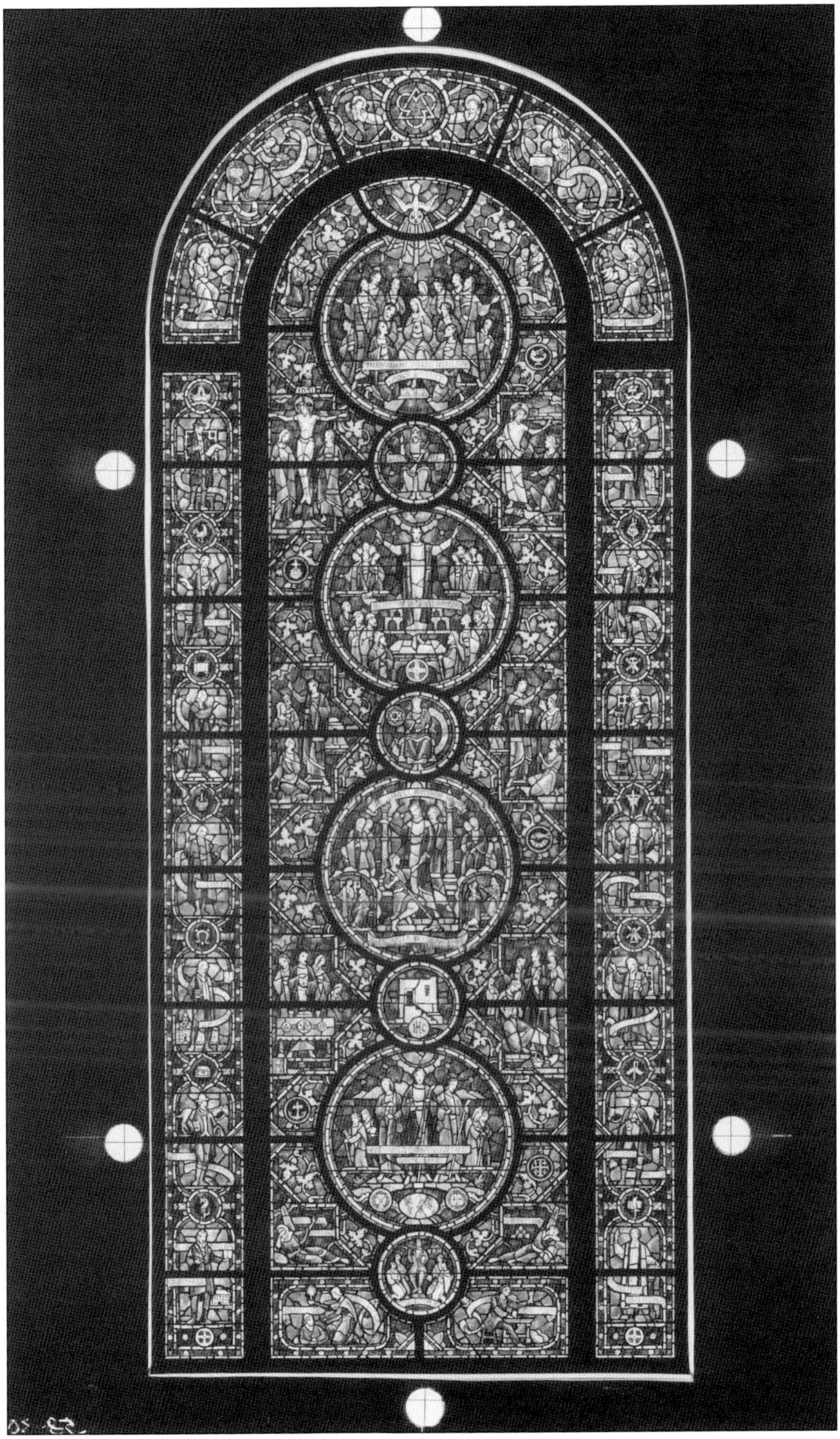

The Upper Room houses a beautiful stained-glass artwork. The 9,000-piece window measures 20 feet tall by 8 feet wide and depicts the story of the Pentecost. (Courtesy of Tennessee State Library & Archives.)

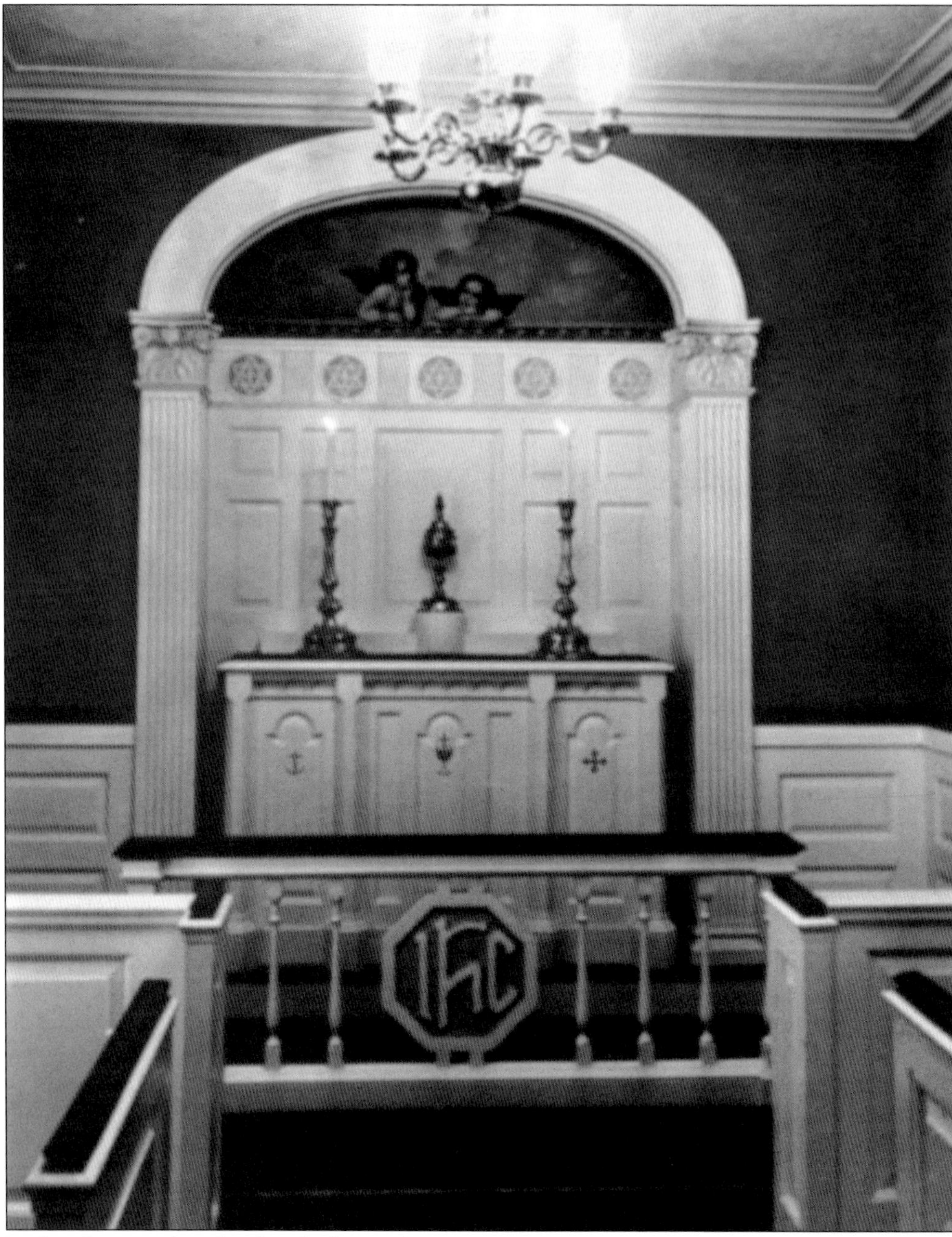

In this photograph is the church altar in the Upper Room. To some Christians, the altar symbolizes God's table. An altar is also important with communion. (Courtesy of Tennessee State Library & Archives.)

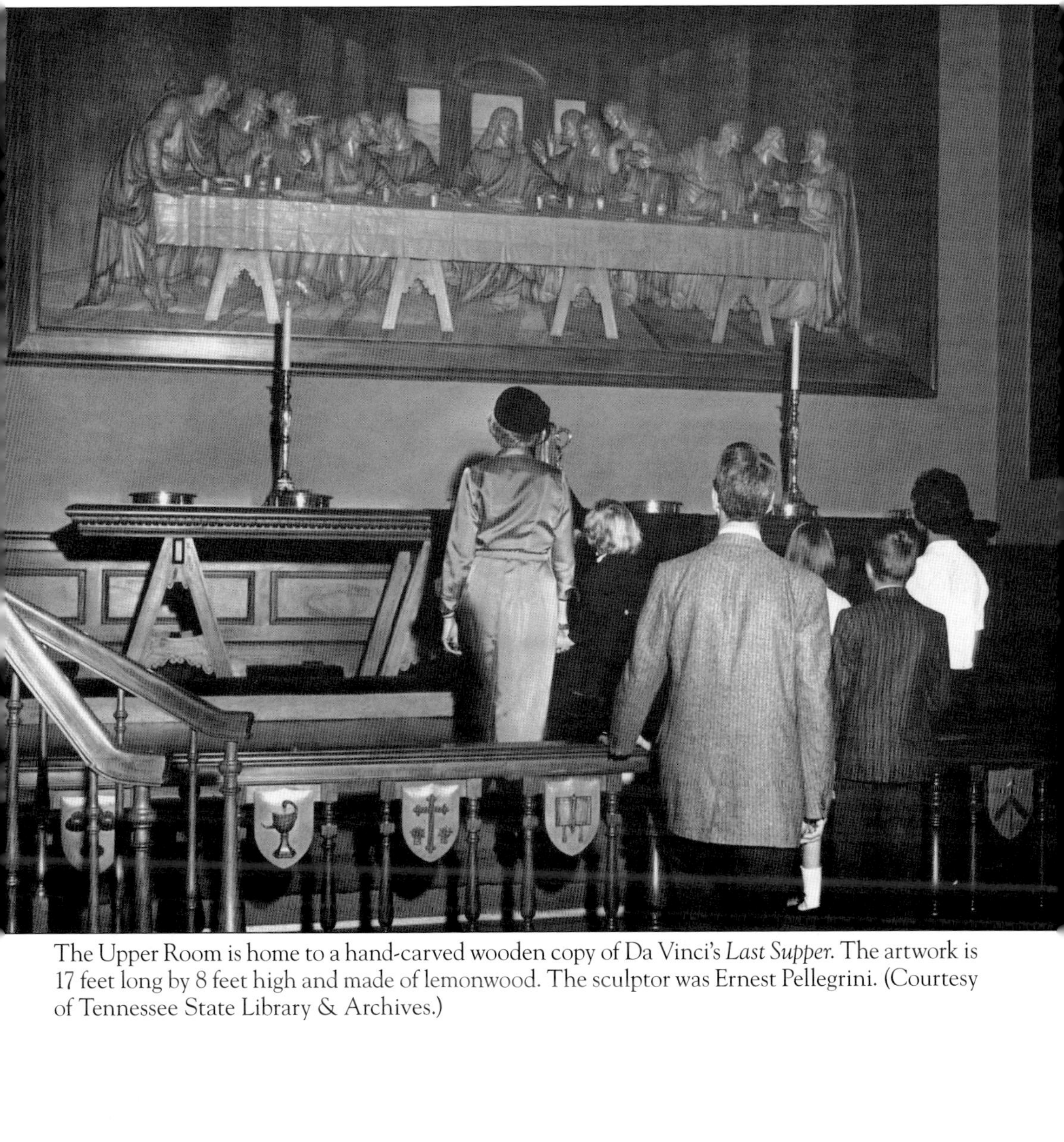

The Upper Room is home to a hand-carved wooden copy of Da Vinci's *Last Supper*. The artwork is 17 feet long by 8 feet high and made of lemonwood. The sculptor was Ernest Pellegrini. (Courtesy of Tennessee State Library & Archives.)

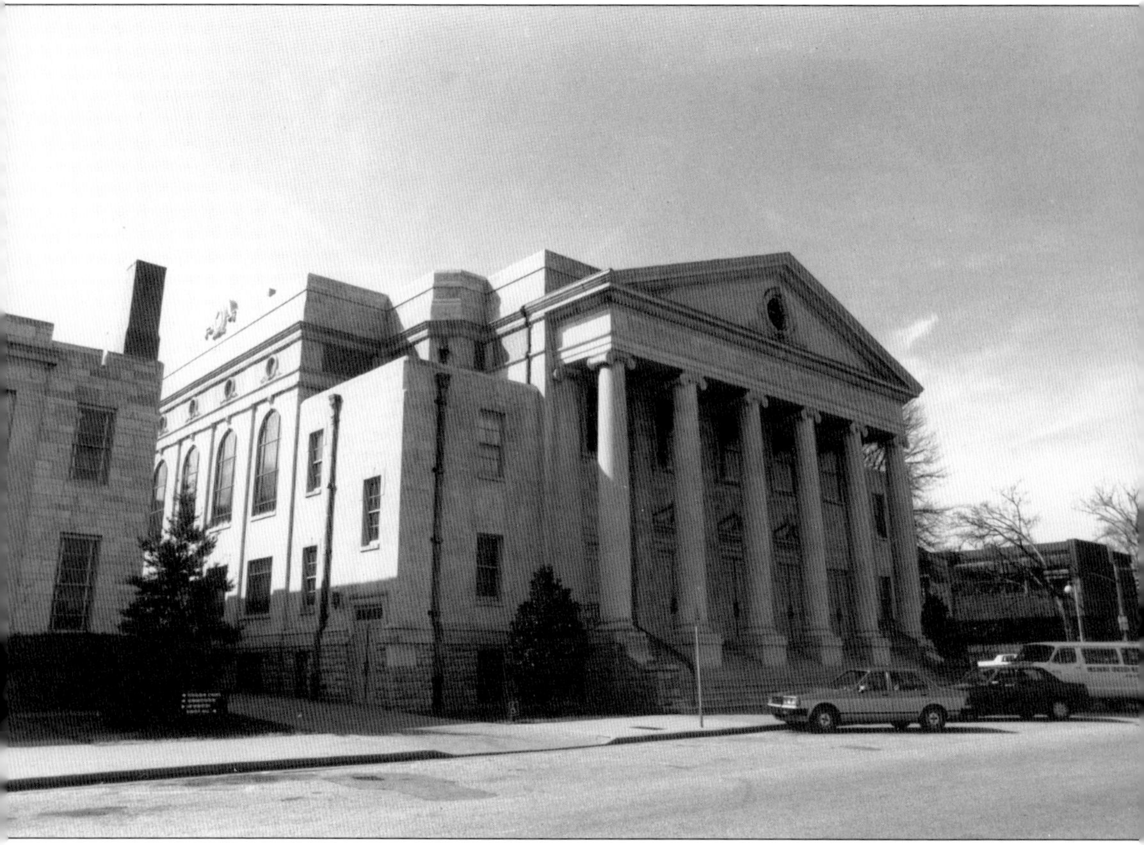

On July 10, 1910, the Belmont United Methodist Church had its first service. The first sermon was held in a tin-roofed frame chapel facing Acklen Avenue. The cost of the first chapel of the Belmont United Methodist Church was $400. Families were moving into the homes in the area. The West End, Vanderbilt, and Belmont neighborhoods were taking shape. People were wanting places to worship close to their homes instead of traveling to other parts of Nashville. Within the first year, the Sunday school attendance had grown from 35 followers to 102, with seven classes. In four years, the congregation outgrew the building. (Courtesy of Metro Archives.)

Seven

Living near the Village

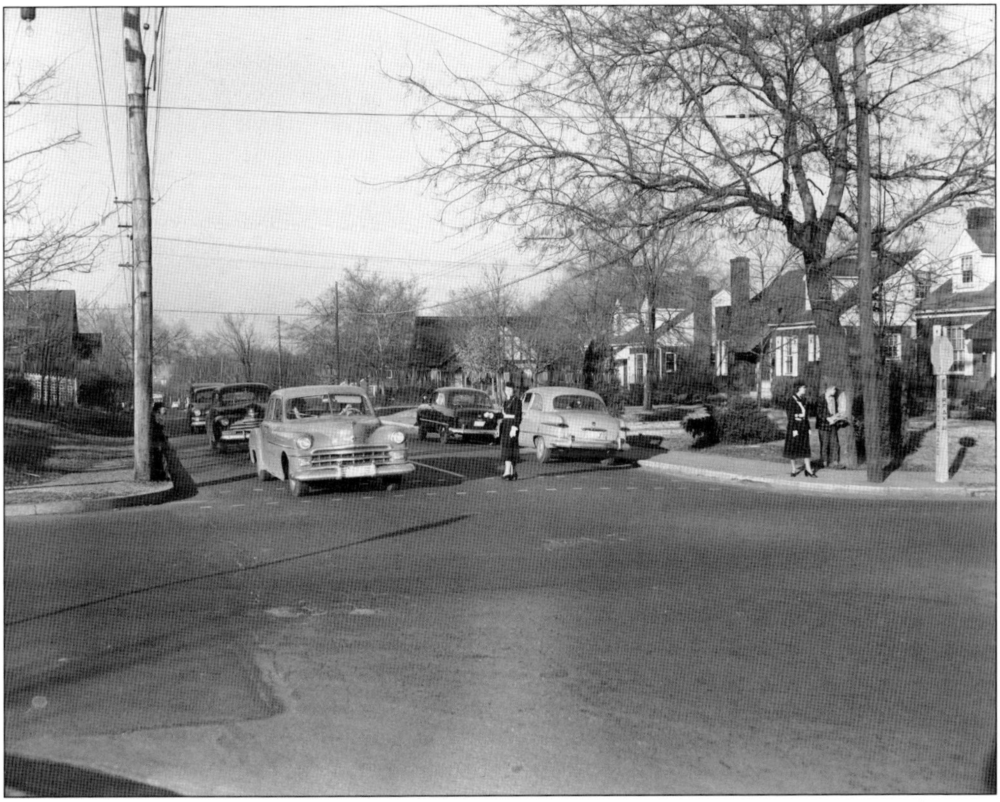

Nashville's public schools have provided crossing guards for students and anyone walking in the school zones. This photograph was taken at the crosswalk at Fairfax Avenue and Natchez Trace. The Nashville police introduced the program in 1951. After Nashville City and Davidson County schools merged to become Metro, there have been as many as 202 guards at 200 schools. (Courtesy of Metro Archives.)

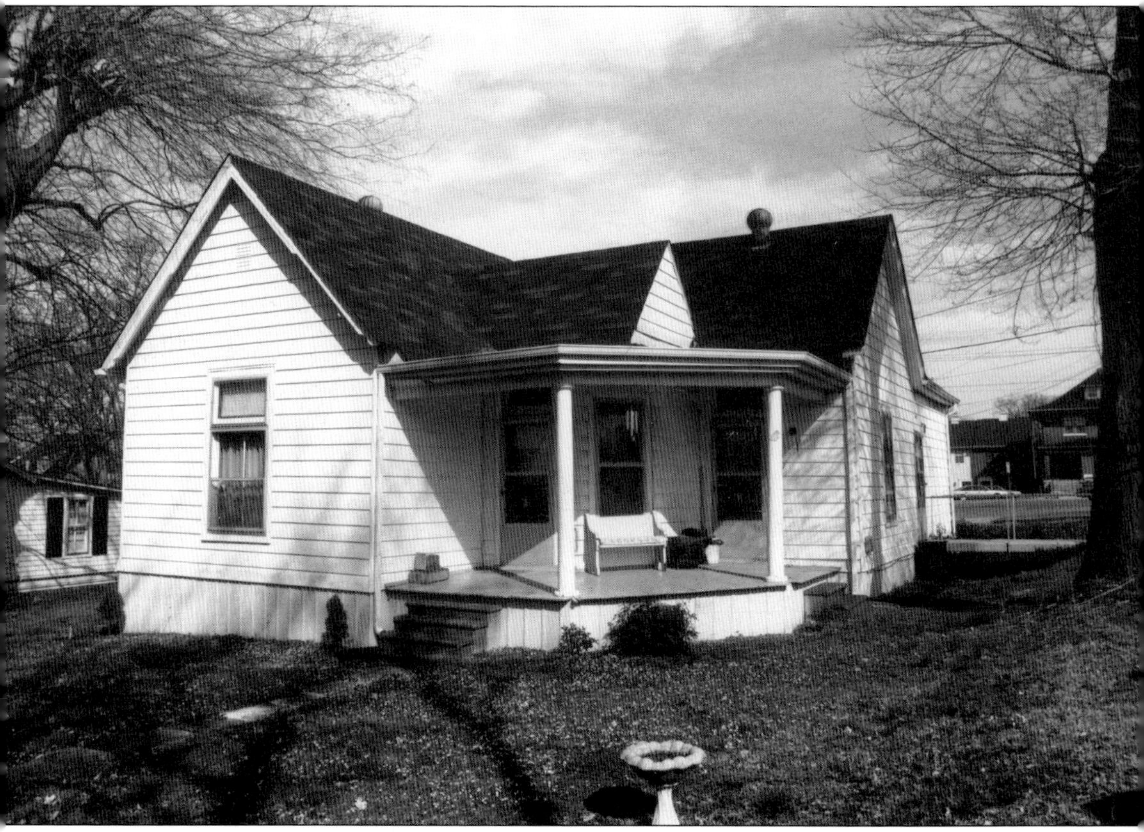

The house in this picture was the tollhouse built in the 1800s. When operating as a tollhouse, the gatekeeper would live there, and at this tollhouse, the gatekeeper was Sterling Pyron. It was common to have a tollgate every five miles. (Courtesy of Metro Archives.)

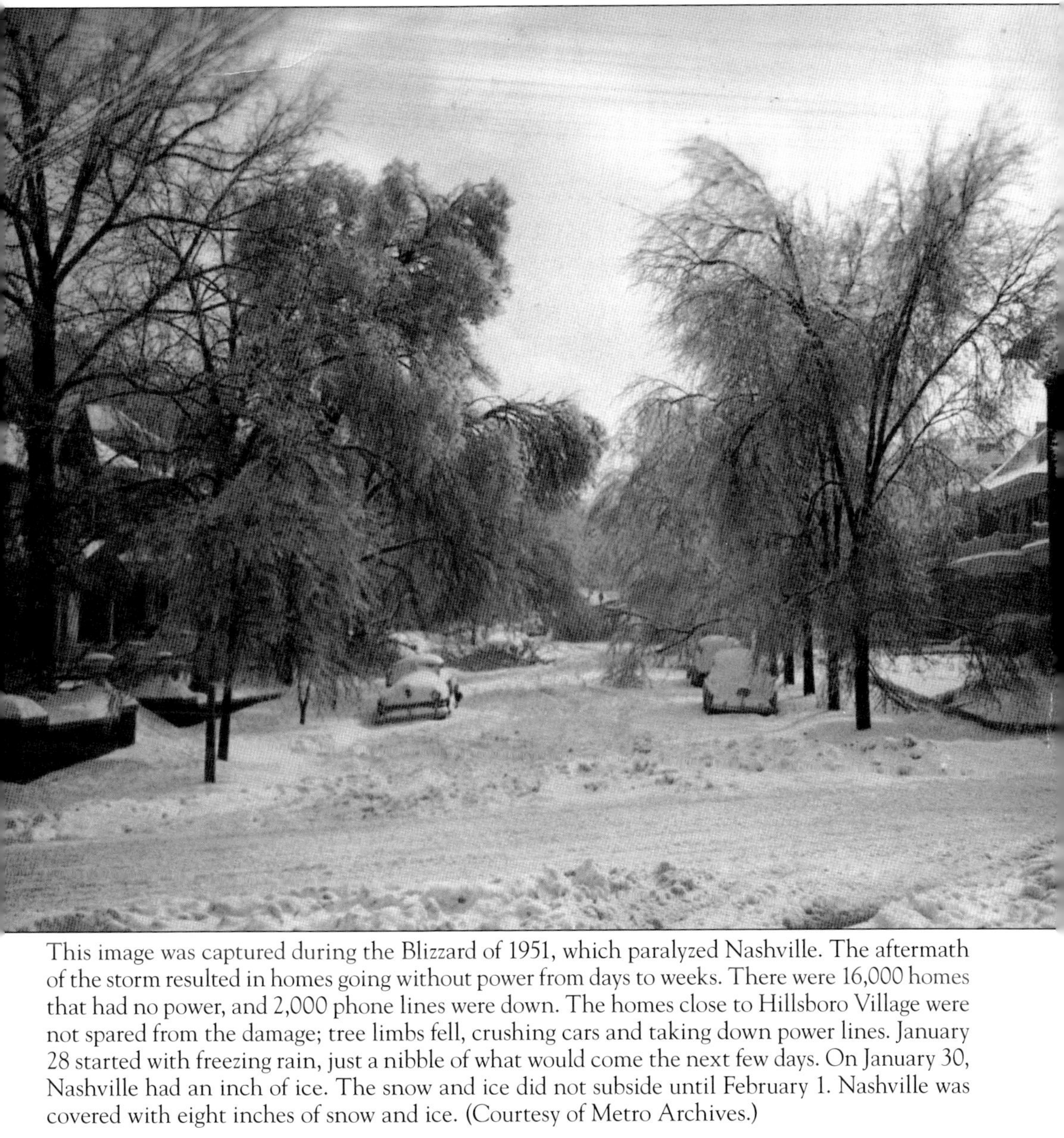

This image was captured during the Blizzard of 1951, which paralyzed Nashville. The aftermath of the storm resulted in homes going without power from days to weeks. There were 16,000 homes that had no power, and 2,000 phone lines were down. The homes close to Hillsboro Village were not spared from the damage; tree limbs fell, crushing cars and taking down power lines. January 28 started with freezing rain, just a nibble of what would come the next few days. On January 30, Nashville had an inch of ice. The snow and ice did not subside until February 1. Nashville was covered with eight inches of snow and ice. (Courtesy of Metro Archives.)

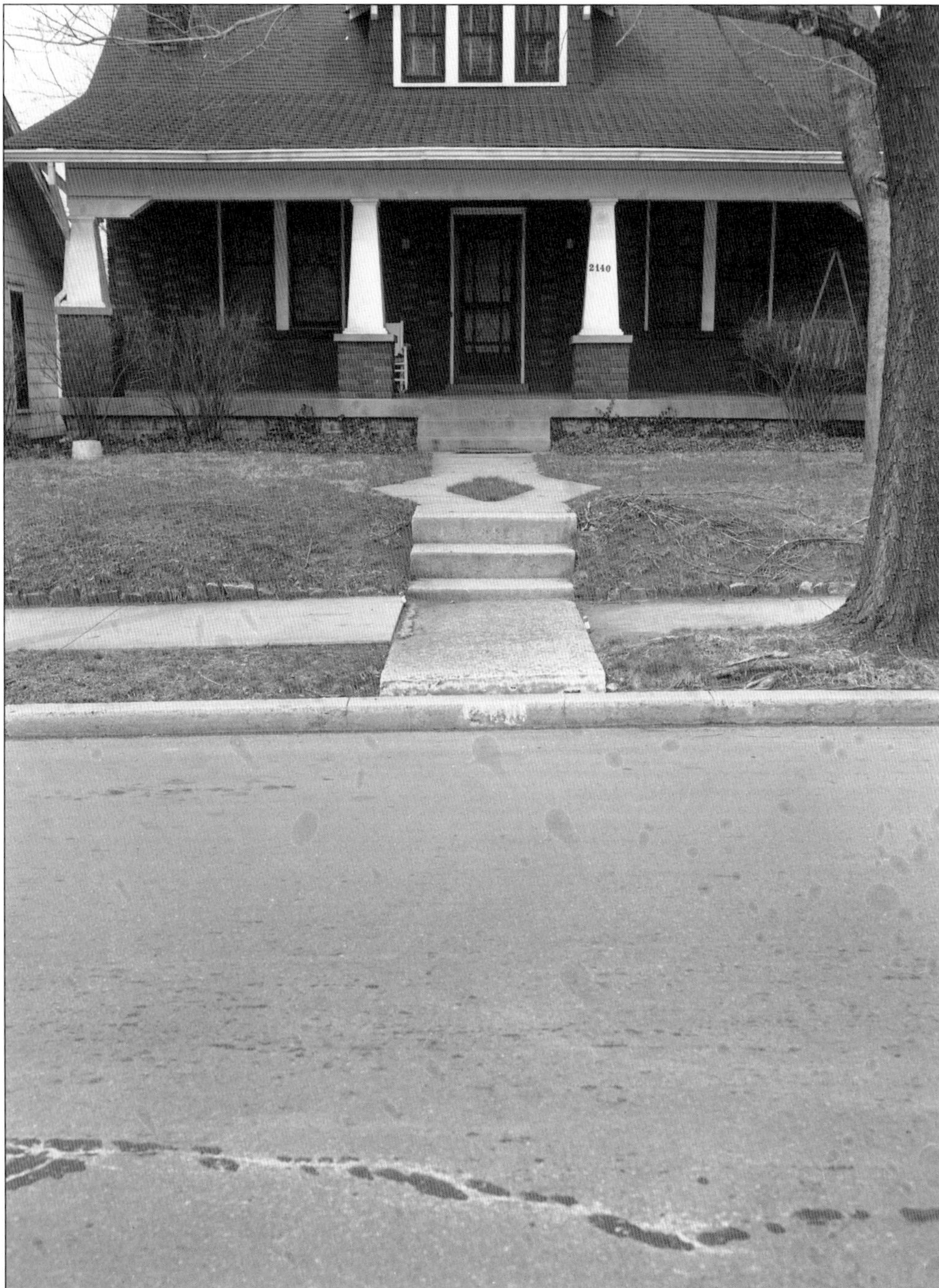

This house was located at 2140 Blakemore Avenue. This is a typical home close to Hillsboro Village. Records indicate the oldest house on Blakemore Avenue was built in 1924. The address of the earliest house on Blakemore Avenue was 2113. Blakemore Avenue is listed in the city directory as early as 1900. This house was a victim of Vanderbilt's growth. (Courtesy of Metro Archives.)

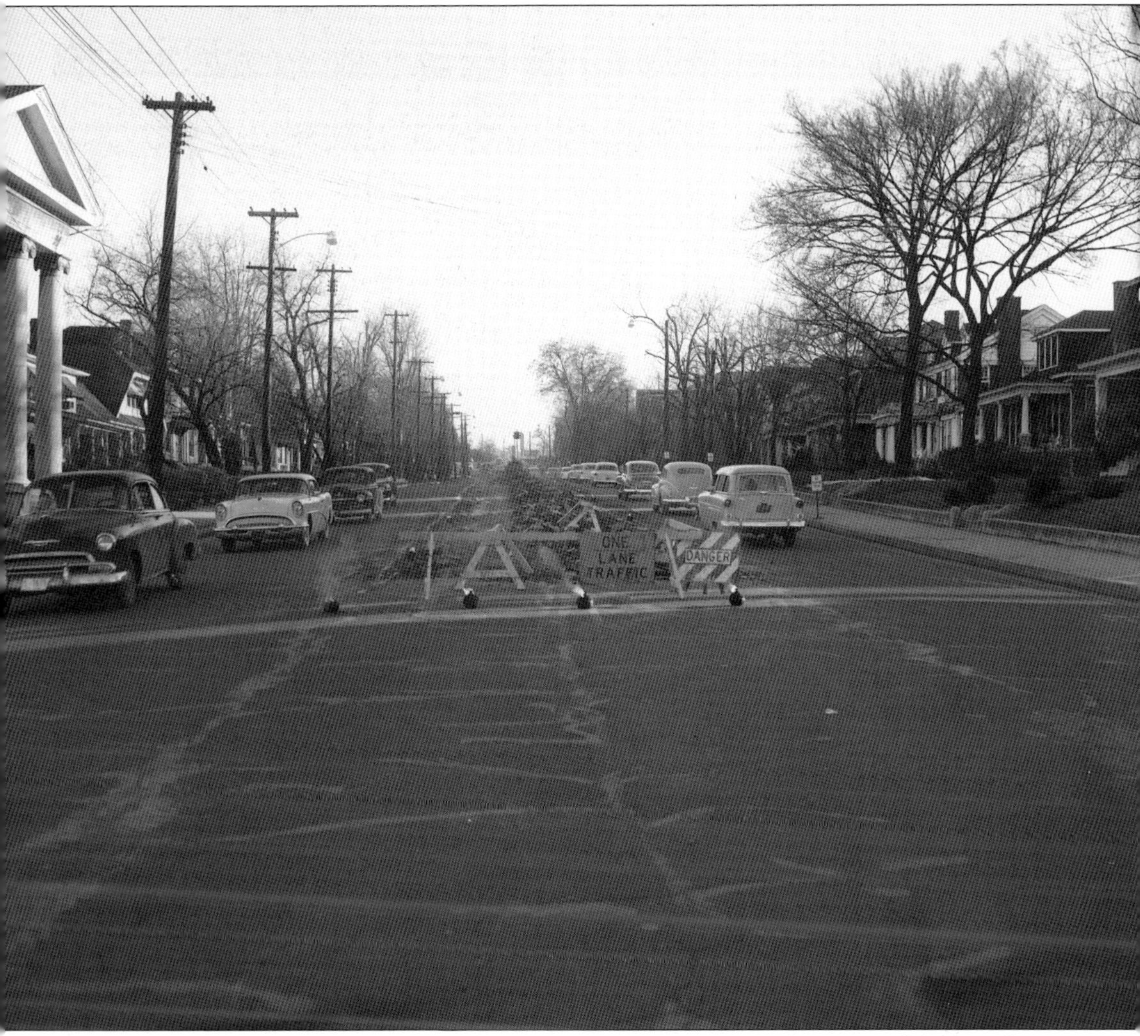

The Belmont Methodist Church is on the left. During the 1960s and 1970s, Hillsboro Village experienced urban renewal. Some of the homes on the right have been converted to commercial buildings. This photograph is an example of how close the homes were to the Hillsboro Village business district. (Courtesy of Metro Archives.)

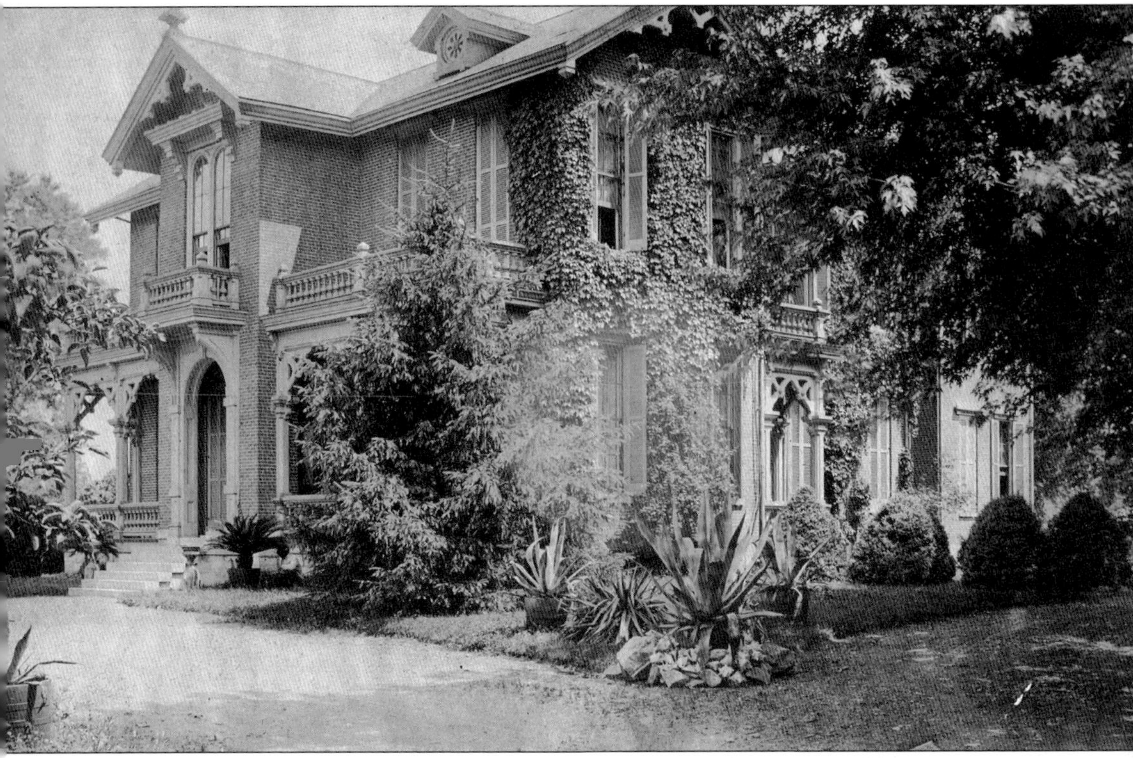

The Edgehill was built in 1879 at the southeast corner of Edgehill Avenue and Twenty-First Avenue South. The brick house was dismantled and reassembled brick by brick in 1911 at 211 Bowling Avenue. The original owners were Edward Thompson and his family, who owned Thompson's Dry Good Store in downtown Nashville, known for high-quality merchandise and super customer service. The property was sold to Peabody College after Peabody acquired the land once owned by Roger Williams University. Peabody Normal College relocated from south Nashville to Twenty-First Avenue South. (Courtesy of Tennessee State Library & Archives.)

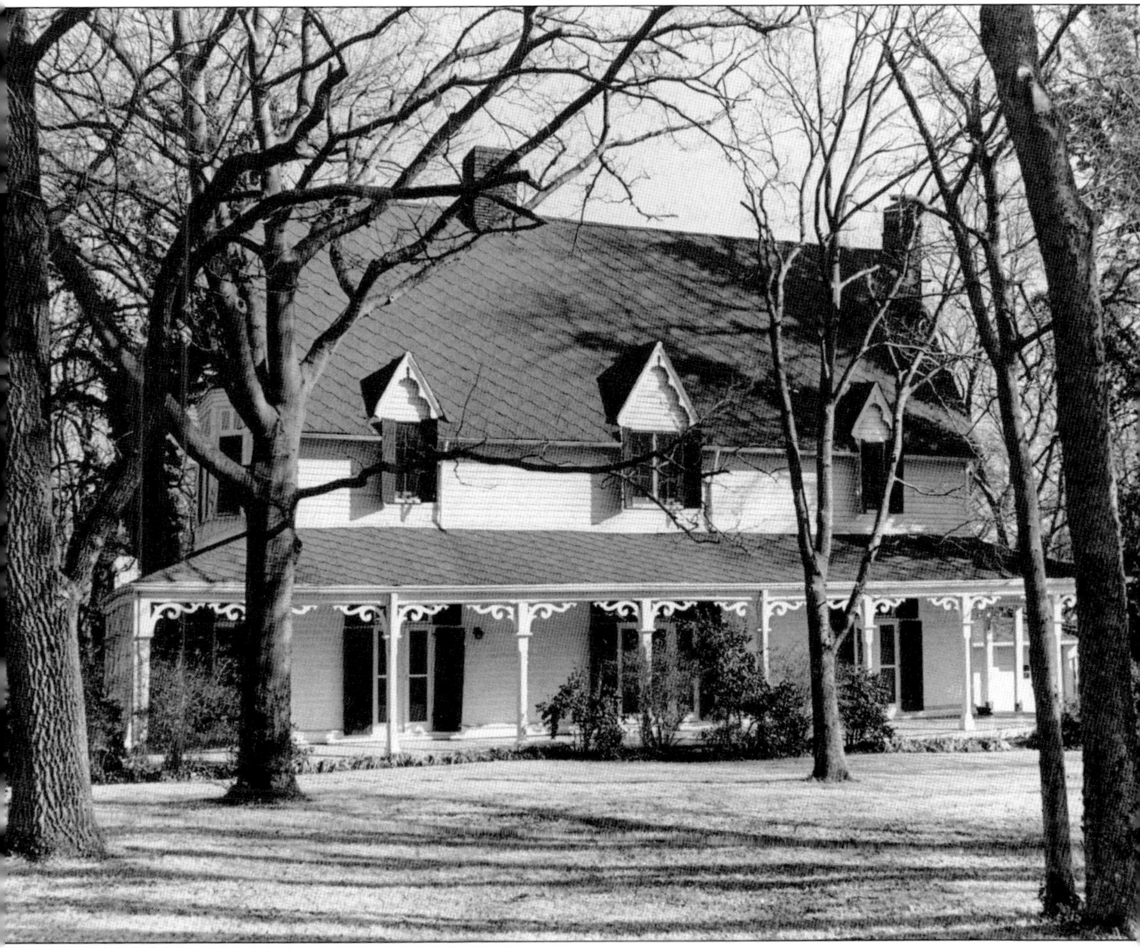

Glen Oak was built between 1854 and 1857 by Rev. Charles Tomes. The estate was named for a grove of oak trees on the property. Glen Oak consisted of 15 acres between Old Natchez Trace Road and Hillsboro Pike. Reverend Tomes was the rector of Christ Episcopal Church; a rector of a church is someone who takes care of the parish. Eventually, Edgar Jones, who was in banking, purchased Glen Oak in 1867. In 1912, Glen Oak was subdivided, and two new streets are the result of the subdivision: Barton and Essex Avenues. Jones Avenue became Fairfax Avenue. (Courtesy of Tennessee State Library & Archives.)

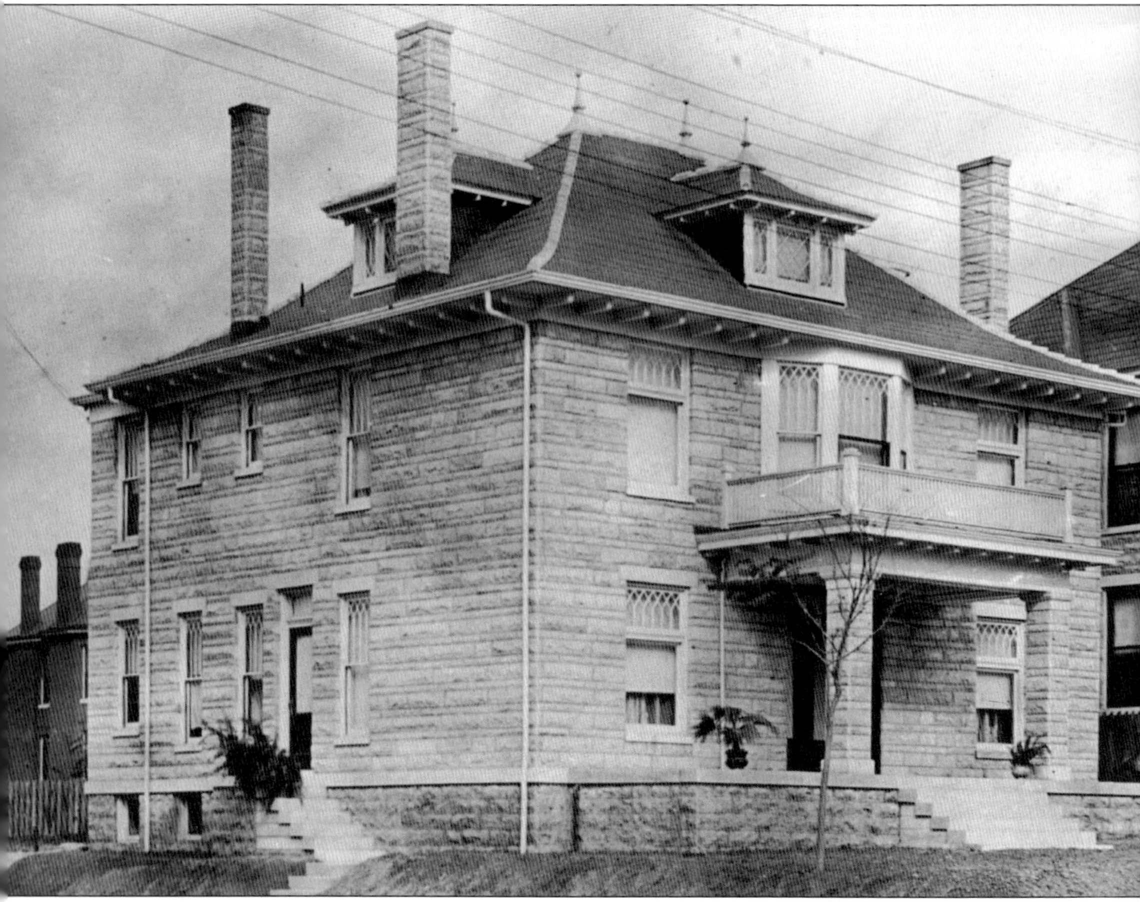

Grainger House, part of the Hayes-Rokeby subdivision, was demolished for the Upper Room. (Courtesy of Tennessee State Library & Archives.)

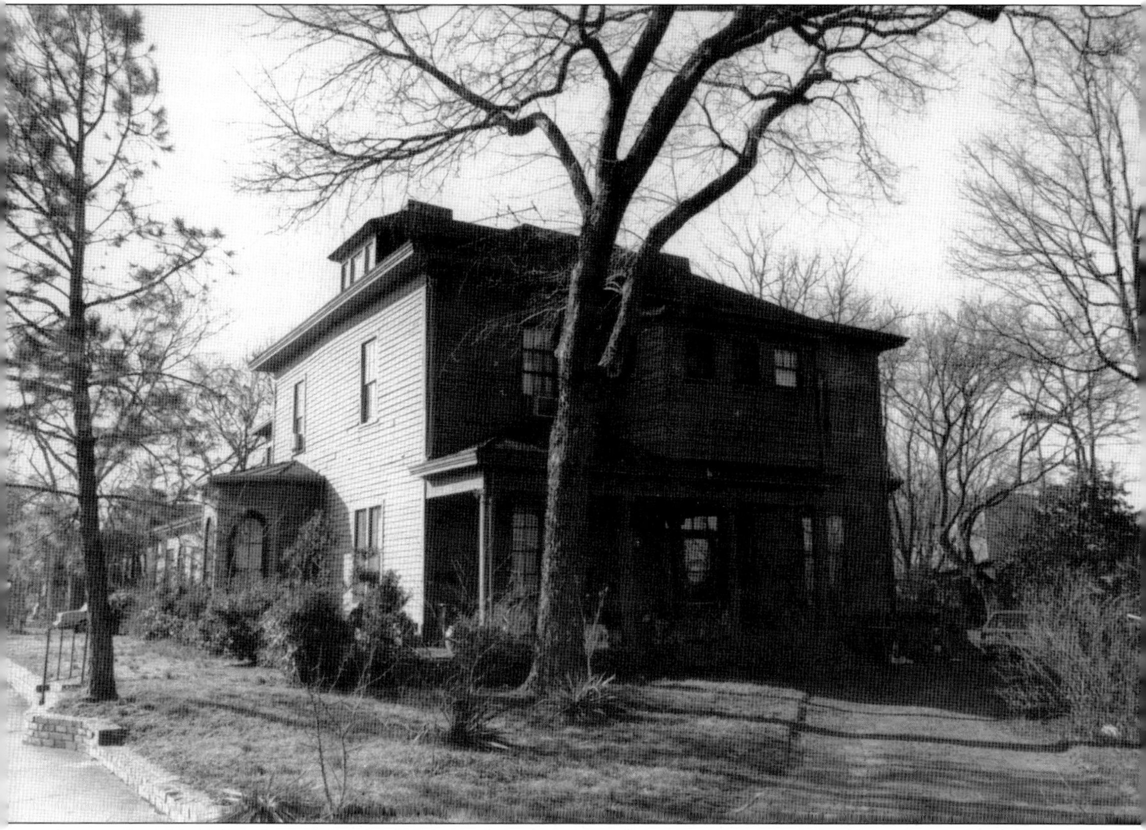

Around 1870, John Burch built the first home on Acklen Avenue. Burch, a lawyer and a state politician, moved his family to Nashville from Chattanooga around 1860. He and his wife, Lucy Newell Burch, had six children; daughter Catherine was an active supporter of the women's suffrage movement. There is confusion about the address of the house, as records indicate the house was built on Jones (Fairfax) Avenue. Around 1900, the house was remodeled and now sits at 2134 Acklen Avenue. Burch was also the publisher of the morning newspaper *Nashville American*. (Courtesy of Tennessee State Library & Archives.)

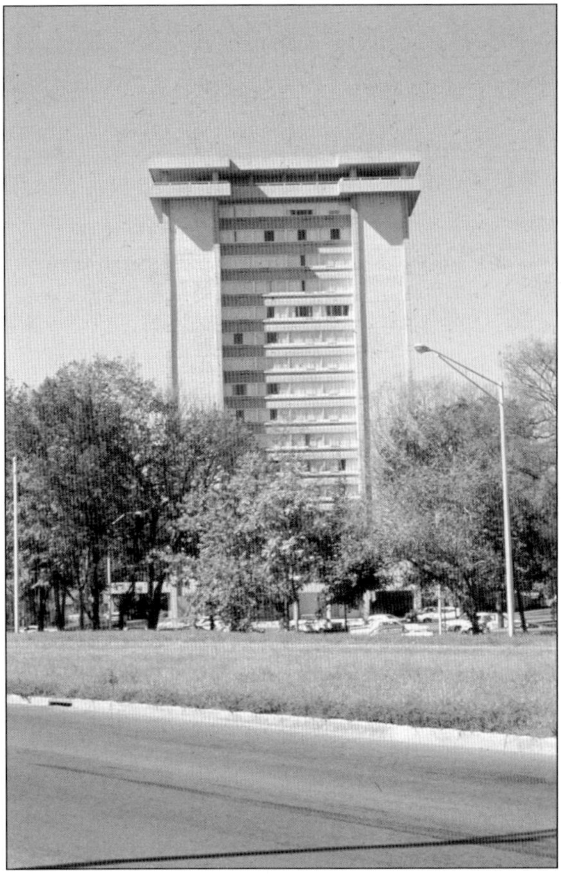

The Leah Rose Residence for Senior Citizens is located at 1900 Acklen Avenue. The facility opened in 1973 as a high-rise apartment building for senior citizens. The 17-floor high-rise is within walking distance of Hillsboro Village. There are some apartments with an awesome view of downtown Nashville. (Courtesy of Metro Archives.)

This is another view of the Leah Rose Residence for Senior Citizens. A feature of the building is the green space so residents can enjoy being outside. (Courtesy of Metro Archives.)

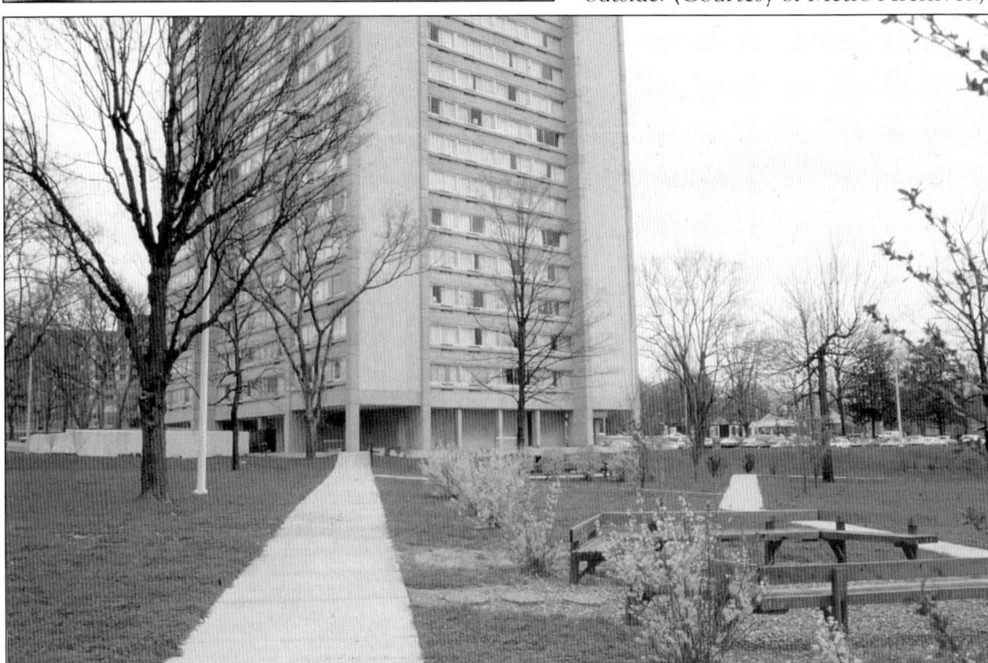

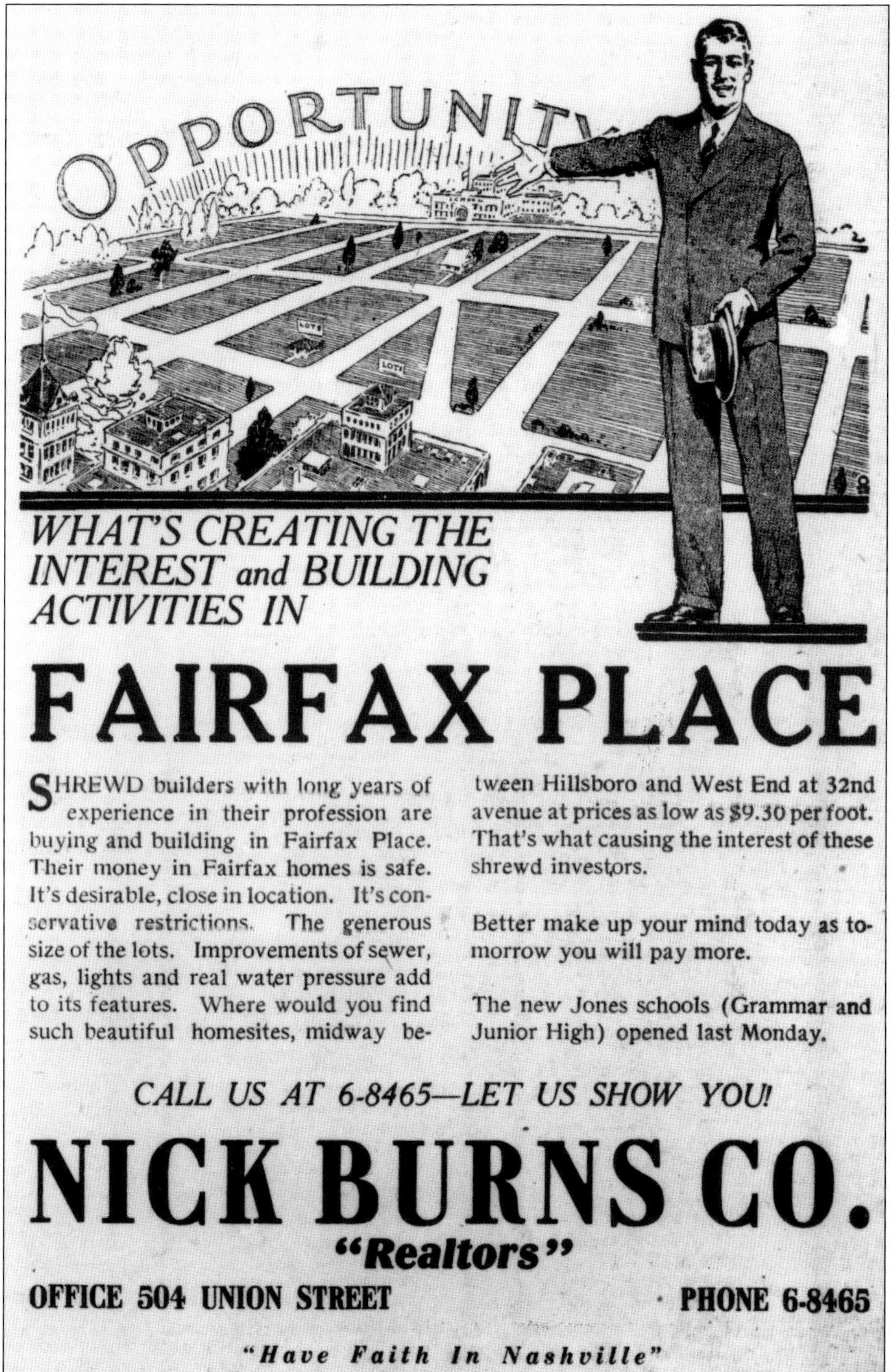

This was a typical advertisement from the land companies selling parcels of property. In the early days of the Hillsboro Village, Eakin School was first named Jones School. (Courtesy of Metro Archives.)

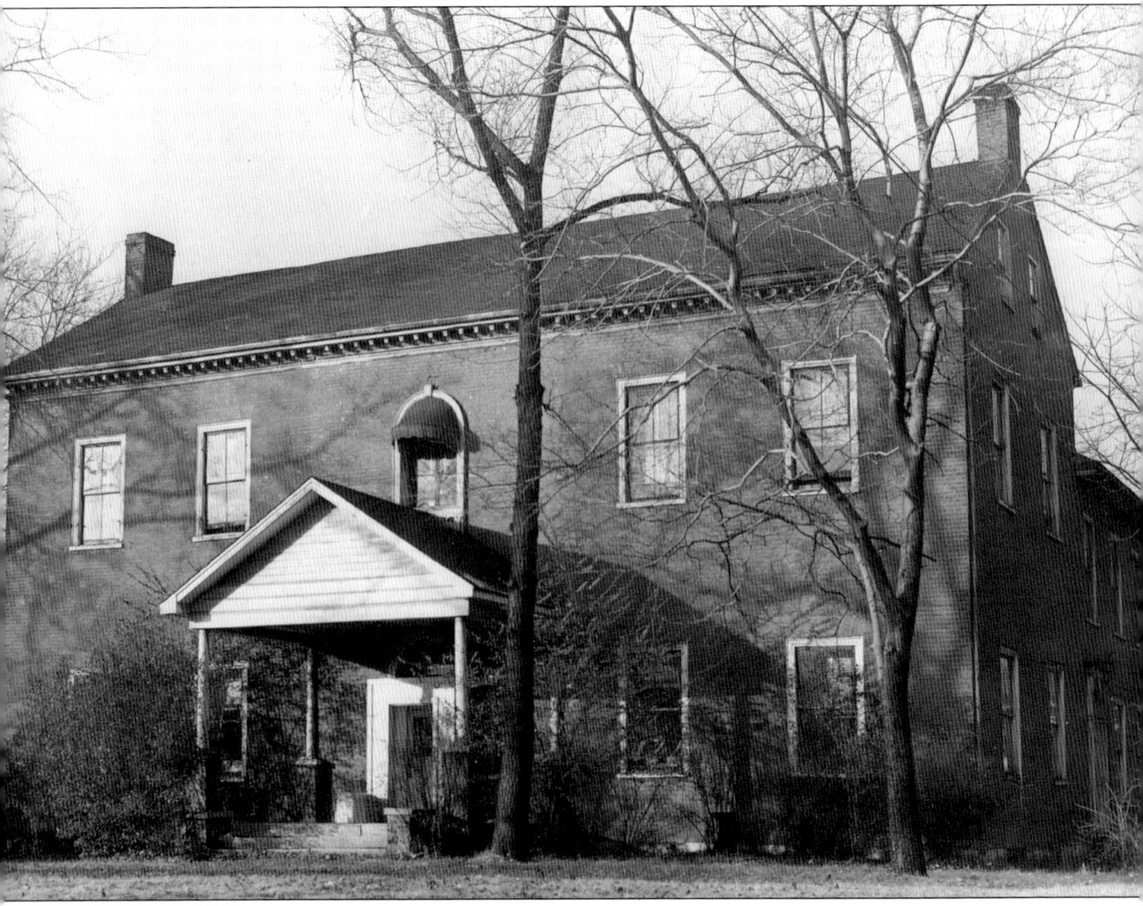

Rokeby became home to two influential families. Elijah Robertson, brother of James Robertson, owned much of the land known close to today's Twenty-First Avenue South by 1791. Elijah's daughter Sarah Robertson married John Childress, who served as the US marshal for the West District. Around 1813, the Childresses lived in Rokeby, a newly built mansion with a large farm just a couple of miles south of Nashville city limits. Accounts of Rokeby describe the main sitting room decorated with the same wallpaper as the Hermitage. Oliver Hayes purchased the Rokeby Farms. The Hayes family moved into Rokeby in 1827. Many of the Hayes children also became property owners in the area. The best known was daughter Adelicia; she and her second husband, Joseph Acklen, were owners of Belmont Mansion. Oliver and Pres. Rutherford Hayes were cousins. Rokeby was believed to have been haunted. Footsteps could be heard while no one was present. Locked doors would open and slam. Faces appeared in mirrors and windows. The story was that during the Civil War, Sarah Hayes left Rokeby unoccupied. She told the troops "Everything in the house was protected by her bodyless guard." After the first night on the grounds, the Union troops would not enter Rokeby. Rokeby was demolished in 1950 to make room for the Upper Room. (Courtesy of Tennessee State Library & Archives.)

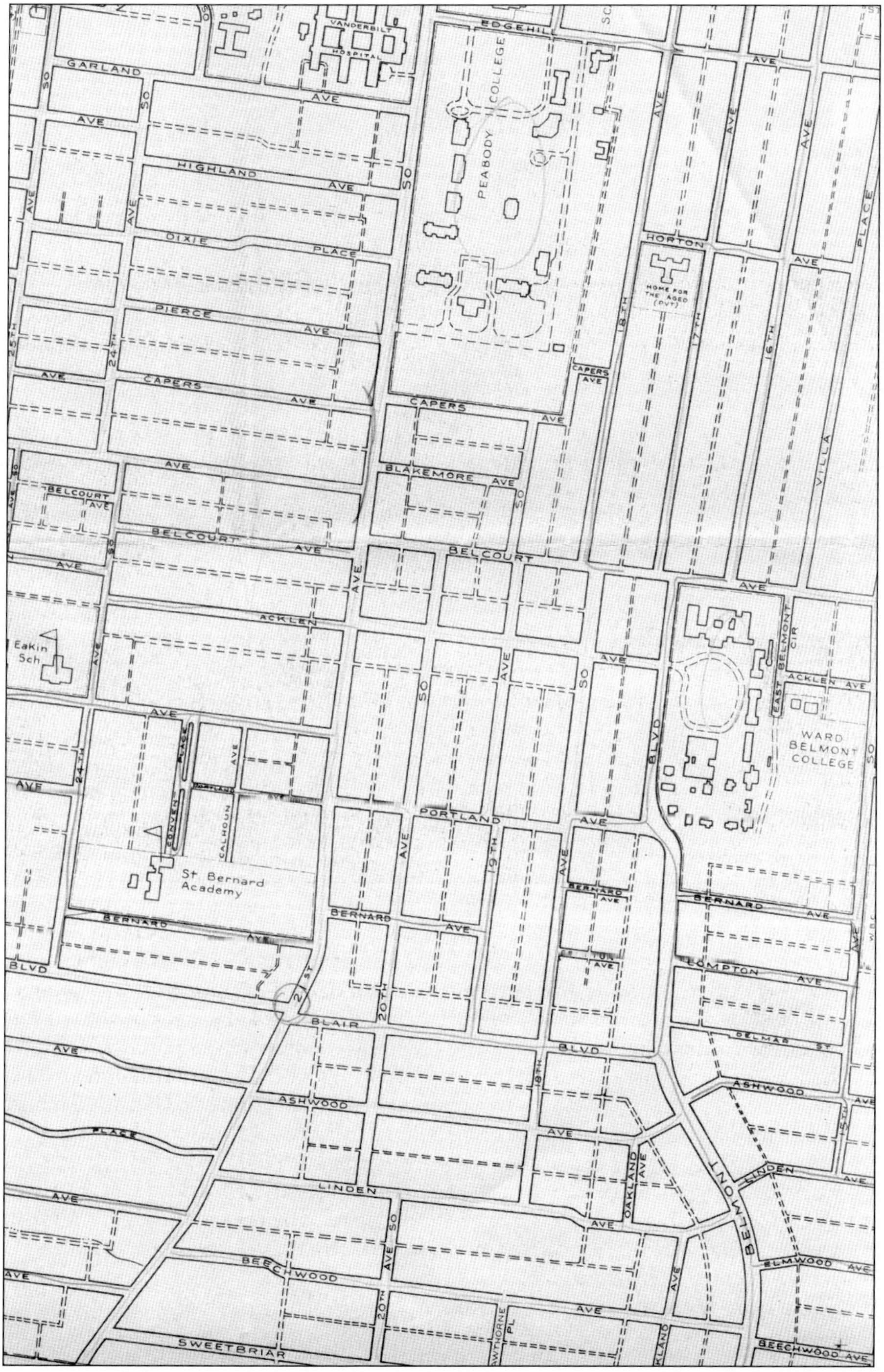

This is a map of the streets in Hillsboro Village during the 1960s. This map shows how the streets did not line up going across Twenty-First Avenue South. A big project was the widening of Blakemore and Wedgewood Avenues. In the 1970s, Blakemore and Wedgewood Avenues were in alignment crossing Twenty-First Avenue South. The streets were widened to five lanes. (Courtesy of Metro Archives.)

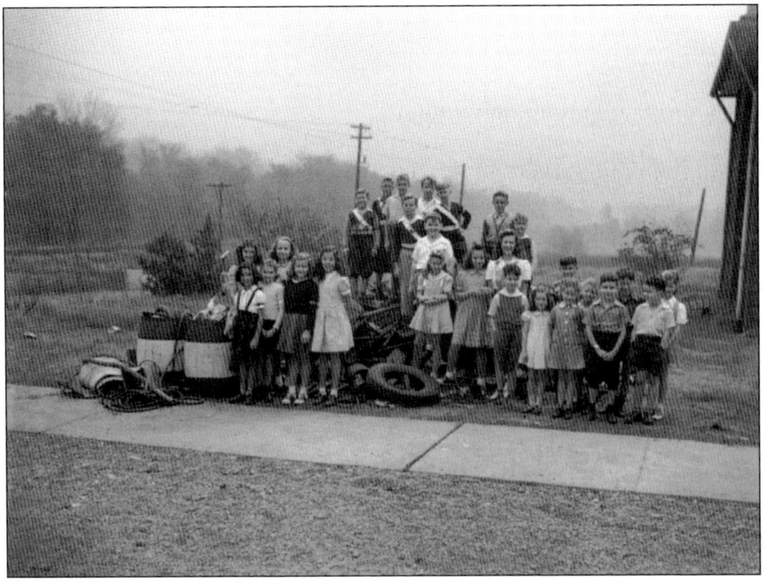

During World War II, times were very hard. The neighborhood children would go door to door collecting scrap metal, rubber, scrap rags, and paper. In Hillsboro Village, Fire Hall No. 16 was a collection area for scrap materials. (Courtesy of Metro Archives.)

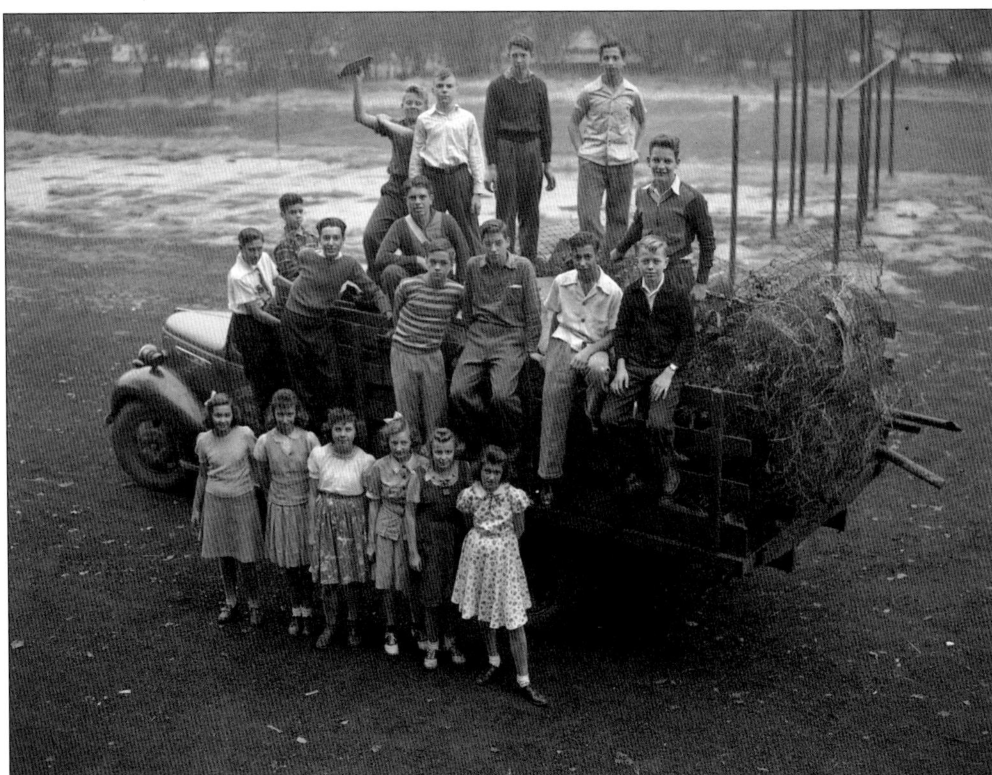

Americans had to deal with rations and neighborhood dark outs. It was a difficult time for the world. In this photograph, the students from Cavert School participate in a scrap metal collection. The collection in this image was part of the *Nashville Banner* newspaper drive. Students gathered 10,000 pounds of metal for this particular drive. (Courtesy of Metro Archives.)

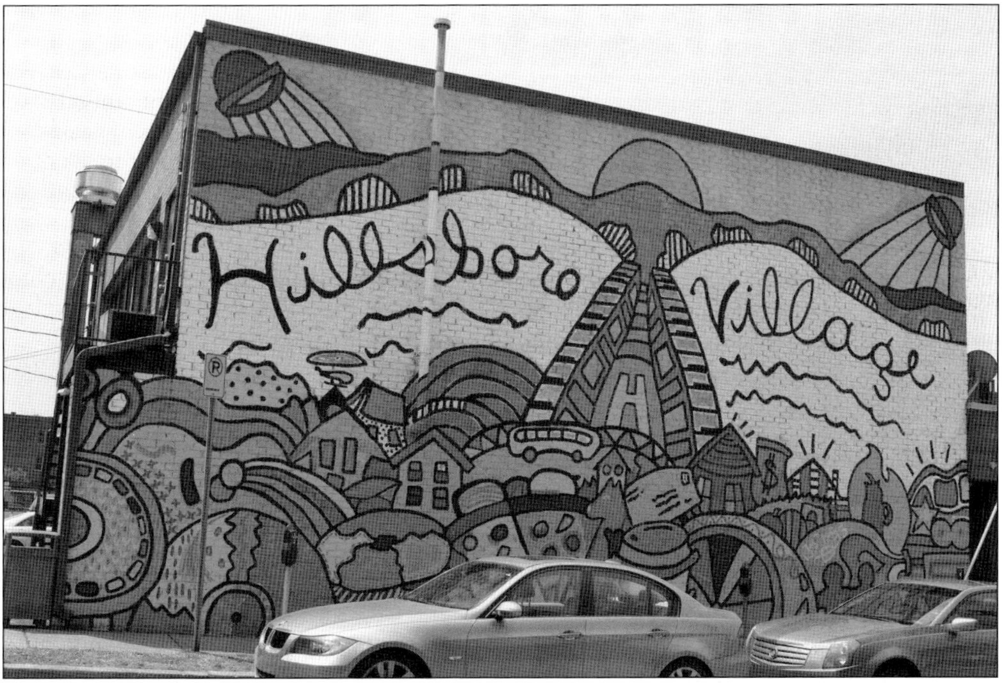

This mural is one of several in Hillsboro Village. Street art is very popular in Nashville, and this mural is unique to all that's part of Hillsboro Village. Hillsboro Village is represented on the mural; some of the symbols include a bus, a dog, and a dollar sign. Also seen are the Vanderbilt Children's Hospital logo and parts of a dragon that looks like it is wrapping itself around other items on this street. This mural is located near Twenty-First Avenue South and the southeast side of Capers Avenue. (Author's collection.)

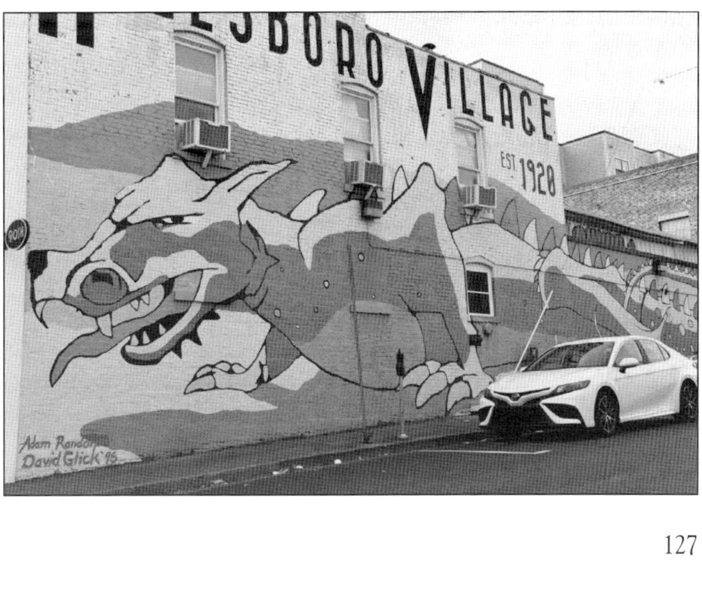

This is another mural in Hillsboro Village, located on the southwest corner of Belcourt Avenue and Twenty-First Avenue South, directly across the street from the Belcourt Cinema. As a result of the sea serpent in Fannie Mae Dees Park, a dragon is considered the unofficial mascot of Hillsboro Village. This street art was created in 1995. (Author's collection.)